THE VISION

It was twelve o'clock. The Angelus rang out from Lourdes. Suddenly Bernadette heard the noise of a great wind. She saw the curtain of branches below the niche in the grotto blowing restlessly. Nothing else was stirring.

Then, in the opening, she saw a light brighter than the sun and yet soft to her eyes. And immediately, as if springing from that light, a young girl, beautiful, radiant, heavenly . . .

"EXCELLENT"—Best Sellers

SAINT BERNADETTE

The Child and the Nun

by MARGARET TROUNCER

A CHAPEL BOOK

Published by
DELL PUBLISHING CO., INC.
750 Third Avenue, New York 17, N.Y.
© 1958 by Margaret Trouncer
Dell ® TM 681510, Dell Publishing Co., Inc.
Reprinted by arrangement with
Sheed and Ward, New York, N.Y.

Nihil obstat:

Barry E. Fontaine
Censor Delegatus

Imprimatur:

†Robert F. Joyce
Bishop of Burlington

December 24, 1957

Dedication:
To Chanoine Guynot
Mère Alphonse-Marie Crapard
Mother Isabel-Eugénie

First Dell printing—October, 1962

Printed in U.S.A.

CONTENTS

PREFACE

When I decided to write this book on one of the two greatest saints of modern times, a kindly Providence sent me helpers all along my path of studies. I must express gratitude to M. le Recteur des Chapelains, of Lourdes, for permission to read books from his library. To M. l'Abbé Caillabère for finding me two patois songs. To M. l'Abbé Laurentin for permission to quote from his book *Sens de Lourdes,* to M. le Chanoine Guynot for moral support and permission to quote from his precious *Souvenirs inédits,* to Reverend Mother Alphonse-Marie Crapard for so kindly sheltering me in a room at St. Gildard's, where the Secretary Archivist lent me all the documents and books I wanted. My gratitude also to the Misses Burn, Murphy and Over who kept house for me as I wrote. Last but not least, my warmest gratitude and affectionate thanks to Mother Mary Bede, librarian of the Assumption Convent, who anglified my own French text throughout, and completely transformed the difficult chapter on false visionaries.

O happy days, too soon gone! I wanted so much to share my discoveries with others. I wanted to write a spellbinding novel, but somehow, this book would not fall into that mould. The dry facts about the apparitions of Our Lady were so arresting in themselves, that they could dispense with the novelist's art.

The editor of a life of a seventeenth century nun said that as he "busied himself with the writings of this virgin, he was captivated by a secret charm, which could not be described, but which is known to those who study the writings of the saints and which is a salary of higher price than all human promises."

That is what I, too, felt.

Good-bye, Saint Bernadette. You have become my dear friend. Now go and become the friend of every one who reads this book! I urge all readers to visit her shrine at Nevers.

Feast of the Sacred Heart. 1957.

BOOK ONE: THE CHILD

1.

THE SOUBIROUS FAMILY
IS RUINED

One morning in the autumn of 1856, François Soubirous and his wife Louise were leading a mule-drawn cart containing their four children and some chattels along the road leading from the village of Arcizac-ès-Angles. François walked disconsolately, his head down. The fine dusting of flour on his black beret betrayed his calling: he was a miller. But he had been obliged to give up his mill at Arcizac-ès-Angles, for the stream was too slack to turn the wheel and customers were too few. Now the family were woefully returning to Lourdes.

At forty-nine François was a handsome man. Strangers thought that he looked surly—he had lost an eye in an accident—but he had in fact a generous, loving nature and was the soul of honesty and proud integrity. Had he been more worldly-wise and insisted that his poor customers should pay their debts promptly, he might not have been in such sorry straits, but he could never bear to see the sufferings of the poor. He let them have credit in the lean time before harvest. Although he was loved for his kindheartedness, some people took advantage of it. The customers who owed him most money were the first to rail at him in his present misfortune. The whole sum of nine hundred francs inherited from his Castérot mother-in-law had been swallowed up in this last venture: now he was ruined and could never hope to have his own mill again.

His wife Louise Castérot, who walked at his side, was thirty-one years old but looked a great deal older. He had married her when he was thirty-four and she was only seven-

teen. When he had courted her, he had been bewitched by
her fair hair and blue eyes, and her gay, gentle ways, but
now constant childbearing, hard work and bereavement
(they had lost three children) had greatly diminished her
good looks. But he loved her as much as ever, for nothing
could daunt her valiant spirit. During his set-backs, she had
never once upbraided him or reproached him, and she had
never put on that martyred expression which can be so trying to a husband. Perhaps she felt herself a little to blame
for their troubles, for the Boly mill which she had brought
him as a dowry had turned out to be heavily mortgaged, a
burden rather than a source of livelihood. Also, in a mis-
guided attempt to attract customers, she had kept open
house, spending too much on refreshment for the gossiping
women who came to have their corn milled. Oh, if she could
have her time over again, she would have learnt to read and
write and add up, and thus keep track of the debtors.

And now they were going back to Lourdes to crowd into
a single room in a hovel owned by a rapacious-looking in-
dividual called Soubies-Pélat.

Louise looked up at her husband, and said to him in the
Lourdes dialect: "I'm glad you got the cupboard in yester-
day. I never feel things can be too bad when I see that cupboard and know that inside it is some decent linen and a
few earthenware plates." (She was a very tidy, very clean
woman, and she and her children were always well-scrubbed
and neatly turned out.)

François said: "You should have seen the admiring look
Soubies-Pélat gave the cupboard: if we get behind with the
rent, I'm sure he'll pounce on it. However, we mustn't look
for trouble. We shan't starve if Maisongrosse occasionally
gives me some work in his bakery, and Cazenave has hinted
that I could look after his horses sometimes."

"And I can always go out and help with the reaping. I
wish one earned more than ten sous a day, washing and
cleaning. It's not so bad in the houses where the mistresses
aren't closefisted and suspicious: if they give me a large
helping for my midday meal, I can always bring some back
for the children. At the Mingelatte's, for a day's reaping
with a sickle, there's soup at ten, the proper meal at two,

and for supper, maize broth, potatoes and cheese. Hey, ho!
But that's unusual. Why are the rich so often mean?"

"That's how they become rich," he replied. "Oh, Louise,
I hate to see you going out to work and breaking your back
with reaping. If only I'd had those sieves mended sooner,
the customers wouldn't have complained about bran being
left in the flour."

"We just couldn't afford it at the time," she said with a
sigh. "I wish my three sisters weren't so cross about it all;
they don't seem to understand in the least. However, I will
say this about Bernarde, for one. With all her scolding
tongue, she's always so kind to Bernadette: I know she'll
take her in, if we're in trouble. Remember the day she came
to Arcizac? She gave one glance at the streams and the
damp walls, and when she heard Bernadette coughing, she
took her back for the winter. It's a pity, though, that the
child got cholera last year: she's never looked well since,
and she's not growing. And her wheezing! She's the weakest
of the four."

"They seem very quiet in the back there," François said.
"I hope they're not up to mischief. When we get to those
poplars, we'll give you a rest and the children some food."

In the cart the little Soubirous were enjoying themselves,
ensconced among the mattresses and leaning against the bat-
tered old trunk full of family linen. The elder sister, twelve-
year-old Bernadette, who was a wonderful mimic, was telling the others a thrilling story, an old Lourdes legend about
an eagle and a trout, and impersonating all the characters in
turn. Ten-year-old Toinette and five-year-old Jean-Marie
were spellbound. The baby, Justin, aged sixteen months and
very sweet with his golden curls, was asleep in Bernadette's
lap.

"Mirat, the Saracen chieftain who held the citadel of
Lourdes against the Emperor Charlemagne, was looking
out towards the Pyrenees one fine day," Bernadette related,
"when he saw an eagle fly overhead and drop a trout into
the castle courtyard."

At this point she fished a dried herring out of a saucepan:
"Here's the trout! Now, if I pretend to be the eagle and drop

the trout, you won't eat it, will you? Because if the trout's gone, I can't go on with the story."

"Not even a tiny nibble?" pleaded Jean-Marie, who was perpetually afflicted with hunger.

"No, not even the tiniest. Well, Mirat sent the trout to the Emperor, with the message, 'Ha, mighty Lord, we can hold out for a long siege, for we have fish ponds.'"

"And did the Emperor believe him?"

"He did, but not so his bishop: he knew that Saracens could be very crafty men, and he suspected a trick, so he called on Mirat and said, 'Ho, great Mirat, if you don't want to give allegiance to an earthly man, why not become the chevalier of Our Lady of Le Puy? She is black like the goddesses of your land. She is a most noble lady: to serve her would be an honour.' And so he did, and his men stuck handfuls of hay to the ends of their lances, and went to pay tribute to Notre Dame du Puy by laying down their lances in her sanctuary."[1]

"And now," said Jean-Marie, "I will have my nibble of herring."

"Oh no you don't!" yelled Toinette, and they started fighting. The cart shook and bounced. Justin wailed, and Bernadette drew him closer to her, to protect him from hammering sabots. Toinette, nicknamed "gendarme," was a fierce fighter. Although two years younger than Bernadette, she was so much stronger that she could beat her.

---

[1] The trout is still on the arms of Lourdes. Mirat changed his name to Larus, which in time became Lorus, then Lourdes. The Comte de Bigorre eventually held the castle, and thus one of the titles of Our Lady of Le Puy was Comtesse de Bigorre.

Prophetic omen, this fish! To the early Christians in the Catacombs, the fish symbolized Christ. In Greek the initial letters of the words "Jesus Christ, son of God, Saviour" spelt "fish." In consequence, a Christian, when speaking to someone he was not sure of, would trace a fish on the ground or table, with stick or finger, and if the other was a Christian, he recognized the sign. It was as if in the turbulent ninth century, that fish falling into Lourdes were foreshadowing the times when to that unknown little town, Christ in the Blessed Sacrament would come to multitudes of afflicted pilgrims. Often during the passing of the Blessed Sacrament among the rows of sick people, many miraculous cures take place.

Louise sprang at the combatants with a switch in her hand and parted them with a few sharp blows. (She did not believe in sparing the rod. Although she never ill-treated her children, she knew how to keep them in order. But she never had any trouble with Bernadette, for, as her father was to say later, this child had never disobeyed him and she was incapable of telling a lie.) "Now then, now then," she said. "Out you all get and we'll have something to eat. Here, Jean-Marie, you can make a fire and grill the herrings, they'll be tastier." She seized Justin and kissed him. The other children jumped out and shook themselves like terriers.

Louise took out a loaf of coarse maize bread (*milloc*) from a white napkin and started cutting large hunks, which she rubbed with garlic and sprinkled with salt before distributing them to her family. But she gave Bernadette a slice of fine white wheaten bread. The child was too frail to digest the *milloc*. Toinette and Jean-Marie cast sidelong glances at their sister, and Toinette gave her a surreptitious kick. Had her parents not been there, Bernadette would not have been allowed to eat her portion at all. The other two always managed to filch it from her, when they could do so unobserved, and as she never told tales, the culprits were never punished.

At the end of this frugal repast Louise, with a gleam of pleasurable anticipation in her eye, fetched half a bottle of red wine from between two mattresses. She gave some to her husband, took a draught from the bottle herself, and then poured some into a mug, with two lumps of sugar, for Bernadette. (For this Toinette gave Bernadette another kick.) Louise was very weary, and the relaxing warmth of the wine spread into her limbs and made her more carefree.

From being out so much in the sun, Bernadette had a brown complexion and fresh rosy cheeks. She had a round, chubby, childlike face, great sparkling brown eyes under dark, strongly marked brows. Her lips were rather full, and her voice, for one with so weak a chest, surprisingly strong. She had tiny, delicate hands. Her beautiful black hair was half hidden under her striped Pyrenean kerchief, knotted on one side. She wore a clean but heavily patched dress which reached to her ankles, a shawl crossed over her chest, and a black apron, in the pocket of which she kept a cheap rosary given to her by her mother. No stockings but clogs. She now gave her head a vicious scratch.

"Praoubo dé you! Poor me!" exclaimed Louise. "I wish I'd washed your hair before we left. The washing arrangements will be very awkward at Lourdes. I'll have to go out to the pump in the street every time I want a drop of water, and in January it will freeze. And as for drying clothes in winter, when you haven't got even a back yard, let alone a field! Well, I just don't know how we'll manage in one room."

"We could stretch cords across the room and make up a roasting fire," said Bernadette. "On washing day, we'll all go to the forest and gather firewood."

"Yes, and steam the place out with Justin's nappies," grumbled François Soubirous. "I'll go out and play a game of cards while all that is going on. Which reminds me, you children had better learn not to make so much noise. Remember, we'll be tenants in someone else's house now, and you can't scream and shout the way you did at Arcizac. We don't want the landlord to turn us all out."

Bernadette looked a little sad. She had loved Arcizac, their little hut surrounded by millstreams, the ditches full of green hellebore in midwinter, the lilies-of-the-valley and violets in the woods, which she used to pick and arrange into careful nosegays for her mother and father. The elders and aspens had sparkled with goldfinches, and there were wide sunsets, glowing with all the tints of the local kingfishers, mirrored in the streams and pools. And the air was sweeter than in Lourdes. It had been the first time they had lived together in the country.

Her father's mill was at Escoubès, a short distance away from their hut at Arcizac. When her mother did not need her for looking after the other children, Bernadette used to trot along with her father, whom she adored, and watch him open the sluice gates and work the mill. She would chase away the mice. It was a never-failing pleasure to see the grains of wheat pouring in and coming out afterwards, transformed into pure white flour. Often she would picture

to herself the fate of one little grain of wheat being ground
slowly to powder by the two immense millstones, and whisper: "I'm glad it is not me." She shared all her father's
anxiety about the tricks the mill wheel played him. Sometimes, when the snows had turned the stream into a destruc-
tive, raging torrent, the mill wheel had to be repaired. But
worse still were the torrid days when the stream dried up
altogether. The former owner, in order to effect a quick
sale, had lied about that stream. Her father would sit down
heavily and let the tears of sheer desperation trickle down
his cheeks. She used to try and comfort him.

François was looking very much on the verge of tears at
this moment. Bernadette went up to him and slid her tiny
hand into his large brown one. "Never mind, Papa," she
said, "the good thing about being together in one room is
that we're still a family."

Just then Justin woke, stretched and looked for his mother. She took him up and suckled him. He gazed up at her
with his blue eyes.

"It'll be dreadful having to cook in the living room fireplace," said Louise, gazing at her baby.

"Who minds?" said Bernadette. "We'll go to sleep by
firelight, and sometimes we'll fry some nice tasty fritters in
the big frying pan before bedtime. We can all gather round
and watch them sizzling."

"Do you children ever talk about anything else but food?"
said François Soubirous in mock despair.

Louise said in a determined voice, "I really will manage
so that we can do our washing in private. Every evening I'll
hang a sheet across the corner of the room where the sink
is: we'll all go there and wash in turns."

"What shall we do if the water freezes at the pump?"
asked Toinette.

"Oh well, if it's snowing, we'll go out and get snow in a
pail," said Jean-Marie.

Louise said, "Whatever happens, we must not forget to
wash. The only way for us all to live together in such a
small space is to be as clean and as neat as we possibly can.
Woe betide the child who leaves things trailing about, it
will have a taste of my switch. Oh dear," she said, glancing

at the sun, "I think it's time we went on again. Hold Justin, Bernata.[2] Somebody untether the mule. He must have a drink and a feed. What a pity he's only on loan."

"Oh, I know something," said Jean-Marie. "You know on market days at Lourdes, when farmers let vegetables drop as they unpack their carts? Do you think if I went to market early with a basket . . . ?"

"Oh misery me!" exclaimed his mother. "You're not going to sink to pilfering, are you? We've got to keep our self-respect."

Jean-Marie continued undaunted: "Oh no. I'd always ask first. There are lots of things you can get for nothing if you know how to look for them."

"Food again," murmured François Soubirous.

"There are blackberries and wild strawberries in the woods," said Jean-Marie "and sometimes whole fields of mushrooms. And trout in the Gave—if *only* I had a fishing rod! And chestnuts in the forest. Nothing nicer than roast chestnuts!"

His mother looked on him with pity. "My poor boy, I long for the day when I can see you sit down to two hot meals again! But God won't allow us to starve. Every night we must say family prayers together and ask for our daily bread. If God can care for the birds, He can look after us. We are more precious than many sparrows."

At last the family reached Lourdes, which was only five kilometres away. Greeted by comments, some friendly, others pitying, a few sarcastic, they proceeded to make their home in the single slum room in the dark street near the citadel, the rue du Bourg. Their situation was one of which they could never have dreamed in the earlier days at Lourdes, when François Soubirous had been the owner of the Boly mill.

Lourdes was a very small, insignificant town at the foot-hills of the Pyrenees, with about four thousand inhabitants. The Gave, its turbulent, rushing river, encircled it before joining the Adour on its way to the Atlantic Ocean. The Gave was fed by the glacial streams and torrents tumbling

---

[2] Bernadette was often called Bernata by the members of her family and her friends.

down from the Pyrenees. One of its tributaries was the Lapaca stream, to the north of the town, on whose banks were
various mills, including the Boly mill, where Bernadette had
been born on January the 7th, 1844. The ancient little
houses with their grey slate roofs huddling around the
twelfth-century church were overshadowed by the citadel
on the rock, which looked like an eagle's eyrie.

Lourdes boasted of a tribunal, a judge, a parish priest
with two curates, an Hospice run by the Sisters of Nevers,
who looked after the sick poor and kept a school for the
children of the town, and a police station near the Hospice.
There was also the Café Français, where the doctors, law-
yers and suchlike met to read the latest Paris newspapers
and air their freethinking views inspired by Voltaire. There
were a very few retired folk with settled pensions, but many
small farmers who met on Thursday, market day, and stone
quarrymen. The only hostelry, the Hôtel de la Poste, catered
to people travelling to the nearby watering places, who
stopped for an hour or so at Lourdes to have a meal and to
look at the castle on the rock.

A little to the south of the town, wood-gleaners took the
road out of the Porte du Baous, past the churchyard, and
went out across the Vallée de Paradis, and then over the
little Roman bridge spanning the Gave. This led to a lovely
walk along the forest road. To one's right could be glimpsed
the island embraced by the sinuous arms of the Gave and
the Canal de Savy, which fed the Savy mill and the sawmill.
Beyond this island, across the Gave to the north, were the
Ribère meadows with their pleasant, lightly wooded hillocks.

Continuing the walk along the forest road, on the left
would be seen the Mont des Espélugues with its promontory
called Massabielle, which means "old mountain mass." Massabielle, looking northwards, had a very ancient grotto, desolate, damp and wild, where fishermen would shelter when
they were caught in storms. Here Samson, the town swine-
herd, would eat his meal whilst keeping an eye on the herd
of swine which he had summoned with his horn in the
Lourdes streets at dawn.

It is a curious fact that at this time there was a kind of
hearsay tradition about Massabielle, preserved by the sac-

ristan, Louis Fourcade, who repeated what he had heard from some of the oldest inhabitants. He declared that a great marvel would be accomplished in that grotto. A long time ago, a child had said: "One day they will build a chapel in the Massabielle grotto." Old Jean Vergès, the rural policeman, said that a curate of Lourdes had said on his deathbed: "In the direction of the forest, something marvellous will happen." Some other old man had also said to the sacristan: "In time to come there will be an apparition in the grottoes of Massabielle."

What could have led them to think this? It was a wild and desolate place with a sinister reputation. When any Lourdes child misbehaved, its mother would say, "You've learnt your manners at Massabielle." The Gave would often flood the entrance to the grotto: the inside had all been silted up by sand and small stones. The ancient rock, which was more like an overhanging cliff, was crowned by wild roses, brambles and box. On the right was an arched opening, not high,[3] hollowed out by the glaciers aeons ago. Below this grew a wild white rosebush over a hundred years old; its hanging branches swayed and tossed in the wind. As, a hundred years ago, the level of the ground was higher than it is now, you could touch the foot of the niche if you stretched your hand out. Near by was a glade of poplars, "quite a forest." In spring the meadow was carpeted with golden saxifrage and lady's smock. Sometimes in early February a few snowdrops filled the earthy pockets in the rocks.

On her wood-gathering expeditions to the forest, Bernadette never got as far as Massabielle until one mysterious day in February, when she was fourteen years old.

[3] About four feet eight inches. Bernadette and the apparition were about the same height.

2

OLD RAGS AND BONES AND
THE LITTLE SHEPHERDESS

Louise relied very much on Bernadette. The child had a gift for handling the other children. She was only eleven when she had had to carry Justin all the way to Mingelatte's field, where Louise was helping with the reaping, to be suckled. The infant was heavy, an exhausting burden for such a small girl. Romaine Mingelatte remembered how Bernadette came to her house and said, very simply and politely, "Would you be so kind as to tell me where your field is? I have to carry my little brother to my mother because he needs to be nursed."

During that hard winter when she had lived with her Aunt Bernarde, Bernadette had been kept so busy looking after her little cousins that she had not been able to get to school. At Arcizac, she had won the admiration of the girl who was to become Madame Viron for the way she kept house and took care of her little brothers during the absence of her parents. Her sister, Toinette, was unreliable: now, in the rue du Bourg, Bernadette often had to scold her for leaving the little boys alone, with the result that Jean-Marie went out and wandered about the streets. Toinette resented these lectures, and occasionally she would strike her sister and urge Jean-Marie to do the same.

Let us imagine the Soubirous at Halloween, a few weeks after their return to Lourdes. Early that morning the children noticed that their parents looked troubled and were talking in whispers in bed. There was nothing to eat, and no firewood. When both parents left the house to look for work, Bernadette suggested, "Let's go to Alexine Baron, the old rag-and-bone woman, with a few things. We can go and look for rubbish in the back streets. I know she wants scrap iron and bones and rags. Look, Jean-Marie, you carry a little basket and we'll collect quite enough in an hour to buy some bread for Mother and Father."

Toinette opened the cupboard which was Louise's most prized inheritance. "Isn't there any in here at all?" she said.

"No," said Bernadette, "the cupboard is empty this time."

"I'm hungry, aren't you?" said Jean-Marie.

"Oh, well, *you* always are," replied Bernadette.

At that moment poor little Justin began to wail. Bernadette picked him up and hugged him. "There, there," she said, "we'll soon have something to eat."

At length, after scouring the streets for any discarded object they might find, the children called at the rag-and-bone woman's with their treasures.

Alexine Baron's lair was very like a witch's den. She was unimaginably grimy, and the place stank from all the horrors that she had accumulated. In the argument which ensued about the value of the articles which the children had collected, Toinette and Bernadette held their own and came off triumphantly with six sous. This was enough to get a fresh crusty loaf from Maisongrosse, a tin of sardines (which was a great treat) and a few onions. The old market woman threw in some garlic free of charge because she liked the look of Bernadette.

Although they were very tired when they reached home again, they had to hurry now with the housework. Bernadette gave Justin a little crust of bread to keep him quiet. When the parents came home at eleven, after a heartbreaking and unprofitable morning, the table was laid with the red earthenware plates and everything was in order. A fire was crackling in the hearth. Louise looked tired out, but she smiled when she saw the preparations the children had made. They all sat down and ate with the silent reverence of the poor, to whom every mouthful is of such importance. After the meal was over, François Soubirous broke the news.

"We've got to leave tomorrow. I can't pay the rent. In fact, I'm already behind with the rent and he—" he said, jerking his thumb towards the ceiling—"he says he's keeping the cupboard as security."

Louise wiped her eyes on her apron. That chest meant so much to her. Bernadette jumped up and threw her arms around her.

"Don't cry," she said. "Where are we going?"

"That's just it," replied Louise. "We went to Cousin Sajous to see if he could let us have the room which was the old prison dungeon, and he says he's got to think it over. He'll let us know this afternoon. I hope he won't leave it too late, because we'll have to clean up there before we can move in. It's in a dreadful state."

"Well, while we're waiting for him to tell us," said Bernadette calmly, "we might as well start packing. Then we'll go to the woods before nightfall to get some firewood. It always cheers a place up to have a fire."

"You good little girl," cried her mother, "always so full of sense! What should I do without you?"

In the meantime, André Sajous was discussing with his uncle the wisdom of having the Soubirous as tenants.

"I'm against it," he said. "Why, I'm poor myself, and my wife is so goodhearted, she'd always be slipping down to give them a loaf of bread. She'll deprive our children in order to feed them. I've got five children—they've only got four."

"Ah, yes," said his uncle, "you've kept your children because you've been properly housed. Poor Louise has lost three of hers because she has been pushed about from pillar to post and ill-fed and overworked. You *know* you'll never get anybody else to rent that room. Why, you've had the poorest tenants—the bell ringer, the blacksmith, the butcher: they all tried to stick it out there and had to give up after a short time. It's that cesspool in the courtyard just outside the window and your manure heap on top of that, and the iron bars at the windows."

"True," admitted André Sajous. "But I did try to improve it. I put in a fireplace and made an extra window."

"Ho," mocked his uncle. "Yes, you made it *palatial*. Only fit for the Spanish workmen who sleep on straw because they have nowhere else. The stench in there is unbearable: and then, those damp walls covered with saltpetre rot and that low ceiling and the depressing slate floor. It's a most unhealthy place. Why, the very look of the door gives me the shivers. You can see it's a prison door, with all its bolts and bars and heavy nails. No, my boy, I should let Soubirous have it. After all, you can't turn him out into the street: you *are* a relation of Louise's. If you do have him in that room, it will at least be kept aired, for they'll have a fire there occasionally, I should think."

In the end, the Soubirous were permitted to occupy the back room on the ground floor of the building.

André Sajous, who was a stone mason, kept the front room looking on the rue des Petits-Fossés for himself: he stabled a cow there. The back room looked on to the court-yard under the very shadow of the citadel and got very little light. A staircase led to the first and second floors, where Sajous lived with his family. He was therefore in an excellent position to know exactly what went on in the Soubirous family. He could even hear them saying their prayers to-gether every evening. Often he must have heard Bernadette having an attack of asthma. She would cling to the iron bars of the windows and beg her mother to "open her chest" so that she could breathe. He was able to testify: "Never would you hear them cry out that they were hungry, and many times I have seen Bernadette, Jean-Marie and little Justin laugh and romp even with empty stomachs!"

The Soubirous' room just held the three beds, one for the parents, one for the boys and one for the girls. There was no room for a table. Bernadette was often seen by her cousin Jeanne-Marie Védère taking her bowl of soup to the stone ledge near the window, overlooking the dung-heap.

The family moved in in November 1856. Louise must have been glad it was not summer, when the merry neigh-bours would be playing Sizette or taking snuff on their door-steps in the cool of the evening. It was unpleasant enough to have to parry the witty sallies of passers-by in the twi-light. When they saw the Soubirous with their push-cart they would call out: "What, moving again!" Yes, and it would be those very people who still owed them money, the ones who had been the first to complain about the unsifted flour.

Louise, aided by the two girls, had scrubbed as much as

she could, though it had meant going backwards and forwards to the street pump for water. One of those odd, antiquated, dark wax tapers, curled round and round like a snake, had been put on the wooden chimney piece.

"Oh mercy me!" cried Louise. "Is that all we've got left for light? If only I had a bit more wax, I could manage. We don't want to go to bed by firelight!"

Jean-Marie slipped out unnoticed. He had just recalled something stored in his memory against just such a time. Severe privations had sharpened the wits of the boy: out of sheer necessity he was practical beyond his years, with the practicality of the very poor.

He ran across to the dark old church with its altar of Our Lady. Here he had often watched the candles dripping at the shrine in front of the golden statue of Our Lady of All Graces and thought: What a waste, that all that wax should lie on the stone floor, to be scratched up and thrown away. Now he had found a use for it.

He went up to the sconce and, thinking that he was alone in the church, started scraping the wax off the floor and putting it into his large red pocket handkerchief. Then he attacked the candles themselves, wrestling with his conscience as he scratched bits of wax from the holders. Finally he went to a sconce of brown wax funeral candles.

"Ssh," said someone from a shadowy corner of the church.

Alarmed, Jean-Marie looked in the direction of the voice and saw Mademoiselle Emmanuélite Estrade, the youngest sister of a tax collector. She wrote afterwards that she saw this child, aged about five or six—ill-dressed, a charming face but sickly, evidently underfed. She thought that she saw him put some of the wax into his mouth.

"Are you eating wax?" she asked.

He didn't speak but made a vague gesture which she took to mean that he was.

"Are you very hungry, then?" she asked. "Wouldn't you prefer to eat something else?"

He nodded several times to say "Yes."

"I left the church immediately," she wrote, "with the little fellow, who had become my friend."

She brought him to her house—at least, to the house in which she had a flat; Monsieur Jacomet, the commissioner of police, lived on the ground floor. She asked the child into the house, but he obstinately refused to cross the threshold. After a while she persuaded him to come a little further into the hall. He sat down on the staircase and would not budge. She went to her kitchen and returned with a tray of food. She looked at him with pity as he ate without a word. "Come again tomorrow," she said.

He smiled, and taking up his handkerchief full of candle wax he went out the door and disappeared silently into the darkness.

When he returned home, where they had begun to be anxious at his prolonged absence, he emptied the wax on to the table and said, "Look, Mother, here's your wax!"

Late into the night Louise sat mending the clothes of her husband and children. Occasionally she would catch her breath with fear when the thought came to her that she might never again be able to buy any new clothing for her family. The last purchase of any importance had been a white *capulet* (hood) from the second-hand dealer outside the church door, and even that had to be put into communal use. It was called *"the capulet."* Bernadette had already washed it several times, and the patterned hem was fading. Oh, if only she could collect some old bits of wool here and there, she could knit another pair of wool stockings for Bernadette. That child was never free from cough or cold nowadays. Even now she was tossing and turning uneasily in her sleep and wheezing as she breathed. (Often Louise had to get out of bed and comfort the child during an attack of asthma.) She went on with her darning, sighing. If only she could knit some stockings for Justin. It was pitiable to see him walking with bare feet in his little clogs in midwinter. . . .

Somehow, with, on rare occasions, the gift of food or clothing from some kind neighbour, the Soubirous managed to keep body and soul together through that winter. It was in March, 1857, that a new and terrible blow fell.

At midday on Thursday, March the 27th, the police were

at the door. It seemed that two sacks of flour had disappeared from the stock of the baker, Maisongrosse, and he was accusing Soubirous. François was always calm by nature, it was a family trait. "This room is my only home," he said to the policemen. "You can search it from top to bottom." And search they did. They opened the beds, pummelled the mattresses, unlocked the trunk and scattered all the clean, well-mended linen on to the floor.

"Whose is that yard over there?" exclaimed d'Angla, the officer in command.

"That belongs to my cousin Sajous," replied Soubirous.

"Do you have the use of it?"

"Oh, I occasionally leave things there."

"Well, we'll have a look round."

They went there, and found a plank leaning against the wall.

"Aha, did you bring that in last night?"

"Yes I did," said Soubirous. "I got up very early in the morning."

"Yes, so we heard. You were up at three. The neighbours told us. What were you up to, at that unearthly hour?"

"We were freezing," he replied, "and I meant to walk to Bartrès to get some sticks for a fire."

"To Bartrès—all that way? Couldn't you find some sticks a little nearer home? And I suppose you collected this plank on the way back?"

"It had been against the town wall for a long time and I thought nobody wanted it."

"Well, you come along with me, my man. You'll have to report to Monsieur Jacomet on this matter."

Poor Soubirous was imprisoned in the room above the Baous Gate until April the 4th, when he was released: they said it would be inhuman to keep him in there any longer, and it would cause hardship to his family: also they could not prove his guilt. One can imagine the misery of Louise and the children during his absence.

But cheerfulness prevailed. One can picture the little Soubirous children playing in the *cachot* at their favourite game one June day. Having discovered a feeding hatch for prisoners on one wall, the children used to flock into André Sajous' room, with his permission, and play at "feeding the prisoner." This time it was Bernadette's turn to be the jailer. She had almost exhausted her supply of tit-bits, with which she was going to feed Toinette, Jean-Marie and Justin, when all of a sudden she heard her name called from the street.

"Bernadette! Bernadette!"

She dropped her basket and ran out, and there was her dearly loved foster mother, Marie Lagües[1] from Bartrès, on her way to market with two huge baskets on her arms.

(When Bernadette was only ten months old and the Soubirous were still living at the Boly mill, her mother, worn out with work and with suckling and already pregnant again, had fallen asleep by the fire, and one of the candle wicks had fallen on to her bodice and set fire to it. Owing to the burns which had resulted from this accident, she had been unable to nurse Bernadette any longer, so she had lent the child to Marie Lagües, who had just lost her first-born son. She paid her five francs a month for Bernadette's care. Marie became devoted to the child, and so did all the other inhabitants of Bartrès. They loved her for her charm and enjoyed holding her in their arms. Bernadette herself had become very much attached to her foster mother. Afraid of losing the child's affection after she had been returned to her own family, Marie Lagües would always slip in and see her on market day, bringing a cake which she had baked at the farm, or some good white wheaten bread, or a few eggs, though she knew, alas, that these gifts might be seized on by the other children.)

"Well here you are, child!" cried Marie as Bernadette appeared. "And when are you coming to stay with us again?"

Although she was a good and devout woman, Marie was rather calculating and parsimonious, and she liked to make use of people. At the back of her mind was the thought that her foster child could make herself very useful at the farm, looking after her growing family.[2] Or she could relieve the

---

[1] Pronounced Laguss.

[2] She eventually had eight children of her own. I have talked with her granddaughter.

maid, overworked Jeanne-Marie Garros, by taking on some
of the farm work or even minding the sheep. No need to
pay her any wages. The Soubirous, especially since the
prison incident, were in such bad straits that they would
accept any bargain.

Since Bernadette did not reply at once, Marie now put
on her most honeyed smile and asked her question again.
To her surprise Bernadette's honest little face looked rather
worried.

"I'd love to come," she said hesitantly, "but you see I
want to prepare for Holy Communion and go to catechism
classes."

"Well, that can be arranged at our place quite easily. I'll
speak to *Monsieur le curé* about it. That would only take
three hours a week."

"And then," added Bernadette, "I haven't been to school
for such a very long time—I still don't know how to read or
write, and I don't know a word of French."

"Well, we've got a school too. You could go to school as
well." (At the back of her mind, Marie Lagües was quite
determined that the child should only go to school if the
weather were too wet for minding sheep.)

Just then there was a rat-tat-tat on the other side of the
feeding hatch. "Aren't you going to feed us, Mister Policeman?" cried the children.

"What's all this?" said Marie Lagües.

"Oh, we're just playing at prisoners. They're Spaniards.
Look, I'll give them a little bit of your lovely cake."

"But I'd meant it for you—you're the one who needs it."

"Yes, I know, but they're so hungry. Just let me give
them a little bit."

And thus it was that arrangements were made for Bernadette to go to stay again with Marie Lagües. The servant
Jeanne-Marie Garros came to fetch her. ("She didn't have
much to pack up," she said later, "and more than once during her stay at Bartrès I lent her my linen whilst she washed
her own.")

After leaving the school of the Nevers Sisters behind,
they turned abruptly up a side road which led uphill almost

all the way to Bartrès. The walk took about an hour. The servant was devoted to the little thirteen-year-old child, who was so undersized that she looked barely eleven. *"Elle était si brave,"* she said. ("She was so gallant.")

At the farm of Marie Lagües there was only a tiny box of a room for the servant, and that was now shared by Bernadette.

An old country woman of the hamlet, whose mother was a contemporary of Bernadette's, told me a delicious anecdote, hitherto unpublished.

Often enough, Bernadette used to go to bed hungry. In truth, her foster mother's heart had chilled a little towards her since she had acquired children of her own. The poor child had ceased to be a member of a family and was now no more than a neglected and unpaid servant girl. Bernadette used to whisper to the maid: "Go and get me some of the little potatoes meant for the pigs." (These were very small potatoes which were boiled in their skins in a pail.) Jeanne-Marie would slip away and fetch a handful of them.

This tiny hamlet of two hundred souls is extremely attractive. Often there is a lightness in the air in the places where saints have passed. Bartrès is completely unspoilt to this very day. It smells of hay, manure and mown grass. The air is pure and sweet. In Bernadette's day, the little church on its knoll was surrounded by enormous beech trees. Next door to it, actually in the churchyard itself, was the tiny school, since demolished. The priest's house was quite near.

The gables of the Lagües house looked out on to the street. Inside, clothes hung on the walls. Flax and wool mingled with hams and onions hanging from the rafters. "Poor Mama," thought Bernadette, as she saw the hams and onions on the day of her arrival. "How I should like to give her a few of these." She felt a little homesick for a moment. On the great wooden chimney piece were small statues of the saints. In the middle was a crucifix and holy-water stoup, with a rosary twined around a palm branch.

Basile Lagües, Marie's husband, did not know how to read or write, but he certainly knew how to make his farm yield a profit and had all the disarming ways of one who is on the look-out for a good bargain. (Later on, when Bernadette was mentioned, he would always exclaim: *"Ah, la pauvrette!"* From his point of view, she had been an ideal person to have about—never any trouble, never any complaints; she never answered back when she was scolded, and she looked after the sheep as well as anyone ever had.) Now he thought it prudent to ingratiate himself at once.

"Well, *la pauvrette,* it seems you want to go to catechism classes? Well, well, well, we shall have to see to that."

The foster mother interrupted. "Now, Bernata, could you run across to the church and look for my rosary under my stool? I think I must have left it there." (Marie was very devout. In her old age, she said her rosary three times a day and belonged to the Third Order of St. Francis.)

Bernadette did not have to be told twice: in her little clogs she ran up the village path. She was greeted by the neighbours, who were always pleased to see her again. There was Domenge Barrère, Marie Pujo and Maria Adias, all at their doors. They loved Bernadette's smile and the lovely expression in her eyes.

Bernadette darted into the church as swiftly as a swallow and looked up at the gilded wooden figures over the high altar. On the left was Our Lady visiting her cousin Elizabeth. Bernadette knew about this story in the Gospel, for she was used to saying her rosary. On the right was the beheading of St. John the Baptist, the patron saint of this parish. The neck bleeding without its head always made her shiver. In the middle, over the high altar, was a statue very like the one in the parish church of Arcizac, the land of waters and millstreams—it was St. John the Baptist baptizing Our Lord in the Jordan.

After she had found her foster mother's lost rosary, Bernadette gave one longing look at the altar and at the golden statue of Our Lady's Assumption.

"Oh, when shall I know my catechism by heart?" she said to herself. "When shall I be allowed to come to Holy Communion?" The catechism was difficult to learn by heart, for it was all in French. She had tried so often to learn off a few phrases and had failed.

Before leaving the church she caught sight of something charming on the front of the altar itself—a tiny little John the Baptist, barely two years old, holding a baby lamb; such a sweet little lamb. "Oh, I must go," she said to herself, "or I'll get into trouble."

From the schoolmaster, Jean Barbet, who left a memoir, we learn something of the religious instruction which Bernadette received at Bartrès.

The curé, *M. l'Abbé* Ader, who had come to Bartrès two years before, was not a typical parish priest for a country village. He divided his time between his church and his presbytery. He was a man of prayer and study, and indeed his heart was not wholly in his parish work, for he felt the stirrings of a vocation to be a religious. He wanted to be a Benedictine monk and was only awaiting the permission of his bishop, Monseigneur Laurence.

Jean Barbet says in his memoir that once in the presbytery after catechism class, in the hearing of Barbet's nephew, the priest turned to his servant and said, "Look at that little girl over thére. If the Blessed Virgin appeared to anyone, she would choose a child like her." The little girl was Bernadette. Indeed the curé said to Jean Barbet himself with regard to Bernadette: "To me she seems like a flower, all fragrant with the divine perfume."

One day the schoolmaster had to take the priest's place at catechism, and when he gave an account of the class to the curé afterwards, he said that "Bernadette found it hard to remember the catechism word for word, because she could not study it, not knowing how to read it; but she took great care to understand the sense of the explanations. Moreover, she was very attentive, and especially very devout and very modest."

The Blessed Virgin Mary had appeared to two children in September 1846 at La Salette, in the mountains near Grenoble. The schoolmaster assures us that the curé never spoke of this to the children, nor did he speak of the newly proclaimed dogma of the Immaculate Conception.[3]

---

[3] The definition of the dogma of the Immaculate Conception, made by Pope Pius IX on December 8, 1854, reads as follows: "We declare, announce and define that the doctrine which states that the Blessed Virgin Mary was preserved in the first instant of her

But by reciting the rosary from her childhood, Bernadette had been preparing herself to receive the message of high mysteries. "The rosary," Père Garrigou-Lagrange, O.P., has written, "is a prayer which gradually takes the form of an intimate conversation with Jesus and Mary. It is easy to see how saintly souls have found in it a school of contemplation . . . the words are a kind of melody, which soothes the ear and isolates us from the world around us, the fingers being occupied meanwhile in allowing one bead after another to slip through. Thus the imagination is kept tranquil and the mind and the will are set free to be united to God."[4]

Unlearned though she was, Bernadette must also have been taught the elements of the doctrine about original sin, by which as a daughter of Eve she had been stained before her baptism.[5]

Near Assumption-tide, in mid-August, Père Lagües, thinking he could economize on the pay of the summer day-labourer who usually looked after the lambs, arranged that the man should help with the harvest while the flock was entrusted to Bernadette. At first Bernadette's heart began to sink when she heard this, for she knew it would mean no more school or catechism. But she must soon have learnt that it was a good thing. So many French saints have been shepherds in their youth, as if living the words of Scripture —"I will lead him into a silent place and speak to his heart."

---

conception by a singular grace and privilege of God Omnipotent and because of the merits of Jesus Christ the Saviour of the human race, free from all stain of original sin, is revealed by God and must therefore be believed firmly and with constancy by all the faithful."

[4] *La Mère du Sauveur* (Paris, Editions du Cerf, 1948); English translation by Bernard J. Kelly, C.S.Sp., *The Mother of the Saviour* (Dublin, Golden Eagle Books, 1949).

[5] The Penny Catechism defines original sin as: "That guilt and stain of sin which we inherit from Adam, who was the origin and head of all mankind." And the Council of Trent, upon whose definitions this catechism is based, said: "If anyone shall assert that the prevarication of Adam injured himself only, and not his posterity; and that the holiness and justice received of God, which he lost, he lost for himself alone, and not for us also; or that he, being defiled by the sin of disobedience, has only transferred death and not sin also, which is the death of the soul; let him be anathema."

St. Vincent de Paul, St. Germaine Cousin, St. Geneviève and St. Joan of Arc all kept sheep. So did the Curé d'Ars.

Until this time, the child had received a severe training. She had had two very bad illnesses, which had left her enfeebled for life. She had known the depths of poverty, homelessness and public humiliation. She had been disciplined to make herself useful in a household and to look after other children. She was practical and matter-of-fact; not at all a dreamy child. She could care for the sick, cook and mend and sew—mend clothes so beautifully that the darns were like embroideries. And now, on the brink of great things, her soul needed a period of solitude and silence, in order to become more attentive to God's whisper. (Many years later, a friend, Julie Garros, said to her that shepherdesses were especially pleasing to God. Bernadette replied abruptly: "How can you prove that?" No, she was no dreamer.)

Bernadette would leave the house at dawn, accompanied by the sheepdog, Pigou. In her basket was some knitting or mending, and the provisions Marie Lagües had given her for the day. These latter tended to be rather meagre, and when she passed by the neighbours' houses, the women (aware, perhaps, of Marie's frugality) always stopped her and gave her some little extra tit-bit, for which she thanked them with her sweet smile. (She was, and ever remained, very grateful, rather like St. Teresa, who said her affection could be captured by a sardine!) Marie Lagües had usually provided roast maize paste with some soup in a pot and a slice or two of bacon. The kindly women would give her white bread or a little tureen filled from their own *pot-au-feu*, and some fruit. She used to say, smiling, "I will eat my maize bread first and leave your good white bread to the last."

The sheep's feet on the road sounded like hailstones falling in summer. She would lead them through the dew to the heath of Puyono, where the wild thyme was delicious for cropping. If it rained, she would go to shelter in the thatched hut, which is still there among the trees, on the wooded slope.

From that height she could almost see the road from

Lourdes, and every day her father, who missed her keenly, would come and see her. She would greet him with a cry of joy (she said afterwards that he was her favourite parent), and if he looked hungry, she would insist that he eat some of her provisions—"It is more than I can eat myself." One day he found her looking very distressed.

"Has anybody made you unhappy, my Bernadette?" he asked anxiously.

"Look, Father," she said, "all my lambs' backs are green."

He tried not to smile. The dealer had just marked them all, but Bernadette did not know this.

"Ah," he replied, very seriously. "Green on the back? That is because they have eaten too much grass."

"Could they die of it?"

"Perhaps."

And Bernadette burst into tears.

"Come now—don't cry," he said, laughing. "It is the dealer who has marked them like that."

(When, many years later, the companion to whom she related this story said: "You were simple to believe such a thing," she replied, "What can you expect? I had never told a lie and I could not imagine that what my father said was not true.")

Small and tranquil as she was, the birds hardly noticed her—the birds of those lovely Pyrenees—and she was able to watch them—the blue and green chaffinches, the red, black, yellow and white goldfinches, the warblers, the kingfishers, the orioles, the wagtails, the thrushes, the blackbirds, the black and green woodpeckers, the bullfinches. The vultures and the sparrowhawks stayed away. She watched the light change in the ashes, the poplars and the sweet chestnuts, and in that part of the world with its immense vistas, she saw a wonderful variety of sunsets.

It was the youngest lambs of her flock which delighted her. The sheep left the mountains at the end of August and went to the meadows. The lambs were born any time between September and May. They were most lively and affectionate, as they frolicked around her, and even mischievous. One can imagine her singing a shepherd's song of the district:

> "U moutou éstélat
> De blanc e négre barragat
> Soy fatigat dou cérca
> E l'abéret troubat?"[6]

She had a collection of tiny cheap medals of the Blessed Virgin, and, generous as she was with everything else, these she refused to give to a little friend, Jeanne-Marie Caudeban, who came to join her occasionally on the heath. (Many years later, Jeanne-Marie told Père Cros that Bernadette was "good, simple and quiet.")

One day she made a shrine to the Virgin Mary under an old chestnut tree. She had just heaped a pile of stones and was putting little bouquets of flowers on it, when all of a sudden she heard a voice behind her: "Well, Bernadette!" and there was Julie Garros, a naughty young friend from Lourdes.

"Oh, Julie, I'm glad to see you! Look at my little lamb. Isn't he sweet?"

"And why do you love him more than the others?" asked Julie.

"Because he is the smallest. I love everything that is small."

The lamb struggled out of her arms and skipped into the air. Bernadette called him gently by his name. He ran towards her. She gave him a little piece of bread sprinkled with salt, which he loved. Alas, he did not thank her for her kindness. With his head down, he started to butt the altar, and everything collapsed.

Bernadette and Julie laughed. Bernadette said, "Yes, he looks very innocent but he's the most mischievous of the flock. Now look, if I call the flock, he always comes ahead of the others, and see how he attacks me." She called the flock and the lamb in question jumped up before the others, rushed at Bernadette and made her fall to her knees.

"Oh well," said Julie, "I suppose that's his way of caressing you."

---

[6] I gleaned this from the aged housekeeper of the present Curé of Bartrès. Her mother was present at some of the apparitions.

"Probably," replied Bernadette, unmoved, "but he's rather rough. However, I reward him all the same."

Pyrenean shepherds tell one how delightful lambs are to watch, hour after hour: they are artful and affectionate, their frolics are ridiculous, and they play in groups, like children.

But most of the time Bernadette was alone in the great summer and autumn silence of the Pyrenees. When the church bell rang the Angelus, the labourers in the harvest fields would take off their berets, make a sign of the cross and say a prayer, and Bernadette would pray too. The peasants of the place were exceptionally devout. They had been taught to honour the sign of the cross by Père Ader. He had a great respect for this. He would say: "You make the sign of the cross most irreverently—much too quickly—as if you were flicking away flies. That is not the sign of our redemption. Do it as I do." And he would cross himself very slowly and majestically, and Bernadette would imitate him.

Suffering and loneliness were her lot at Bartrès. Basile Lagües was closefisted: and there is evidence to show that he dealt roughly with her if she made a mistake with the lambs. Her foster mother now treated her coldly. Marie's brother, the newly ordained Abbé Aravant, noticed this and spoke to the couple about it when he stayed there, but without much result. Bernadette never complained to her father: she said to her cousin, Jeanne-Marie Védère: "If you but think: God allows it—then you don't complain."

The evenings were the most trying time: her foster mother, seeing her grief at being kept away from catechism class, would try to teach her the catechism from seven till nine, but she never had any success because the child was by then too weary. Sometimes in despair she would throw the book down and say: "You'll never know anything," and Bernadette, in tears, would hug her to mollify her.

Abbé Ader left the village in November to become a monk, and he was not replaced for some time. There was nobody else to teach the child. Bernadette grew desperate. When Aunt Bernarde, her godmother, came to see her in November, Bernadette drew her aside and whispered in her ear: "Aunt Barnarde, I must learn the catechism. They promised to send me to catechism here, and to school, and I've hardly been at all. I must make my First Communion next year. Can't you ask them at home to fetch me back again?"

"But my poor child, there is hardly anything to eat at the *cachot*. Here, at least, you've got a certain amount of good food and pure air. It's so unhealthy at home for you with your asthma and your cough. Try and be patient."

"Oh, do tell them, Aunt Bernarde! I don't mind about the food and the air. What I want is Holy Communion."

But Aunt Bernarde was unable to persuade Louise, who had said some time before that Marie Lagües could have more of her children, besides Bernadette.

A little before Christmas a woman from Lourdes was passing by the heath and came to see Bernadette amongst her lambs. Bernadette said to her, "I'm sick of being here. Please tell my parents and ask them, if you please, to come and fetch me. I want to return to Lourdes, to go to school and to prepare for Holy Communion."

Christmas passed: the parents ignored this appeal. During the second half of January, 1858, the maidservant, Jeanne-Marie Garros, told Bernadette that she was going in to Lourdes.

"Oh," cried the child, "beg my mother to come and fetch me!" When the servant returned that evening, Bernadette whispered in her ear, "Well, is she going to fetch me?" Jeanne-Marie shook her head. "I don't think so. She wants you to stay here." Before she went to sleep that night, Bernadette had made up her mind. On the following Sunday she went bravely to her master and asked his permission to go to Lourdes. He said, "You may go, but you must come back tomorrow."

Bernadette's father proved easier to persuade than her mother, for he had once heard Marie Lagües speaking sharply to his little girl, and had never felt easy since. She did not return to Bartrès until the Wednesday. Great was the wrath of the Lagües family when she calmly announced, "I must go back home. *Monsieur le curé* is going to prepare the children for their First Communion, and if I go to Lourdes I will be able to make mine."

She left, very probably, on Thursday, the 28th of January. "He hath filled the hungry with good things and the rich He hath sent empty away." This sickly, undergrown, ignorant little girl, who sprang from a poverty-stricken family which had lost its good name, was soon speeding down the wintry road to fulfil her spiritual destiny.

3.

BERNADETTE GOES
GATHERING FIREWOOD

Thursday, February the 11th, 1858, the great day, the first day of the apparitions. All Bernadette's short life of fourteen years had been one long preparation for that day. She had been prepared by every kind of suffering. First, the searching, searing pain of poverty—Léon Bloy, above all, has shown how this can sift a soul through a very fine sieve. She had known successive humiliations, sharp descents from plenty to want. She had known disgrace through her father's arrest; she had known loneliness and neglect; she had known frustration, and the bewildering pain of the loss of the affection which a second mother had shown her when she was a small child. Very young she had learned to be responsible for others; to look after her brothers, to find food for the household. She had learnt the meaning of tasks much above her strength and her tiny stature. And throughout it all, the long hopelessness. Sometimes she felt certain that she would never be able to replace the clothes she wore, that the family could never buy new ones. It was just as well that she had stopped growing.

And so, on this cold winter's morning, about a fortnight after her return from Bartrès, she was ready for her destiny.

A thick fog filled the little town, a drenching fog like a fine drizzle. As the morning wore on, thin rays of sunlight pierced through. There was not a breath of wind. It was a school holiday and the feast of St. Germaine Cousin, the shepherdess. François Soubirous, weakened through giving up his share of food to his children, remained in bed. He might as well stay there instead of dissipating his ebbing

strength, particularly as there was no prospect of work anywhere. The hearth was empty and there was no fire. The
night before, Mère Soubirous had said: "If it's a fine day
tomorrow, I will go and fetch a bundle of faggots." Towards eleven o'clock she was just preparing to go and glean
in the woods, when her pet aversion appeared on the door-
step, little Jeanne Abadie, a school-friend of Toinette's,
from the rue du Bourg, a vindictive, rather coarse-tongued
child, nicknamed "Baloum" by her parents. She often came
to spend the day with the girls when she was in charge of
her little brother—"as if the place weren't overcrowded
enough," thought Louise to herself. A pity, too, that a passage connected Jeanne's street with the rue des Petits-Fossés,
lying parallel.

"Where are you off to?" asked Jeanne.

"I'm going to the woods," she replied shortly. Jeanne exclaimed, "We'll go, too!" glancing at the Soubirous girls.
Bernadette, who had lived a very outdoor life up till now,
was delighted at the prospect of escape into the fresh air.
Unfortunately, she had a cold that day. Her mother turned
to her and said: "I'd rather you didn't go out in this bad
weather." (When Jeanne made it evident that she would
join the expedition, Louise had decided that she herself
would not go.)

"But Mama," she replied, "I was out in any weather at
Bartrès."

"Very well, then, but on condition you wear the hood,
and your stockings too."

"Yes, Mama," replied the child, "and I will take a basket
to pick up any bones we might find on the way."

With clogs clacking on the cobblestones of the slimy
street, they made their way to the forest through the Porte
du Baous, along the chemin du Bois and across the Vallée
de Paradis, till they reached the old Roman bridge over the
Gave. They picked up sticks and old bones as they went.
Under the bridge, just as they were about to cross it, they
saw a distant relation of the Soubirous', an old woman nicknamed Pigouno (Magpie). She was washing some mysterious messy stuff in the river. She looked up and said to them:
"What are you doing here on such a cold day?"

"We're looking for wood."

"You should go to Monsieur de Lafitte's meadow. He's just cut some trees. You'll find some wood there."

Bernadette said, "Oh, no. We'd only be taken for thieves." Then she put her arm around Pigouno's neck in a friendly way and said, "Tata, who are you washing these guts for?" and Pigouno replied, "For Monsieur Clarens."

Pigouno assured them that the gleanings in Monsieur de Lafitte's meadow were communal property and that they wouldn't be thieving. They bade her farewell, crossed the old bridge and made their way towards the field. This could only be reached by crossing a footbridge over the stream by Savy's mill, which was next to a sawmill. The meadow, planted with poplars and beech trees, was practically surrounded by the Gave and the millstream. This millstream joined the Gave at the extreme westernmost point of the field, under the rocky promontory of Massabielle.

Bernadette now came to Massabielle for the first time.

On that day of all days, the water-mill was being repaired, so the sluice gates were closed and there was very little water in the stream. The miller, Nicolau, said to one of his sons: "Who are these children?".

"They are the little Soubirous girls, with their friend. They must be going to pick up wood."

"Oh, we'll let them go. They can't take a lot and we'll always have enough for ourselves."

Bernadette pointed to the millstream going towards Massabielle and said to Toinette, "Supposing we followed it along its course?" Toinette replied: "And if it goes as far as Bétharram, will you follow it as far as that?" There was plenty of dead wood under the poplar trees, but Bernadette had not yet collected much.

At length they reached the grotto of Massabielle. They stood on the tiny tongue of land facing the millstream, which separated them from the grotto. Jeanne spied a bone inside the grotto. "Oh, there's a lovely bone," she cried, "I must go and fetch it." She took off her clogs, and so did Toinette. Then both the girls threw them across the millstream.

The ground inside the grotto rose gently, as in an amphitheatre, the floods of the Gave having formed large steps covered with sand and pebbles. There was also a huge stone very like a table, and other blocks of stone just outside. It was a wild place. There were no great trees there, but in front of the grotto, on the other side of the Gave, there was a row of tall poplars. (Oh, how Bernadette grew to love those poplars!)

Bravely Toinette and Jeanne stepped into the millstream, icy cold from all the snows. Toinette, who often behaved in a wild way, lifted her skirts up to her knees. "Put your skirt down," ordered Bernadette.

"Oh, how icy it is!" cried both the girls, tears coming to their eyes. Bernadette shivered at the prospect. She already had a cold, and she was frightened in case the shock of the icy water might bring on an attack of asthma. She called imploringly to her sister: "Heave some big stones into the water." Toinette took no notice. She was seated on the sand of the other bank and had wrapped her feet in her skirt to try to warm them up a little. So Bernadette called to Baloum, who was so strong and hearty. "I say, Jeanne, help me to cross the canal." Jeanne replied, "He! *Pèt dé périclé!* You can do the same as me; otherwise stay there, if you want to."

"Oh, Baloum," said Bernadette, "if you want to swear, you can go away from here." But the two girls took no notice of her. Already they were picking up sticks on the opposite bank of the Gave. They were going to take themselves off for the next quarter of an hour.

The little sick girl was left behind, and seemingly in no mood for ecstasy, preoccupied as she was by the wholly practical problem of how to cross the millstream. "Ah, well," she thought, "I'll have to do as they did, and risk a worse cold."

It was twelve o'clock, midday. Just then the Angelus rang out from Lourdes. Leaning against the rock a little to the left of the niche, Bernadette at length resolved to take off her sabots and stockings. She was just beginning to remove her first stocking, when suddenly she heard the noise of wind such as heralds a storm. The sound seemed to come from all the neighbouring hillsides, and just as suddenly it seemed to fade away in all directions at once. She turned to look at the poplars and beeches of the meadow. They were motionless. Without letting her glance rest on it she had, however, vaguely glimpsed a movement of branches and thorns in the direction of the grotto.

She went on taking off her stocking, and she was just putting a foot into the water when she heard the same rushing sound. She raised her eyes and saw the curtain of branches and brambles below the niche in the grotto blowing restlessly hither and thither. Nothing around it was stirring. All was still.

Then suddenly, behind these branches, in the opening, she saw a light brighter than the sun and yet soft to the eyes, like the light at sunset. And immediately, as if springing from the light in the niche, a very young girl hardly taller than herself, whose face was as white as wax. Instinctively Bernadette felt frightened. How had the girl reached such a spot? she wondered. She had an oval face of great sweetness of expression. Her eyes were blue.

Ever afterwards, when Bernadette was asked if this lady was beautiful, she seemed to go into an ecstasy. She said that to have any idea of her beauty one would have to go to Heaven. Many years later, when she was very near her death, a child of five asked her in the infirmary, "Was the Lady beautiful?" and Bernadette replied, "So beautiful that to see her again one would be willing to die."

The girl was young. Bernadette used to say, *"Elle est bien mignonette,"* which is a literal translation of the *"muy niña"* of St. Teresa of Avila, who said: "It was exceeding great, the beauty that I saw in Our Lady . . . clothed in white, in most resplendent light. Our Lady seemed to me a very young child." Or again, we have our own English fourteenth-century anchoress, Dame Julian of Norwich, who says in *The Revelations of Divine Love:* "I saw her ghostly in bodily likeness, a simple maid and a meek, youthful of age and little grown above a child, in the stature that she was when she conceived."

Bernadette wanted to call out to her sister and Jeanne, but she had lost her voice. The girl greeted her graciously, holding out her arms to her, and stretching her hands out, as if inviting her to come a little nearer. (Bernadette always remembered this gesture.) But she dared not move. She began to think she must be seeing something that was not there. Several times she rubbed her eyes, but no, the girl was still there, smiling at her most graciously and always seeming to invite her to draw near. Bernadette was still afraid. But it was not a kind of fear that she might have had at other times in her life, because now she could have remained there always, looking at "that one" (*aquéro*);[1] whereas, when you are frightened, you go away quickly.

And then she was inspired to pray. She slipped her hand into her pinafore pocket, took the rosary which she usually carried with her, and knelt down. She tried to make the sign of the cross, but she could not raise her hand to her forehead. The lady, however, moved and placed herself so that she could be seen from the side, and turned towards her. A lovely rosary of white and gold had been hanging from her right arm; this she now held in her hand. She made the sign of the cross, as if she too were about to pray. Bernadette's hand trembled. She tried again to make the sign of the cross, and this time was able to do so, after which she was afraid no more. She said the Aves. The girl let her rosary beads slip through her fingers, but she did not move her lips. As Bernadette recited her rosary, she looked avidly at the vision. "*Je regardais tant que je pouvais!*—I looked as hard as I could." All her soul was in her eyes. She gazed and gazed and gazed. (St. Peter Damien declared that to see the Blessed Virgin on earth was to enjoy in this world the greatest bliss which the blessed have in Heaven, after that of the Beatific Vision.)

Afterwards, under cross-examination by the Lourdes police, Bernadette said, "I cannot explain these things to you, but what I can say for sure is that she is real and alive, that she moves and smiles and speaks just as we do."

Bernadette had never seen anything so beautiful in all her

[1] At first Bernadette called the lady of her visions "*aquéro*," then "*petite demoiselle*," and finally, "*la dame*," influenced, it would seem, by the reverence of those who had immediately jumped to the conclusion that it was indeed the Virgin.

life. Her hungry eyes took in all the details: the lady's rosary
was unearthly in its beauty, the chain was golden, and the
beads white, quite large and widely spaced; the material of
her white robe was quite indescribable, spun in the looms
of Paradise whereon are fashioned lilies of the valley, rain-
bows and the robes of archangels, of whose clothing Joan of
Arc would not speak to her tormentors. (Later, after much
cross-questioning, Bernadette granted at last that tulle had
some slight likeness to the airy texture of the material, but
even so, she said, the comparison was poor.)

The robe reached to the girl's feet and only the toes were
visible. On her feet, golden roses, "such as one never sees on
earth."

(The Jesuit Père Cros has said that these roses symbolized
that mystical and living Rose which leaves in its wake the
perfume of its virtues, in particular the virtue of charity of
which she is queen.

The Song of Songs cries: "My dove, in the clefts of the
rock, in the hollow places of the wall, show me thy face, let
thy voice sound in mine ears, for thy voice is sweet and thy
face comely." To mystical souls drawn to contemplative
prayer, a riven rock often symbolizes the cleft side of Christ,
revealing His heart. The Virgin too was mingled in this great
symbolism of grace which had been prefigured in the Old
Testament, when water gushed from the rock for the Israel-
ites, and in the New Testament when Christ told the Samari-
tan woman to ask Him for the living water.)

Bernadette went on drinking in all the details of the lady's
appearance. Her gown was closed high up at the neck by a
white draw-string. A thin white veil, covering her head so
that very little of her hair could be seen, came down over
her shoulders and arms, almost to the hem of her dress. The
broad blue girdle of her robe was not knotted, but simply
tied, and fell below her knees.

(It is not surprising, considering how young the lady
looked, that Bernadette had no remote intimation that she
might be the Virgin Mary, and referred to her at first simply
as "that one," until she was reproved. Only two years previously Mgr. Malou of Bruges had said that Mary, in this
mystery of the Immaculate Conception, must be represented

"in her first youth, at the age of fourteen or fifteen, in the period which precedes the Annunciation. It is not surprising that so many have found this youth in her so disconcerting and have tried to elude it."

Many have said that probably Mary appeared in a spiritual body—that body of which St. Paul speaks in his First Epistle to the Corinthians,[2] but Père Laurentin has declared that "divers reasons bring me to believe that the Virgin appeared to Bernadette in her own body and in no other manner." Again, he says: "The apparition of Lourdes is the Virgin 'younger than sin.'" He speaks of "that childlike leap towards God" which the world had in the beginning.)

The girl and the child fingered their beads to the same cadence and rhythm, but when the girl reached the "Gloria Patri" she bowed and her lips moved.

(The risen body has the power to deceive the eye of the onlooker. Mary Magdalen on Easter morning thought Our Lord was the gardener, and the disciples walking to Emmaus on Easter Sunday evening did not know that the Lord walked with them. The rosebud encloses substantially within itself the full-blown rose. The Church in the Office of Our Lady says: *"Juvenili videbatur aspectu"*—"in face she seemed young." *"Juvenilis"* is a well-chosen word, for with the Latins and with the French, it refers to adolescence.)

When Bernadette had finished saying her rosary, the girl greeted her, smiling. She withdrew into the niche: after a while the light faded and then vanished altogether.

When Toinette and Jeanne had first disappeared along the Gave on a little path covered by brushwood, they had turned their heads. Toinette saw Bernadette kneeling on the stones and said to Jeanne: "Look at Bernadette over there saying her prayers," and Jeanne replied, *"Dévote!* Let's leave her alone. That's the only thing she knows how to do." And they went on picking up wood for the next quarter of an hour.

On the way back to the grotto, they glimpsed Bernadette as she was coming to the end of her ecstasy. They saw her

[2] "It is sown a natural body, it shall rise a spiritual body" (I Cor. xv. 44).

through the bare shrubs, still on her knees and looking towards one side of the niche. Toinette called her three times, "Bernadette! Bernadette! Bernadette!" She did not reply and did not turn her head. As Toinette drew nearer still, she twice threw a little stone at her sister; once she struck her shoulder. Bernadette did not move. She was as white as if she were dead. Toinette got frightened, but Jeanne said: "If she were dead, she'd be lying down." But Toinette, full of anxiety, wanted to cross the stream.

All of a sudden Bernadette seemed to come back to earth. She looked over at both girls. Toinette said, "What are you doing there?" Bernadette answered, "Nothing." Toinette said, "How stupid you are to pray there." Bernadette answered, "Prayers are good everywhere," and she stepped into the brook to cross over to them. As she did so, she was astonished to find that the water was lukewarm, although the other two had shuddered with cold as they had crossed it a quarter of an hour before.

When she reached the other side of the stream Bernadette sat down on a rock, without appearing in the least chilly, and put on her stockings. Then she said to the other girls, who were romping and fooling in the grotto: "Did you see anything?" They replied, "No. Did you?" She answered, "No, nothing." Then Jeanne Abadie started to scold and grumble. She said to Bernadette, "You should have stayed at home. You haven't done any work. You'd have done far better to pick up wood than go down on your knees and pray."

Toinette pressed her sister to explain herself, but Jeanne just scoffed at her. "She hasn't seen anything, she just didn't want to pick up wood. Your mother will scold you." Toinette said to Bernadette, "You've been frightened."

Jeanne was in a hurry to go home, so she now set off ahead of the two little Soubirous girls, carrying her bundle of wood on her head and the basket of bones on her arm. She climbed the steep path on the right. Toinette and Bernadette divided their faggots into two equal heaps. They too decided not to go back by the meadow.

As they climbed, Bernadette, usually so fragile, seemed to possess surprising energy and agility. (The Jesuit mystical theologian Père Poulain, in his great book, *The Graces of Interior Prayer,* has invaluable observations to make on the revivifying and strengthening effect of ecstasy on health.) It was the strong Toinette who was unable to climb the ridge and who dropped her bundle of sticks three times. Her sister went back to fetch her and carried it for her. Toinette exclaimed, "I am stronger than you, and yet I cannot carry my sticks!" They placed their bundles on their heads.

When they were on the road, Bernadette could not contain herself any longer. She said, "I will tell you something, but I don't want you to speak of it at home, because Mother would scold me." Toinette promised and Bernadette went on: "I saw a lady dressed in white with a blue sash, and a yellow rose on each foot." Toinette exclaimed, "You're saying that to frighten me, but I don't care, now that we're on the road." Bernadette said no more until she got to the sawmill, and then she said, "I'm tired, let's have a little rest." So they both sat down by the wayside. Bernadette said to Toinette, *"Mon Dieu,* how I should love to go back again to the bank of Massabielle."

At that, Toinette took a twig from her bundle and struck her sister with it, she was so angry with her for talking nonsense. Bernadette said, "It's perfectly true. I couldn't make the sign of the cross until the lady did, and then something made it possible for me to lift my hand."

They started to walk again. Between the old bridge and the rue des Petits-Fossés, Bernadette hardly spoke. Toinette noticed that her face was somehow different: more serious. It was evident that she was wholly absorbed in her own thoughts.

When they got home they stood their bundles of sticks against the door. The whole family was at home. François Soubirous was still in bed. Toinette went to the cupboard and helped herself to some maize paste. Bernadette took a piece of bread. She went back to the passage to eat alone, as if she hated to be with the others.

Louise seized Toinette to comb her unruly locks. Three times Toinette cleared her throat, as if she were starting to say something, then deciding to hold it back. Her mother said, "Why do you keep doing that? Are you ill?" Toinette hesitated, then said, "No. But listen: I have something to tell you that Bernadette told me." Her face turned to the window, she repeated everything in a whisper to Louise. When Louise had heard her out, she cried, "Oh, unhappy woman that I am! What's this you're telling me?" and she called angrily to Bernadette to come into the room.

Bernadette then told her mother what she had told Toinette. Louise started to upbraid them both, then she seized a stick and gave each of them a few whacks. Toinette turned on Bernadette and cried, "This is all your fault," but Bernadette made no reply. It was as if nothing could really matter any more.

Louise's anger left her as suddenly as it had come. Looking at Bernadette's designed face, she softened towards the child. (After all, she was never known to have lied to her parents.) "Your eyes deceived you," she said. "It was a white stone that you saw."

"No," replied Bernadette, "she had a beautiful face."

Louise said, after a silence, "You must pray to God. Perhaps it is the soul of one of our relations in Purgatory."

From his bed François said to Bernadette, "You're already starting to do stupid things at your age," and he gave both the girls a scolding. (Actually he was rather disturbed: he feared that the lady might be something evil.)

In the afternoon, Jeanne returned with her basket of bones, and all three children went to Alexine Baron to sell them. With the proceeds they were able to buy a loaf of bread, which they took back to the house to eat. It was only then that Jeanne Abadie heard Bernadette's story.

Bernadette knew her Credo, her Pater Noster and her Ave Maria. She was also in the habit of saying a prayer the full meaning of which she did not yet realize: "O Mary, conceived without sin, pray for us who have recourse to thee." That evening, as they were all kneeling by the fireside to say their prayers, no sooner had Bernadette spoken those familiar words than she began to weep. Louise was so much upset that she went out to tell the neighbours.

When quiet had been restored, Louise said to Bernadette,

"You must promise me not to go back to the grotto. We are quite unhappy enough here without all your tricks." And poor Bernadette promised. (Her father said later that she had never disobeyed them in her life.) She went to bed heavy-hearted, and she did not sleep.

4.

ECSTASY

On that evening of the 11th of February, Jeanne Abadie was unable to hold her tongue, in spite of her many promises to keep the secret. She told all her little friends in the rue du Bourg, where she lived. The next morning, Friday, all the schoolgirls who attended the Hospice run by the Sisters of Nevers were in the know. One of the more sensible girls warned Bernadette that she would do well to tell a nun about it. She replied, *"You* tell Sister Damien." The girls did so, all speaking at once in higgledy-piggledy and inaccurate fashion, so that Bernadette had to keep interrupting and saying, "I did not say that—but this." Sister Damien realized that the child was completely sincere. However, she said to her, "Bernadette, my child, don't speak about this. They'll only make fun of you." A murmur of approval arose from some of the children, who despised poor Bernadette for being so backward, for not knowing any French and for being unable to learn her catechism. As soon as Sister Damien's back was turned, the chemist's nine-year-old daughter, Sophie Pailhasson, went up to Bernadette and hit her in the face. But Bernadette was as calm and as unmoved as ever. She was living in a world of joy; she had her treasure, turning it over and over in her mind, and she did not care what happened to her.

Rumours of what had happened at the grotto spread among the boys, and when Jean-Marie went to the Christian Brothers' school he was asked by Brother Léobard, "Will you tell your sister that I shall be very pleased to see her?"

Bernadette went that very afternoon and told him all that had happened at the grotto. However, she was very discreet and reserved with everybody else.

By Saturday morning she felt drawn to return to the grotto. (This strange attraction was to last to the end.) She said to Toinette: "I feel as though something were calling me back to Massabielle." Toinette noticed that she was more serious. (Usually she was a very gay and mischievous child —so mischievous, indeed, that Frère Léobard was a little shocked by her account of the happenings at the grotto, and for a long time could not believe in the reality of her vision.)

On Saturday evening, she went to the parish church of St. Pierre to Abbé Pomian's confessional. Mademoiselle Perard of Lourdes, who later became a Sister of St. Vincent de Paul, overheard her speaking very loud, describing her vision. Abbé Pomian, who was Bernadette's confessor, was a plump, energetic, kindly and charming priest. During the cholera epidemic, he had distinguished himself by his zeal. He taught catechism to the pupils at the Hospice and trained a very good choir at the parish church. He listened carefully to the little girl, whom he could hardly see on the other side of the grille and whom he did not recognize; then he asked her permission to tell his pastor, the Abbé Peyramale. Bernadette said "Yes."

The Abbé Peyramale was a typical French curé of the old school, harsh and authoritative in his bearing. Bernadette was frightened to death of him.

Sunday, February the 14th, was the last Sunday before Lent, and usually a day of festivities in Lourdes. All the Soubirous went to High Mass at the parish church. After Mass, the parents went home, leaving the older children to amuse themselves as they saw fit.

About a dozen fellow pupils surrounded Bernadette. Their names were: Toinette and Jeanne; Augustine Sarrat, Catherine Mengot, Marie Hillot, Pauline Bourdeu, Justine Soubies, Thérèse Courreau, Antoinette Cazalas, Annette Courèges, and Catherine Grammont. They all cried out: "We want to come to the grotto and see the lady too!"

Bernadette replied, "I want very much to go, but I daren't ask my mother."

"Oh come on," they said. "We'll come with you and persuade her." So they trooped off like a little band.

At the *cachot* Louise was already at work, preparing a good soup whose ingredients were rye bread, bacon, cabbage and goose fat. François was out, grooming Cazenave's horses to bring in a few sous. Louise was bending over the fire when the tiny room was invaded by the children. She turned around a little impatiently when, all talking at once, they asked if her two daughters might go to Massabielle. "No!" she said. "You'll fall into the river—it's unsafe around there. Besides, that might be an evil spirit. It's risky to have anything to do with such things."

"Oh please, Mère Soubirous!" they all cried, and one of them added, "We won't fall into the river, we promise you."

"But you'll be late for Vespers if you go," Louise objected.

"No, we promise we'll come back in time."

"Mind that you do," Louise said automatically. Overwhelmed by the swarm of children in her tiny room, she was losing control of the situation. Now she recovered herself and said to Bernadette, "No, I don't really think so. Go and ask your father. He's in Cazenave's stable."

François Soubirous said, "No." But Cazenave, who was within hearing, said gently, "Let the child go. If the lady is carrying a rosary, she can't be an evil spirit."

François Soubirous, who seems to have been, from the first, more impressed and upset by the whole thing than he had let anyone see, was now almost in tears. Finally he said that they could go for a quarter of an hour. The children complained that that was not enough and begged him to give them more time. He made a despairing gesture and the little group ran back to the rue des Petits-Fossés.

"We can go!" Toinette and Bernadette cried to Louise.

"Oh well," said Louise with a sigh, "if your father says so."

Suddenly Toinette had a scruple. "But supposing it is something evil?"

"Ah," said Marie Hillot. "Let's take some holy water."

Louise searched the cupboard. "Here's a little flask," she said. "Get it filled."

They all ran to the church, where they filled the flask

from the holy-water stoup. Then they set off in two groups for Massabielle.

This time they took the steep road instead of going by way of the meadow. On the way they were joined by Marie Labayle and Cyprine Gesta. These two walked with Jeanne Abadie, who stayed a little way behind the others.

Many years later, Toinette said: "There were about twenty of us—all poor, and all the others a little older than I was." For the most part they were silent, tense with eagerness to discover whether Bernadette had spoken the truth. They were a little anxious; in fact some of them were secretly afraid.

When Bernadette and her companions arrived at the corner of the wood path where you turn to go down to Massabielle, they heard some men cry out to them: "Don't go any further, the Virgin will get you." (This was the first time that Bernadette had any notion that it might be the Virgin.) The incident increased the girls' fear.

As Bernadette neared the sacred spot, she went faster and outdistanced the others. When she got to the perpendicular slope, she ran down the zigzags, while the others behind her clung to shrubs. When they got to the grotto, Bernadette was already kneeling there. She made all the others kneel down and take out their rosaries. There was a hushed expectancy amongst the kneeling girls. What was going to happen? All of a sudden, after having said twelve Ave Marias, Bernadette cried out, "There's a shining light." (She thought all the others could see just as clearly as she did. The lady was there.) After a moment she added, "Look at her. She has her rosary twisted round her right arm. She's looking at us."

Marie Hillot gave the flask of holy water to Bernadette and said to her, "Throw some at her." Bernadette rose from her knees, walked a few steps towards the niche and was almost touching the wild rosebush, when she sprinkled the lady, crying out loudly, "If you are from God, come closer."

Marie Hillot asked, "Is she there?" Bernadette replied, "Yes, she's smiling." Then she went on to describe how the lady was dressed. (She had not dared to say the second part of the exorcising prayer to guard against evil spirits: "If you come from the Devil, draw back.")

The lady responded by bowing, smiling graciously and making the sign of the cross. Bernadette drew back and knelt again among her friends. Then her ecstasy began. She was silent and motionless, her eyes drinking in the vision. She hardly dared blink, let alone look away for one single fraction of a moment. Still that hushed expectancy, not unmingled with fear, among the little girls.

And then something dreadful happened. A huge stone, as large as a basket, suddenly hurtled down from the top of the rock and fell near Bernadette. She started, and then seemed to take no further notice. All the little girls cried out in fear; some ran away as fast as their legs would carry them; and others, seeing Bernadette with such a fixed gaze and such a pale face, thought that the stone had killed her and cried out: "She is dead! She is dead!" Pauline Bourdeu, who had from the outset been amongst the frightened ones, was the first to flee, and she did not dare come down again. "Ah," she thought to herself, "it must be an evil spirit."

It is most important at this point to read the mystical theologians on the phenomenon of ecstasy and its effect on Bernadette's appearance, in order clearly to distinguish it from the phenomena of hypnosis, trance and hysteria or even hallucination (of which more later). St. Teresa of Avila says that the soul seems to leave all the organs which it quickens, vital heat is lowered, accounting for the pallor, the alabaster transparency, of the ecstatic's face. Usually the body is immobilized in the attitude it was in when the rapture seized it, and the eyes are fixed on the object of contemplation. Ecstasy makes the homeliest face beautiful. Blessed Angela of Foligno, who heard Christ saying to her one day, "I love you more than anyone in the valley of Spoleto," became so beautiful during her ecstasies—her face was so illuminated and her eyes so dazzling—that her companion was almost afraid to walk with her. We have two important witnesses to Bernadette's appearance during ecstasy. Her cousin, Jeanne-Marie Védère, has written that,

". . . after giving a slight start she raised her hands and her whole being seemed to be drawn upwards. Her face, which became paler, and transparent, yearned towards somebody above her. Her cheeks were very pale, but seemed to be illuminated. There was a touch of color on her cheek-bones and lips. Her eyes, looking upwards, were wide open and seemed to spend all their strength in a longing, radiant, enraptured gaze, without a flicker of the eyelids. Two tears glistened on her cheeks, and she looked as though she were about to leave the earth. The people round about tried to read on her face what they were unable to see, and found in her ravishing beauty a pale reflection of what she was contemplating."

Abbé Laurentin, in his marvellous book *Sens de Lourdes*, points out that certain saints give us the impression that we have in some way encountered Christ, because they live Him, because their gestures, their attitudes, their whole demeanour are a reflection of the habits and ways of Christ. He says that the Apostles were imbued with this divine manner of being, which all Christians are invited to imitate. He adds that in the same way those who saw Bernadette during the apparitions had the feeling of having seen the Blessed Virgin. . . . "No doubt the Apostles unconsciously modelled their behaviour on that of Christ, long before, in the depths of their being, they lived according to the divine point of view." Similarly, Bernadette: ". . . from the first moment becomes the mirror of the Immaculate." This was seen from the very first vision, when she could make the sign of the cross only after the Virgin herself had done so. The movements and ways of Mary took possession of her. People used to say to her: "How do you make the sign of the cross?" and she would invariably reply, "I don't know. The Lady makes the sign of the cross and I do as she does."

Abbé Laurentin again says: "The gestures made in *imitation* of Mary constitute the very texture of the apparitions. They used to make all the witnesses marvel and left them with the profound impression of having seen something that was not of this world."

But we cannot blame those simple little schoolgirls for

being unable to recognize from Bernadette's strange appearance, the phenomena of the marvel of ecstasy and mystical experience.

It was Jeanne Abadie who had thrown the stone from the height. She had done it to show her resentment at being left behind. She suddenly appeared on the scene. "Oh Jeanne," cried the others, "you've killed Bernadette!" Jeanne reported many years afterwards: "Her face was shining. We were all crying." They were frightened by her pallor; she seemed like an angel. She looked as if she were dead. They started to shake her, but without effect. She continued to smile. "What shall we do?" they said to one another. "Well, we'd better try to carry her home." The strongest tried to lift her and to carry her up the steep slope, but it was impossible. No good going the other way, for the mill was working again and the stream couldn't be crossed. One of the young girls thought the best thing to do was to run back to Lourdes and tell Louise that Jeanne Abadie had killed Bernadette. They all thought that it was fright, caused by the crashing stone, which had put her into that state.

It was now about a quarter to one, and a few of the girls who had remained decided to enlist the help of the miller's mother, Madame Nicolau, and her sister, Marie. They both went down to the grotto and tried to drag Bernadette away, but they could not budge her. Then Madame Nicolau thought of her son Antoine, a sturdy young man of twenty-eight. He was just about to leave for Lourdes to enjoy the carnival revels when his mother and her sister came to fetch him. Here is his account:

" 'Bernadette Soubirous is at the grotto,' they said. 'We don't know what she can see there, but we can't get her away from the place. Do come and help us.' I immediately followed my mother and my aunt as I was, bareheaded and without a jacket, taking the dangerous little path down the cliff to the grotto. When I got there I found three or four poor girls and Toinette and Bernadette Soubirous. The latter was kneeling and was very pale. Her eyes were wide open and fixed on the niche. Her hands were joined and she was holding a rosary. Tears were running down her cheeks, but she was smiling and looked more beautiful than anything I had ever seen. I felt a mixture of sorrow and pleasure, and the whole of that day, whenever I thought of it, my heart was stirred.

"I stayed for some time without moving, just looking at her. The girls were with me; my mother and my aunt were also carried away by the sight. In spite of her smile, I was worried because she was so pale. In the end I went up to her because my mother told me to take her so that we could help her to our home. I took her by the arm, but she resisted because she wanted to stay. Her eyes were fixed on a spot above her. Not a sound came from her, but after the effort to withstand us she was rather breathless. I lifted her up first by one arm and then by the other: my mother also took an arm. As I raised her I wiped her eyes and put my hands in front of them to prevent her from seeing. I also tried to make her lower her head; but she kept lifting it up and opening her eyes again, smiling. . . . It was very difficult to make her climb the path. My mother held her by one hand and I held her by the other, and we both had to pull her along, while my aunt and the girls came behind. She was trying all the time to go back, but without saying a word. You needed to be strong to drag her. Although I'm pretty tough, I should have found it a difficult business by myself.

"All the time she was climbing, Bernadette's face remained quite colourless and she still continued to gaze upwards fixedly. When we'd reached the top I was in a sweat. My mother and I went down the wood-path as far as the mill, still dragging her after us. We asked her questions, but she didn't answer. I was upset and nervous. Her face and eyes were just the same as they had been in the grotto. Tears were rolling down her cheeks, all the time. From time to time, I put my hand in front of her eyes, and I wiped away her tears, but they did not stop until we reached the mill. Then, as she crossed the threshold, she lowered her eyes and the colour came back to her face. We took her to the kitchen and made her sit down. . . . I asked her what she could see in the hole in the rock. Something nasty? 'Oh, no,' she said, 'a beautiful lady with a rosary hanging from her arm and her hands joined.'

"As she said this, Bernadette joined her hands.

"I then went into the town, and I met in passing her god-mother [Aunt Bernarde], who kept an inn. I told her the whole thing, and she said, 'What in heaven's name is the child thinking of to be going there?' "

Père Poulain, in his fascinating book *The Graces of Interior Prayer,* speaks of the condition of ecstasy. It cannot be induced by man; it is a state given freely by God, and therefore no human being can possibly intervene or interrupt it. Often only the voice of religious obedience from a superior can bring it to a close. He also describes how it can be discerned as coming from God and not emanating from some nervous disease. True ecstasy always produces an effect of calm and dignity. (At the Sâlpetrière Hospital, on the contrary, you often see convulsive and repulsive movements among the lunatics.)

What is most remarkable about this ecstasy of Bernadette's on the 14th of February is that the Virgin Mary seems to have deigned to follow her in mid-air until she reached the mill. St. Ignatius Loyola, the founder of the Jesuit Order, and himself very knowledgeable in the discernment of spirits, tells us of a similar grace he received when he made a pilgrimage to Jerusalem: "As I was coming down from the Mount of Olives, a servant sent from the convent to follow me, came towards me, his face red with anger, an enormous stick in his hand, with which he threatened to strike me. He contented himself, however, with seizing me sharply by the arm, and he dragged me towards the town. Now, as I was going forward held fast in this way, my soul was flooded with consolation, for it seemed to me that I saw Jesus Christ all the time going before me in the air, and the vision lasted until the instant when I went into the convent."

Meanwhile the messenger despatched to Lourdes had found Louise Soubirous at the house of a neighbour and said to her: "Bernadette is at the mill. She sees a lady following her. Do come and fetch her." Louise said, *"Mon Dieu!* And I'd forbidden her to go there!" She appeared, accompanied by Cyprine Gesta, with a switch in her hand.

Jeanne Abadie, whose conscience was not clear, took to flight as quickly as her legs would carry her. As it was, the mill was crowded with people, not only those on their way to Lourdes for the carnival, who had met Bernadette being dragged to the mill, but those returning. Louise found her daughter sitting at some distance from the fire and in tears again. She started to scold her in the local dialect. *"Petit drôle"*—(which, in the Lourdes dialect, means little girl)— "so you're making everybody run after you." Bernadette stayed quite calm and replied, "But, Mama, I didn't ask anyone to follow me." Her mother lifted her switch as if to strike her. Madame Nicolau said quickly, "Louise, what are you doing? Why are you going to strike her? Your daughter is an angel from Heaven."

At these words, poor Louise collapsed into a chair and wept. After a while she took Bernadette by the hand and both of them went back to the *cachot*.

By this time the town, crowded with people, was in a turmoil. Not only the little girls who had witnessed the ecstasy, but all the others who had been at the mill and on the path started talking at once. By evening every inn was in a hubbub. Antoine Nicolau played his part in spreading the news. By nightfall the story was known in farms and hamlets as much as four miles from Lourdes. The curé of Omex heard about it from two people who had seen Bernadette in tears on the way, and some of the older inhabitants nodded their heads and remembered the prophecy that great things would take place one day at the grotto of Massabielle.

5.

THE PROMISE OF
ETERNAL BLISS

And now the child who had been on the threshold of Paradise came down to earth again. She went into the *cachot* with its damp, dirty, sweating walls. The place was overcrowded with the rest of the family.

"Now, my girl," said Louise very firmly, "this is the last time you go to Massabielle. Is that quite understood?" Just then a knock was heard at the door. Aunt Basile appeared.

"Louise," she burst out, "I beg you, keep your daughter at home!" Then, turning to Bernadette, she said, "You're going to make us all ill with the annoyances we shall have to put up with having you talked about." François then declared, "You can rest assured, Basile, that our daughter will never go to Massabielle again." Bernadette's heart sank, but she said nothing.

On Monday morning she went to school as usual and was told by the Superior not to take any notice of these illusions.

On that same Monday, in a comfortable house of Lourdes, a certain rich widow called Madame Millet was talking to her dressmaker, Mademoiselle Antoinette Peyret, whom she had engaged for four days, Monday to Thursday. Madame Millet was not a popular woman in the little town for several reasons. Some years ago there had been much chatter about her morals, though now she was beyond reproach; otherwise a good, practising Catholic like Mademoiselle Peyret would never have come to work in her house. Madame Millet had been a servant and had married her master who, when he died, left her with a tidy little fortune. Her situation in the town was now somewhat equivocal, since she was unable or unwilling to mix any longer with the servant class, to which she belonged, and was quite incapable, through lack of social training and education, of associating with the bourgeoisie. (When, two weeks later on March 1st, the Prosecutor of Lourdes wrote to his colleague at Pau with regard to the events in Lourdes, he said of her: "Her idleness and ignorance made her very impressionable and likely to indulge in every sort of caprice and whim. So it is not surprising that she should be the first person to listen to the gossip bandied about in Lourdes.")

On that Monday, February the 15th, she sat down on the well-padded low chair then fashionable in this most comfortable of reigns, and went prattling on about a lady in a white dress and blue ribbons, and so on, getting it all wrong, as people do when they hear things at third—or fourth—hand. Mademoiselle Peyret, who was arranging flowers on the crinoline skirt of the tailor's dummy, pricked up her ears when she heard the word "blue sash" and said, "Ah! I think I know who that might be. Supposing it is the ghost of our dear Mademoiselle Elisa Latapie, President of the Children of Mary, who died last November? Perhaps she has come back to ask for prayers."

Now Elisa Latapie, who had died at the age of twenty-eight, had left a reputation of genuine holiness. Besides this, she had been really beautiful. The Children of Mary, of whom she was the President, wore in their processions a white dress and the medal of the Immaculate Conception hung on a blue ribbon, so it is understandable that Madame Millet got muddled between the ribbon and the sash. The Children of Mary also carried their rosaries over their arms or in their hands during processions. On her deathbed Elisa had asked to be dressed with great simplicity after her death, and her last triumphant words were: "Glory to God in the highest!" Abbé Peyramale had written to his bishop that he had given her a splendid funeral, which was attended by everybody in the town, and that, in the eyes of all, she was a saint.

Plump, overdressed, idle, chattering Madame Millet stared into space. "You may be right, my girl, you may be right. Strange, however, that Elisa should choose a little beggar-girl like that Bernadette Soubirous as her confidante." Wholly wrapped up in worldly concerns herself, she would be among the last to grasp the meaning of the declaration that "He hath filled the hungry with good things and the rich He hath sent empty away." Why, she *knew* Louise Soubirous, she sometimes employed her to do laundering and cleaning for her!

Her thoughts turned to the good meal she was going to put before Mademoiselle Peyret, who, as a humble dressmaker, certainly was not used to lavish boards. Yes, a nice little roast chicken, stuffed with good country butter and finely chopped-up parsley—she knew exactly how it should be done—and some crisp *pommes allumettes*, such as she had served to her late master; the hearts of several lettuces carefully dressed; perhaps some chestnut croquettes, and then a nice *crème au chocolat*, a liberal allowance of the local herb liqueur, and a cup of really strong, aromatic coffee. After this, since her cheeks went rather purple after meals, she would take a well-earned siesta.

But the thought of little Bernadette Soubirous pursued her the whole day long. Supposing the child were lying? Ah! *She* was the one to find out.

And so on Tuesday the 16th, a little after midday, she sent her servant to the rue des Petits-Fossés, asking that Bernadette should be sent to her—she wanted to speak to her. Bernadette went to see her on the way to school and answered all her questions. In the evening, the idea came to Madame Millet that she should really go to Massabielle herself to verify whether the child were lying or not.

On Wednesday evening, the 17th of February, after dark, Madame Millet and Mademoiselle Peyret went together to the home of the Soubirous, in the rue des Petits-Fossés. Mademoiselle Peyret remained outside, no doubt because there would be no room for her in the overcrowded little prison, but Madame Millet went in. She found the parents quite decided in their minds. No, their daughter should never again go to the grotto. Madame Millet said, "No doubt you're quite right to be prudent and not let Bernadette go to Massabielle at midday in the middle of a noisy group of little girls, but what harm would there be if she went before daybreak, under the protection of two responsible persons like myself and Mademoiselle Peyret, who as you know is a Child of Mary?"

The poor, who must depend on their employers, cannot argue. The Soubirous had to agree. We really should be grateful to Madame Millet, this strange instrument whom God chose to further His glorious end.

And so on Thursday, February the 18th, a little before five-thirty in the morning, both women came to knock on the door of the *cachot*. Louise had already left to start a day's laundering with Mademoiselle Fanny Nicolau. Bernadette replied from inside that she was not up yet, but she dressed quickly and joined them. All three went to the first Mass.

It was very cold and dark when they came out into the streets, and there was a heavy mist. Under her long cape, Madame Millet had a blessed candle. (This would be the first of countless millions to be lighted in the grotto.) Mademoiselle Peyret, who was not a bailiff's daughter for nothing, carried in her pocket a sheet of white paper, a pen and an ink pot, borrowed from her father's office. Being of a legal turn of mind, she had quite decided to ask the apparition to write down her needs: perhaps she wanted people to have Masses said for her; perhaps, having died with such a reputation for sanctity, she had not had Masses said for the repose of her soul, and was now in the flames of Purgatory.

All the way they lectured poor little Bernadette: "If you're telling lies, God will punish you, my girl. Now take care, you can't deceive us. We'll have our eyes on you." Directly they got to the path which led to the grotto, Bernadette disappeared down the slope, as sure-footed and as swift as a chamois. The two ladies could only follow her by sitting down and sliding, happily protected by their fashionable crinolines.

On that dark misty morning, what silence, what peace, broken only by the murmur of the Gave. But what a desolate place! Not a soul to be seen.

Abbé Laurentin, in his book *Sens de Lourdes*, has marked

the striking contrast between the visions of Fatima, in full sunlight before an enthusiastic crowd with southern temperaments, and Lourdes: "At Lourdes a land of mists, in winter, a crowd of mountain people, slow and inflexible in mind and character—more secretive, more tenacious, modelled on the surrounding rocks." And whereas the basic elements of Fatima are fire and light, those of Lourdes are earth and water.

At last the two women reached the grotto, where Bernadette was already kneeling in the dark. They knelt on either side of her. Madame Millet lit her candle and put it against the rock to shelter it from the icy wind. All three had taken out their rosaries, all three were looking towards the rosebush. All of a sudden Bernadette cried out, "She's there!"

"Hold your tongue," said Madame Millet, who could see nothing and was still incredulous, and Mademoiselle Peyret, who saw nothing either, said, "Let us recite the rosary."

Antoinette Peyret finished her rosary first. Then she said to Bernadette, "Go and ask the lady what she wants." Bernadette, who had not fallen into an ecstasy this time but seemed able to hear what was being said to her, took the writing materials which Mademoiselle Peyret gave her and went towards the rosebush. And then all of a sudden, according to the account Bernadette gave afterwards, something extraordinary happened. "That one" made her a sign with her finger to draw near. Bernadette obeyed instantly. She got to the far end of the grotto, right inside. The lady had withdrawn into her niche and apparently let herself slip through the opening which pierces the vault of the rock. She now drew near to Bernadette and spoke to her.[1] (Bernadette, of course, knew little of the powers of the risen and glorified body and how it could appear first in one place and then in another, in humanly inexplicable ways.)

Bernadette put down the writing materials on the table-shaped stone which occupied the centre part of the back of the grotto.

Mademoiselle Peyret's account is as follows: "We were preparing to follow her, and we had already taken two or

[1] This reminds one of when the Lord spoke to Moses face to face, as a man speaks to his friend (Exodus xxxiii. 11).

three steps after her when, without turning round, with her right hand she made a sign to us to move back, and we with-drew behind the fold of the rock at the bottom of the path, where we knelt down."

The child now stood on tiptoe, presenting the paper and the pen to the lady. She spoke, and as it seemed to her that she spoke quite loud, she thought that the others could hear her, but they didn't hear a word. Bernadette said: "Mad-ame, would you be kind enough to write your name?" And for the first time Bernadette heard her voice, which she de-scribed later as *"Délicate. Délicate."*

(To Abbé Pène of Lourdes, asking her about this voice and whether she heard it distinctly, Bernadette replied: "Oh yes. Very. Only it seems to me that her voice comes to you here," and as she said this she put her hand on her chest.

The great St. Basil said: "The voice of God is something very special, something I know not what; a lively image; a clear, perceptible vision which impresses itself in the spirit of men." St. Teresa, in chapter fifteen of her Autobiography, has written: "Before I had experienced it myself, I never thought that there was any means of hearing, other than by bodily ears; but indeed, the words heard according to some other fashion are heard more clearly than if they had been heard by the bodily ear.")

The courteousness of that lady! To start with, she didn't address the poor child as *"tu"* or "thou," as you do servants, but used the more polite *"vous"* or "you." Secondly, she spoke to her in the dialect of Lourdes. Bernadette, who was very proud of being a native of Lourdes, said triumphantly afterwards, "And it was in dialect, the Lourdes dialect, that she spoke to me." Père Laurentin, with several specialists in the local patois, has reconstructed all the words exactly for us, in the appendix of his book.

At Bernadette's request that she should write her name, the lady laughed. How delicious this is, the Queen of Heav-en laughing!

And then the lady said to Bernadette: "What I have to tell you, it is not necessary to put into writing."

Bernadette moved back and repeated these words to her companions. Then Madame Millet said: "Go again and ask her if we can come nearer." (No doubt the memory of her past was troubling her.) When Bernadette returned she said: "There is nothing to prevent you from coming." The two women went forward and knelt down.

In her gentle voice, the lady made her first request: "Would you do me the favour of coming here for fifteen days?"

These words in the dialect of Lourdes practically defy the translator, and they are so full of regal courtliness that, in quoting them afterwards, Bernadette laid herself open to the sneers of people like Madame Jacomet, who marvelled that the Queen of Heaven should ask Mademoiselle Soubirous for a favour. Père Laurentin, in studying the patois of the phrase, was told by the native expert of Lourdes that the form *"boulet aué era gracie"* almost certainly meant more in current usage than "favour." It is "more gentle, more motherly, more smiling, more gracious." The word *gracie,* he says, is less strong in the Pyrenean dialect than the French word *grâce.* "A chaplain of Lourdes used to tell me that he could remember, when he was a child, his grandmother using this term when she asked him to run an errand."

So when the lady said: "Would you do me the favour of coming here for fifteen days?" Bernadette replied: "After I have asked my parents' permission I will come." And then the apparition said words which altered the whole of Bernadette's life:

"I do not promise to make you happy in this world, but in the next."

An eternity in return for fifteen days!

After she had said that, the lady floated up towards the roof of the grotto and disappeared. Bernadette went back and knelt by her companions. Before she rose, she whispered in Mademoiselle Peyret's ear: *"Aquéro* looked at you, smiling." But at that time, Mademoiselle Peyret did not believe in the reality of the apparitions. All the way back to Lourdes, both the women kept saying to Bernadette: "Take care. If you're lying, God will punish you."

They were met on the path by Louise in a state of great agitation. She and Mademoiselle Nicolau had been talking, over the washing. "Why do you let your little girl go to the grotto like that?" Mademoiselle Nicolau said. "You will have trouble with the police." The very word "police" always made poor Louise go pale. She had thrown down her washer-woman's beetle and run home, only to find that Bernadette had left some time before. She had then run towards Massabielle and so met the three returning. Madame Millet managed to calm her.

"Mama," said Bernadette, "the lady has asked me to go for fifteen more days. You will let me, won't you, Mama?"

At this point Madame Millet was invaluable. "Louise, let the child go," she urged. "I will go with her, and you will come too. We won't be noticed by anybody, for it will be tomorrow early in the morning, before Bernadette goes to school. In the meantime, to avoid meeting anybody, and to rest and be out of your way, let her come home with me. I'll make her comfortable. Let her come and spend the night when she gets back from school."

When Bernadette got to school, her teacher advised her to ask the lady to help her learn her catechism.

The sun was now shining brilliantly, driving away the mists, and all the people from the neighbouring hamlets came in to market, that delightful market which one can see today little changed, with all the live rabbits and hens, the baskets full of flat cream cheeses, the pretty little bou-quets of flowers and the piles of new-laid eggs. The appari-tions at the grotto were being talked about at every stall, and the policemen watching the crowds kept hearing scraps of these conversations. Finally, they questioned some of the passers-by who seemed to be in the know, and when they got back to barracks that evening they made a first report. M. d'Angla told his superior at Argèles, and he in his turn, on Saturday, February the 20th, sent a note to the police station at Tarbes.

It is intriguing to speculate on Bernadette's first stay in a comfortable house. One can be quite sure that Madame Millet, who was by then half convinced of the authenticity of the child's experience and full of admiration, would lavish hospitality on Bernadette. She must, for the first time in her whole life, have sat down to a properly laid table, eaten a rich meal, had some fortifying wine of good quality, and then at night been led to a room comfortably upholstered in plush, with a bed with linen sheets, an eiderdown and a fat French down pillow. She must have washed herself in a china wash basin with a can of hot water brought by a maid in a white apron. She must have caught a glimpse of herself by candle-light, in one of the new fashionable wardrobes with looking-glasses along the front. Her poor little feet would sink down into warm, deep-piled carpets. Probably, as the weather continued very cold, a fire had been lit in the grate, and the child could warm herself by the leaping flames before she got into bed. But no doubt her heart was elsewhere. It was with the *petite demoiselle* of the grotto, and she lived only for the morrow.

Next morning, Friday February the 19th, was so cold that the protective Madame Millet put a little black hooded cloak over the child's white hood. After Mass, they passed by the *cachot* to fetch Louise. There were several other women prepared to follow them, of whom one, Josèphe Baringue, a shoemaker's wife, bore witness afterwards to these events. The dawn had not yet broken. On the way, they knocked on Aunt Bernarde's windows. She came out holding the blessed candle which belonged to Aunt Lucile, who was a Child of Mary.

As usual Bernadette reached the spot before all of them. The shoemaker's wife found her there, kneeling on the little strip of sand, holding the candle in her left hand, and with the right hand letting her rosary beads slip through her fingers. Directly the apparition appeared, "her smile became sweet and her face changed. She motioned to her in greeting with her hand and with her head; it was a pleasure to see her. It was as if all her life she had had nothing else to do but learn to greet people." As for Aunt Bernarde, she said: "To see her face like that made one weep." To all the watching women she seemed a being from another world. She was whiter than the candle she carried. To some she seemed on the point of death. "How beautiful she is like

this!" one of them cried. Another exclaimed, "She's dying!
Ah, the poor little thing!" Aunt Bernarde sobbed. "Unhappy woman that I am!" she cried, and Louise Soubirous,
now for the first time witnessing the event, cried out to
Heaven, "My God, I beseech you, do not take away my
child!"

The vision lasted for half an hour, and when it was over,
Bernadette fell into her mother's arms. It was not through
fatigue, but, as she was to relate many years afterwards to
her Superior at Nevers, because "When she came out of the
vision, her eyes felt as they do when one passes from full
sunlight to darkness."

And on that woodland path going back to Lourdes, on
that path on which Bernadette so often recounted what had
happened during the apparitions, she told the listening wom-
en something very strange. All of a sudden, in the silence of
the dawn, terrible sounds had arisen from the Gave. There
were bawling shouts, voices challenging one another, interrupting one another, roaring like the clamours of a crowd
in tumult. And one voice, more enraged than all the others,
dominating them all, howled, "Flee! Flee! *Sauve-toi! Sauve-
toi!*" But the lady had turned her eyes towards the torrent
with great majesty, and the turmoil ceased as suddenly as
it had begun.

These howls remind one of the devils cast out by Christ
from the possessed creatures. St. Louis Marie Grignion de
Montfort, in his *Treatise on True Devotion to the Blessed
Virgin,* has said: "Mary must be as terrible as an army in
array to the Devil and his followers." And he quotes Genesis iii. 15: "I will put enmity between thee and the woman,
and thy seed and her seed. She shall crush thy head, and
thou shalt lie in wait for her heel . . ." "And in some ways,"
as the same writer goes on to say, "Satan fears Mary more
than God, firstly, because in his pride he suffers infinitely
more from being conquered and punished by a small and
humble handmaid of God; her humility humiliates him
more than the power of God. Secondly, because God has
given Mary such power over evil spirits that, as they themselves have often unwittingly admitted through the mouths
of the possessed, they fear but one of her sighs for a soul,

more than the prayers of all the saints, and but one of her threats more than all their other torments . . .

"But Mary's mastery of Hell will shine forth, especially in the latter times, when Satan will lie in wait for her heel, that is, for her humble slaves and her poor children whom she will rouse to war against him. In the eyes of the world they would be little and poor, and like the heel they would be lowly in the eyes of all, down-trodden, persecuted. . . . But to compensate this they will be rich in the grace of God. . . ."

The Evil One must have foreseen that many sinners would leave their sins behind in the grotto of Massabielle.

Bernadette passed by her Aunt Basile's house. Looking very joyful, she cried out to her: "Good-day, Aunt." Basile called her in and started to scold her. "They're talking a lot about you. They say all kinds of things. You must not go there any more."

Bernadette asked her to go to the grotto next day. Basile felt a shiver run down her spine. But she consented to go to the grotto the following morning at six o'clock.

Half an hour later the child was hurrying to school, carrying her shabby little satchel, which contained her spelling book and a small crucifix, a crust of bread and her knitting. At the recreation period, she enjoyed herself, as usual. She liked playing with other children, as far as her asthma allowed, and she was always the life and soul of the group (although Julie Garros said that she was always rather timid, and had to be fetched to join in the games).

The fifth apparition took place on Saturday, February the 20th. Bernadette left Madame Millet's house extremely early. It was very cold. Aunt Basile came, and so did Bernadette's mother; Louise Baup, who moved in better society, came with her maid: hitherto, it had been the poor women of the town who had come.

Madame Baup said that when Bernadette had knelt down, holding her candle and rosary, after a time her face became "full of laughter"—*"tout riant."* The handful of devout women who were onlookers exclaimed, "Now she sees her!" Occasionally she looked pensive; sometimes a long sigh would come from her lips, as if she were saying "Yes," a low and prolonged *"yes."* Another witness, Rosine Caze-nave, who was very sceptical, said: "Even prejudiced as I was against these happenings, I could not help admiring what I saw: her face, her smile, and her beautiful move-ments of greeting." And another, Romaine Mingelatte, said, "Only to see her eyes was enough to bring you to your knees." Louise Soubirous cried: "I don't know my daughter any longer!"

It was during this fifth apparition that the Virgin Mary taught Bernadette patiently, word for word, a secret prayer for herself alone, which she was to repeat to nobody else and which she recited every day of her life. She recited it at all the subsequent apparitions.

In the meantime, at Tarbes, the chief of police said to his secretary: "Extraordinary things are happening at Lourdes. The people are going to a grotto to be present at some vis-ions. We're going there this afternoon."

The sixth apparition took place on the first Sunday in Lent, February the 21st. There was an icy east wind, and Bernadette appeared this time escorted by her mother and her Aunt Bernarde. There was a huge crowd because it was Sunday: housewives who had been unable to come during the week were there, and women who worked in the fields, and plenty of men—shopkeepers, workers in the slate quar-ries, field labourers, all free because it was Sunday. The press and the clergy were absent, and this, the first of the really great crowds at Lourdes, was primarily composed of working people. The bourgeoisie seemed to show more reserve.

It was not idle curiosity which had brought these people. In a strange, inexplicable way, from the very first, they were all convinced of the supernatural character of the happen-ings at the grotto. These simple people all believed that the little Soubirous child *really* saw Somebody. No name was mentioned, but many hearts whispered the unspoken words: "If it were she!"

Three police sergeants came, their gold stripes gleaming. They stood about fifteen feet away from Bernadette, whom they could distinguish by the flickering light of her candle.

And here for the first time was a most important witness, Dr. Dozous, a kindhearted man who was not, however, a churchgoer, and who, the night before, at the tables of the Café Français, had said that Bernadette Soubirous was a neuropath and boasted that he was going to catch her out properly. His written testimony is of the utmost importance.

He noticed that when the strong wind blew out her candle, Bernadette passed it to the person nearest her to light again. He himself took her pulse. He noticed her easy breathing, and that she showed no signs of nervous overexcitement. He saw that at one point her expression of perfect happiness gave way to sadness, and two tears ran down her cheeks. When the ecstasy was over, he asked her the cause of her tears, and she replied: "The lady looked away from me for a moment into the distance above my head, and then she looked back at me because I had asked her what saddened her. She replied 'Pray to God for sinners.' I was soon calmed down by the kind and peaceful look which I could see on her face again, and then immediately she disappeared." The doctor observed that Bernadette went away from the grotto in the most simple and unassuming manner, without taking any notice of the public ovation of which she was the object.

6.

THE POLICE AUTHORITIES BEGIN TO TALK

The commander of the gendarmerie, M. d'Angla, has given an account of the character of the inhabitants of Lourdes in 1858, from which we learn that they were typical stolid peasants, not especially devout but enjoying pomp and show, not at all interested in the abstract but in facts, and then only in facts of local importance.

The keen air of the Pyrenees has some affinity with the Spanish character, with its highly-strung and spontaneous nature. There was a good sprinkling of passionate Spaniards at Lourdes, as it was so near the Spanish frontier. In the past, Spain had brought to Lourdes her devotion to Our Lady. But Spain had also brought an unruly element, and this was very obvious in the Place Marcadal on the morning of Sunday, February the 21st. After Mass, all the quarrymen, both French and Spanish, who had been to Massabielle before dawn, were now arguing noisily with their comrades. Those who had been too late to get there shouted mockingly at the enthusiasts who had not missed the sight. No one had come to blows as yet, but of course, with southerners, you never knew. All this was observed by the mounted police of Lourdes who were stationed in a corner of the Place Marcadal. M. d'Angla, handsome in his uniform with his sword and cocked hat, was there, chatting to his men.

There was also an unusual stir around the mayor's house. All sorts of official personages, free of their usual engagements because it was Sunday, were meeting to discuss this business of the little Soubirous child. Among them were the

mayor, M. Lacadé, the imperial prosecutor, M. Vital Dutour, and the chief of police, M. Jacomet, the very sight of
whom would set any Soubirous quaking.

There was no one to equal M. Jacomet for getting a male-
factor to confess—laying traps into which he would fall
headlong, making him contradict himself. And yet he was
popular among the people of Lourdes, because he was very
kind to the poor. M. d'Angla, who liked him very much, has
described him as "an attractive-looking man, with a high
forehead, black hair, and a distinguished bearing; well-bred,
gay, charming, and open. He had strong religious principles,
and these were borne out in his speech. He was a churchgoer and his private life was blameless." The people of
Lourdes had never forgotten his devoted service during the
cholera epidemic, how he used to tend the sick and the dying
and make the cowardly show more courage. He never swore,
he never told doubtful stories, he was friendly with the
clergy, always going to call on them when he came to a new
place. The parish priest of Lourdes, Abbé Peyramale, used
occasionally to dine with him. The novels about Lourdes
have often made him out to be a dragon, forgetting that it
was not his responsibility to sift out the evidence of the supernatural, but only to keep order in Lourdes. That was his
only duty.

On this day, the 21st of February, order seemed to be
gravely endangered, with all this fresh turbulence in the
streets; these groups of men arguing; the road of Massabielle overcrowded. "What's all this?" M. Jacomet muttered.
"All because of the little Soubirous child from the rue des
Petits-Fossés? Why, I knew her father. Clapped him into
jail myself last year. No doubt he's using her to make
money. The poor often use their children like this."

"What do you think's the best thing to do?" asked the
mayor.

"Leave it to me," said Jacomet. "If I cross-question her,
I am sure to make her contradict herself."

"Well, I think I ought to have priority," said M. Dutour.
"Have her brought to me at the tribunal." (This was at the
corner of the rue du Tribunal and the rue des Petits-Fossés,
where the Soubirous lived.)

Now forty-one-year old M. Dutour was a good Christian; his two sisters were nuns, he was intelligent and upright, respected and loved by everybody. If he gossiped with the men who frequented the Café Français, he did not share their scepticism about the miraculous, and he took no notice of the anti-clerical newspapers from Paris which littered the tables.

A fire was lit in the clerk's cold office at the tribunal. M. Dutour took out François Soubirous' dossier. Oh yes, that was last year. The unfortunate little affair about the plank being stolen on a winter night. It was not surprising at all that Soubirous should use his daughter to make some money; as it was, he had already profited; hadn't the Soubirous child spent three nights at the house of the rich Millet widow? Perhaps he'd wangled things in such a way that the girl would inherit from her, in which case it would be easy to have the girl up for exploiting charity and playing a confidence trick.

The clack, clack of small sabots in the corridor outside announced the coming of the child criminal: she stood at the door with the hood of her black Pyrenean cloak thrown back over her shoulders. How very tiny she looked, and yet how dignified! He was astounded to find what an attractive and likeable little person she was. He had expected someone rather crafty and glib, and also not too clean. He was agreeably surprised to notice that she was spotless. He didn't tell her to sit down and she stood leaning against his work table. He wrote later: "Her face was calm and confident, neither timid nor overbold. . . . Her spotless cleanliness showed self-respect and dignity in poverty. . . . Wrapped in a cloak of the same material as her head-scarf, she reminded one of a statue rough-hewn by the sculptor's chisel. This material was so heavy that, instead of protecting her, it only seemed to make it more difficult for her to breathe, suffering as she did from chest trouble. When she spoke, her unaffected language and her quiet self-possession impressed me. When her thought soared higher, or she said something out of the ordinary, she had a charm which struck one all the more because of her simplicity."

Now he cleared his throat, saying to himself, "No! No! No! This won't do at all." And putting on a severe tone which was very far from expressing what he felt, he started to ask for her name and age, and so on. He took rapid notes while she, at his request, told him about the first apparitions.

"And so you intend to go to the grotto every morning?"

"Yes, monsieur. I promised to go there for fifteen days."

"But the Superior of the Hospice and the Sister Superintendent, who are both very devout women, have told you that you mustn't pay any attention to this, that your vision is a dream, an illusion. Why don't you follow their advice? In that way you would do away with all this publicity."

Bernadette replied: "I feel too happy when I go to the grotto."

"You could stay away . . . and you could also be prevented from going."

"Something I can't resist seems to make me go."

"Take care! Many people suspect that you and your parents are trying to exploit people. That is what I am tempted to believe myself. Your family is very poor. Since your visits to the grotto, you have been given luxuries which you didn't have before, and you may expect even greater ones. . . ."

"I don't expect any benefits in this life."

"That's what you say, but haven't you already accepted Madame Millet's hospitality? Don't your parents hope to improve their position by making use of you and your visions, although perhaps they are only dreams, or, what would be worse, lies?"

"It was Madame Millet who wanted to take me to her home. She came to fetch me. I gave in to her just to please her. I was not thinking of myself. I have not told lies to her nor to anybody else."

Bernadette looked so sincere that all M. Dutour's suspicions vanished into thin air. He let her go. *Ciel!* What would Jacomet say when he found that he had not succeeded in trapping her?

How useful to the biographers of the saint these civil functionaries are! They have provided us with the first historical documents. As Mgr. Trochu has said: "The traps which they laid before the ignorant simplicity of the Soubirous child provide her with the opportunity of bringing triumphant proof of the truth of her visions."

Quite calmly Bernadette left M. Dutour's office and went home for the midday meal. True, it was all very different from Madame Millet's abundant and hospitable table, but it was good to be home again with the others. Louise had collected some money the week before by her laundering for Mademoiselle Nicolau, and also by helping to serve wine in her brother-in-law's shop. He had given her a bottle of good red wine and she had bought a large, coarse maize loaf. She had prepared some delicious hot onion soup; in each of the earthenware bowls she had put a slice of bread and a thin sliver of goat's cheese, which she had managed to buy very cheap from a friend of hers, and she had stoked up a good fire. Since there was no communal table for them to sit at, they all perched in various places about the room. Bernadette was on the stone ledge near the window. As usual they ate in reverent silence. Occasionally both parents would glance up uneasily at their elder daughter, but still they said not a word. After the meal was over and the girls had helped their mother to wash up and thrown the washing-up water down the little hole which served as a drain, Bernadette went to Vespers with her two aunts, Lucile and Bernarde.

Pierre Callet, a naive, engaging policeman, had been asked by M. Jacomet, who was dressed in civilian clothes, to point out Bernadette as she came out of Vespers. When she came out towards the end, between her aunts, Callet said to M. Jacomet, "There she is."

"Which one?" asked Jacomet.

"That one," said Callet, pointing to Bernadette.

Then Jacomet walked up to Bernadette and touched her on the arm, saying, "You've got to come with me."

Bernadette replied, "Yes, monsieur, whatever you wish." She already knew Jacomet, just as everybody else did. Her aunts said nothing, but Lucile Castérot ran to the rue des Petits-Fossés to tell François and Louise.

In the meantime Jacomet, followed by Pierre Callet, led the way to his own flat, which was in a building quite near the church in the rue St. Pierre. This was the house, it will be recalled, to which Mlle. Emmanuélite Estrade, the sister of the revenue officer, had brought Jean-Marie on the night when she saw him scraping up wax in the church. In addition to the Jacomets and the Estrades, the other tenants were M. Pène, one of the curates of Lourdes, and his sister, Jacquette.

On the way, the crowds said to Bernadette: "Poor Bernadette. They're going to put you in prison." And she replied laughingly: "I'm not frightened. If they put me there, they will let me out again." And then, to Jacomet's irritation, the crowds followed her.

Pierre Callet hero-worshipped M. Jacomet for his tremendous arrogance. Now he stayed in the little sitting-room outside Jacomet's office with Mme. Jacomet, who kept pressing her ear against the door of the office to hear what was happening during the questioning and looking back at him with conspiratorial smiles. "Oh yes," thought Callet. "I'm sure M. Jacomet will be able to cope with the *whole* situation." And he went off into a daydream about his hero —so charming, his whole appearance so pleasing, especially when he was dressed up in his top hat. Why, you would have taken him for a general! He'd never had his equal for making a rogue confess or bringing a knave out into the open. Oh yes! A most distinguished man, and human as well, thought policeman Callet. It was typical of his wife, Mme. Jacomet, to look upon the whole thing as a joke. Why, at parties in the town she used to laugh about this unknown lady who would bestow the honour of an invitation on a . . . Mademoiselle Soubirous.

Jacomet ushered Bernadette into his little office looking on to the courtyard and made her sit down, in case the interview proved to be long. "Ho-ho!" he thought to himself. "I'm sure the Abbé will be glad if I settle this stupid business once and for all."

M. Jacomet could not know that by his zeal in this affair he would make himself so unpopular in the town that it would have been easy to find two hundred women only too ready to throw him into the Gave. One author has even

suggested that the distress he felt at the judgment published
on him even in his lifetime led to his death at the early age
of fifty-two! It cannot have been pleasant for him to read
in M. Henri Lassere's book that he was "pleased with himself but discontented about his position . . . and this account-
ed for a certain bustling pride and an anxious desire to make
himself conspicuous" . . . "He was like a night bird, which
can see only in the dark, and in the daylight blunders into
trees and walls." (When he read these lines Jacomet hurried
to the bishop, Mgr. Laurence, who, however, prevented him
from taking legal action.)

As for Bernadette, she afterwards told her childhood
friend Julie Garros: "I wasn't frightened; I could feel something inside me giving me strength."

In the meantime, Mme. Jacomet had suddenly remembered that she had promised her neighbour, Mlle. Estrade,
that she would let her know when Bernadette was being
questioned, so she fetched her. Very quietly Mlle. Estrade
set the door into M. Jacomet's office ajar. But she had hardly
come when she regretted that her brother was not there too.
"I left the sitting-room at once and went quickly to call him.
He was writing, at that moment, and was very much set
against coming. I took him by the arm, pushed his chair,
shoved him. He had to give in in the end, and we went into
the sitting-room."

M. Estrade, who was later to become such an invaluable
witness, made a sign to Jacomet to explain his presence
there and then went to sit in a place from which he could
see and hear the young visionary. (He said, in his account of
the affair, that she looked only twelve years old. "Her face
was fresh and plumpish. She had a gentle, simple expression. Though her voice was loud, it was pleasant. She sat
in a perfectly natural attitude, with her hands crossed on
her knees and her head slightly bent. Her clothes were poor
but clean.")

Perhaps to impress the onlookers and eavesdroppers, or
perhaps to put the little rogue, as he thought her, off her
guard, Jacomet now smiled a sweet smile and adopted a

tone of the most insinuating good nature. He said, "Now don't be frightened. I've been told about an extraordinary lady who has appeared to you in the grotto of Massabielle. As you know, people are saying all sorts of things. I wanted to hear everything for myself." (He used the familiar "*tu*" of the superior to the inferior.)

M. and Mlle. Estrade took notes on the interview, which have been preserved:

"What's your name?"

"Bernadette Soubirous."

"And what's your father called?"

"François Soubirous."

"And your mother?"

"Louise . . . Louise Castérot."

"And what do you do at home?"

"I go to the Sisters' school. I help my mother in the house. I look after my little brother."

"Tell me what you have seen at Massabielle."

Bernadette told her story once again. Jacomet kept interrupting her.

"Is this lady very beautiful?"

"Oh yes, monsieur. Very beautiful."

"Is she beautiful like Madame X? like Madame Z?"

"Oh, more than that. They just can't be compared."

"Is she young?"

"Yes, very young."

"Can you see her feet?"

"No, not much of them. The dress and the roses hide them, except the toes."

"Can you see her hair?"

"A little, under her veil."

"Do you say it is the Blessed Virgin who appears to you?"

"I don't know if it's she. She has never said so."

"Have you spoken to your parents of what you have seen at Massabielle?"

"Yes, monsieur."

"And what do your parents say?"

"At the beginning, they said that I had been mistaken, and that I mustn't go back to Massabielle."

"Yes, Bernadette, you mustn't go back there. Everybody's laughing at you. It's all imagination. This lady you thought you had seen didn't exist in reality."

"But, monsieur, I have seen her several times. I can't always be mistaken."

After each answer, M. Jacomet took notes. "You see," he said, "I am putting into writing everything you say. It will be very serious for you if you are lying."

"Monsieur, I haven't lied to you."

In the meantime, the people who had seen Bernadette carried off by the police and had followed her were still waiting outside. The mutter of the crowd could be heard quite clearly in the room. Some began to kick the door of the building. M. Jacomet felt a growing irritation. He was self-conscious under the gaze of the two who could see him from the other room. However, he refused to be worsted by this good-for-nothing little vagabond. The insinuating tone of good nature was dropped, and he became menacing: "If you don't tell me the name of the person who has egged you on to tell this story, I will prosecute you as a liar."

"Monsieur, do as you wish."

Then, as if talking to himself, he said, "Oh well, it can't be helped. She has asked for it, and she will be punished." He proceeded to read aloud to her the lines he had written, packed with mistakes. Each time a mistake occurred, Bernadette interrupted sharply, "Monsieur, I did not say that to you."

Finally Jacomet lost his temper completely. "Yes you did," he kept insisting, and she would repeat, "Oh, no," and then they would argue for several minutes. This continued for an hour to an hour and a half:

"You said to me first that it was a woman as beautiful as Madame X."

"No, monsieur, I said that she was more beautiful than all those ladies."

"All right. And that she had appeared at the back of the grotto."

"No. Above the bush."

"That her hair fell backwards like a veil."

"No, I said that she wore a veil, a white one, very long. Her hair can hardly be seen."

"She had a yellow rose at her girdle."

"No, monsieur, you have changed everything I said. She had a blue girdle and there was no rose at her girdle. There was a yellow rose on each foot."

At this M. Jacomet glanced up at Bernadette, his eyes flashing. Then he lifted a hand as if to strike her, but the child continued imperturbably with her story.

In the end he said, "This play-acting must stop. Will you promise not to go back to Massabielle?"

"Monsieur, I promised to go there for fifteen days."

"You want to go there again? Well, then, I will fetch the policeman. Get ready to go to prison."

(Bernadette was so calm that she noticed something which amused her immensely: Jacomet's hand was trembling so that he could not find the hole of the ink pot, and the tassle he wore made a sound like "tin-tin.")

"Yes," he insisted, "you'll have to go to prison."

Bernadette replied calmly, "All the better. I will cost my father less, and in prison you will come and teach me my catechism." (Cheek!)

Things were looking black for the child, when all of a sudden François Soubirous appeared at the half-open door and declared, "I am the father of this child."

"Oh, it's you, Father Soubirous," said Jacomet. "You did quite right to come, for I was just going to have you fetched. You know the play-acting that your daughter has been indulging in for several days? All this would merely be ridiculous if it weren't for the fact that the peace and good order of the town are being disturbed. We must put a stop to it. Your daughter is a minor and you're responsible for her."

"M'sieu le commissaire," he replied, "I ask nothing better than to put an end to it. We are tired, my wife and I, of all that's going on, and of seeing so many people come to our place. I will make use of your authority to keep them away."

"Now we're getting somewhere," said M. Jacomet. He led them out by another door. Eventually the crowd dispersed and went home.

Jacomet was still fuming. When he returned to his office he said to M. and Mlle. Estrade: "All this, I can quite see, is just a stupid trick."

That very evening, the major of the cavalry squadron, before going back to Tarbes, left orders for the Lourdes mounted police: "You will send a policeman every morning to that famous grotto."

The mayor and the police commissioner told their men that young Bernadette Soubirous must be strictly watched, and that all the rumours going about amongst the crowd which followed her should be collected.

From that night onwards the Soubirous in their home in the rue des Petits-Fossés had no peace. There were policemen at the door looking through the keyholes into the passage, peering through the windows, climbing into the back yard, listening to conversations. That night Bernadette sobbed herself to sleep. It was not for herself that she cried, but for her unfortunate mother and father, so poor, so tormented, so very much afraid of the word "prison." And all because of her.

The first person to suffer materially from the apparitions was little Jean-Marie Soubirous. When Mlle. Emmanuélite Estrade came to the Soubirous' home to see Bernadette, she saw Jean-Marie and realized that the little boy she had been feeding all this time was none other than the brother of the visionary. But from that day onwards, she saw him no more. Bernadette must have seen to that, for she was adamant when it came to making any material profit from the apparitions. The poor family showed immense dignity throughout, refusing absolutely all gifts, even legitimate things like the food which they needed so much. This was particularly heroic since, during that time, because of the crowds which came to the house, and the turmoil, both parents were less able to earn money than before, and often sheer starvation faced them.

Monday, February the 22nd, was a sad day for Bernadette from all points of view. First, she was not allowed to go to Mass, for her parents were frightened of what she would do afterwards, and then she was absolutely forbidden to go near the grotto. When she got to school, a horrid little girl, who had heard that she had almost been taken to prison, led the others in a chorus: "It serves you right, it serves you right." Perhaps the chemist's odious child who had smacked Bernadette's face was hovering in the background, sniggering. And then the nuns, shocked that a pupil of theirs should be involved with the police, were especially severe that morning. The Superior herself had met Bernadette at the school entrance and said, "I hope you've given up all this pantomiming." Bernadette answered nothing and remained calm. She set herself to learning Monseigneur Laurence's catechism with special industry.

In the meantime, two women who had hoped that Bernadette would go to the grotto that morning were very much disappointed, so they went to see her mother in the *cachot*. One was Anna Dupas, who kept a shop, and the other Marie Segot, a devout old spinster who often went to work for the Christian Brothers. They found Louise at her door, holding on her arm a pretty little boy with curly fair hair—Justin. They asked, "Where is Bernadette?" Louise replied, "She is at school, and I don't want her to go to the grotto."

Bernadette came back for the frugal midday meal. The family again said that she must not go to the grotto. She didn't say much, and when she left home she had the full and firm intention of going straight to school. But, as she was to say later to Mlle. Estrade, who became one of her trusted confidantes, no sooner had she come into the forecourt of the school, than she lost control of her legs: she could not make them go anywhere except to Massabielle! So she resolved, instead of passing through the town, to make a circle round the citadel.

At the end of the path leading to the Hospice is the police station. From the window Bernadette was seen by two policemen and they, as we remember, had had strict orders to follow her every movement. But of course they had no orders to arrest her. They came out. They were fully dressed in official uniform, with epaulettes, shoulder-knots and yellow cross-belts. She walked between them quite calmly. Of course the very sight of two policemen attracted attention. A number of people followed her, crying out, "It's she, it's she!" One policeman muttered into his moustache, "And to think we're living in the nineteenth century and they try to make us believe in such superstitions!"

When Bernadette reached the grotto, there, alas, was M. d'Angla. (He was not to believe in the reality of the apparitions for another twenty long years.) She knelt down. M. d'Angla tapped her on the shoulder and whispered in her ear, "If you weren't a little fool, you would know that the Blessed Virgin, if it is she, is not frightened of a policeman;

she has nothing to be frightened of, so why are *you* frightened of them? Is it by any chance because you have got a guilty conscience about telling lies? I am looking just as hard as you are and I don't see anything at all. Look, you can't see anything more than I can."

Alas, this time the lady, who had asked the child to come fifteen times, did not appear. (Actually, she had not promised that she herself would appear fifteen times.) The crowds began to murmur, "Yes, that's the end of these apparitions." (The sceptics in the town, when they were told of what had happened, sneered: "The lady of the grotto is frightened of the police. She won't come any more.")

Bernadette's aunts, Lucile and Basile, led their niece away. "So you've not seen her?" they questioned. "No," moaned Bernadette, "I don't know in what way I can have failed her." Her face looked very drawn, so her aunts took her to the Savy mill to rest. Louise hurried there immediately, for she had heard what her daughter had been up to. Other women from Lourdes also went in to the Nicolaus, among them Mlle. Estrade, who wrote the following account in her *Mémoire:*

"Bernadette was seated, and a woman near her, I didn't know at the time it was her mother . . . The poor woman was pale, and from time to time she looked at the child anxiously. I asked her if she knew the little girl: 'Ah, mademoiselle, I am her unfortunate mother!'

" 'Unfortunate!' I said to her, 'and why?'

" 'You see what's happening. They're threatening to put us into prison. Some people are laughing at us and others jeer at us. Some are sorry for us. They say "Bernadette is ill." '

" 'And what about you?' I asked, 'What do you think of it?'

"She replied, 'The child doesn't tell lies. I know that she is quite incapable of taking us in deliberately, and she isn't ill either. When I ask her if she feels ill, she says, "No." I'd forbidden her to go to the grotto. She has gone all the same. But she is not really disobedient. She tells me that something she can't explain makes her go.'

"The poor woman made one feel quite sorry for her."

When they got home, the mother and aunts insisted that she should not go back to the grotto. Very sadly Bernadette replied, "I can't bear it. I must disobey either you or the lady." Aunt Basile said, "But if they put you in prison, you'll be obliged to disobey her." Bernadette replied, "Ah, that's very different. If I am not able to go, I won't go."

This absence of any apparition on February the 22nd gives the lie to so-called scientific men who talk about hallucinations. If the child had indeed been out of her mind, she would have invented the object of her dream as usual. It is quite obvious, too, that she was not a puppet in the hands of intriguing relations. In the darkness of that deprivation, Bernadette still believed in the light. She must not lose faith in the lady, who would give her true happiness. And she, whose mission was to pray for sinners, had now to begin to expiate in their place.

The next morning, Louise and François Soubirous knew that it would be useless to prevent their daughter from going to the grotto, and so they gave their permission.

Before dawn on Tuesday, February the 23rd, about a hundred of the inhabitants of Lourdes had made up their minds to go to the grotto. "To hell with the police," they said. Many of them were carrying lanterns, and as they glanced at one another, exclamations of surprise were heard, for now the simple country folk were joined by people like Dr. Dozous (who was making his second visit), a lawyer and former mayor, M. Dufo, M. Laffitte, the senior commissariat officer and the captain of the citadel, and M. Estrade, the revenue officer. M. Estrade had been persuaded, much against his will, to attend in order to protect his sister and other ladies, who said that at such a time of day and in such a deserted spot it would be most improper for ladies to be unescorted. When he spoke to Abbé Peyramale about the plan, the Abbé said, "Do go along with the ladies. There has been so much talk that I shan't be sorry to have a few reliable witnesses present."

The Estrade group arrived in the grotto devoid of any great spirit of contemplation. A number of country folk and townsfolk were already there, kneeling with their ro-

saries in their hands, putting the behaviour of certain others
to shame—a party of curiosity-seekers bent on mockery:
"Have any of you brought holy water? Have you got your
opera glasses?" and suchlike fooleries. (When, before Bernadette arrived, all these clever people searched the grotto
thoroughly, they were driven to the surprising conclusion
that Bernadette could not have been the victim of any opti-
cal delusion caused by a play of light.)

At last an indistinct sound of voices in the distance
warned the crowd at the grotto that Bernadette was coming
down the slope. She arrived: the devout went to kneel down
by her side. And here is the invaluable account of M. Estrade, who was among those who had come there to mock:
"All of a sudden, as if she had been struck by lightning, she
gave a gasp of wonder and seemed to be reborn. Her eyes
lit up and became sparkling, her face was illuminated by
heavenly smiles, she was completely transformed by indescribable grace. It was as though the visionary's soul were
trying to break through the prison of the body in an attempt
to show its rapture. Bernadette was no longer Bernadette!

"Quite instinctively we men who were there took off our
hats and bowed down like any woman."

Then he noticed her in a listening attitude. He said that
she looked as if she were afraid to lower her eyes for fear
of losing sight of the ravishing beauty they contemplated:

"Usually the ecstatic finished her prayers by bowing in
the direction of the hidden lady. I have been around in the
world, too much perhaps! And I have met models of grace
and distinction, but I have never seen anybody bow with
such grace and distinction as Bernadette.

". . . If they make the sign of the cross in Heaven, it can
only be as she made it.

"The ecstasy lasted for about an hour. Towards the end,
she went about on her knees, going from the place where
she was praying until she was just under the rosebush hanging from the rock. . . .

"In vain the lady of the rock might veil her presence. I
could feel it, and I was convinced that she had looked on
me with a mother's love. It was indeed a solemn moment in

my life! I was deliriously happy to think that I, who had
been so full of mocking scepticism and self-assurance, had
been allowed a place near the Queen of Heaven. . . ."

When it was over, the Estrade group was crying out: "It's
extraordinary! It's unearthly! It's divine!"

And as usual, on the way home, Bernadette confided in
her aunts, her mother and her neighbours. She said that this
time the lady had told her a secret for herself alone.

In all, the lady confided three secrets to Bernadette, but
we do not know how many were confided on the same day.
Bernadette has written: "In the space of those fifteen days
she entrusted me with three secrets." Probably the sad secret was communicated to her during the seventh apparition,
and there is a great probability that one of the secrets con-
cerned her vocation as a nun. But the vocation itself was
not a secret. Neither was it a secret that the lady had told
her she would die young.

That afternoon Mme. Anna Dupas went to see her again.
She tells us that one of the other women who came to ask
Bernadette questions wanted to kiss her, and Anna said: "I
shall not have the pleasure of seeing the Blessed Virgin. Let
me kiss you, since you do see her."

Mme. Anna Dupas goes on to say: "I would very much
like to have given her something, but I was not rich. Apples
had been scarce the year before; but I still had one beautiful
one left. I went to fetch it from the cupboard, and I offered
it to her. She thanked me but did not want to take it, and
although I pressed her she consistently refused."

After this, their cousin Sajous, seeing the crowds of people who came to see Bernadette the whole time, let her use
a room on the first floor. The poverty and the stench (despite
Louise's best efforts) of the *cachot* would have been far too
much for the visitors. And it was in that room on the first
floor, on the evening of February the 23rd, that Mlle. Estrade saw Bernadette "near a fire that was half out, and
with a little child on her knees. By her side I recognized our
guest, Jean-Marie, and it was not without very keen joy
that I saw that this link had already connected me for some
time with a family beloved of God."

On Wednesday, February the 24th, between four and five

hundred people came to Massabielle in the early morning.
A swaggering police sergeant began to strut back and forth
in front of Bernadette in her ecstasy. She remained utterly
still, giving no sign that she saw him. The crowd protested,
and after that there was a dead silence. The child had hardly
said twelve Ave Marias of her rosary when they saw: "a
slight movement of her whole body, leaning forward, as if
she saw something which carried her out of herself." Then
all of a sudden, after five or six minutes, she came out of
her ecstasy. She stood up and began to weep. "Who has
touched the bush?" she cried. (A young girl had parted the
branches to see Bernadette better. To Bernadette the rosebush on which the lady rested her rose-covered feet was
utterly holy and must not be touched. Perhaps she feared
that the lady would fall if it were moved.) Then she knelt
again and she moaned, and somebody said in a whisper
"pauvre chou." A girl called Dominiquette Cazenave has
written: "Suddenly her whole being seemed to light up, and
a soft 'Ah!' came from her lips, as though she were saying,
'Oh, what bliss! There she is!' And as I looked on I thought
to myself, 'That little girl is not making it up.'" And then
she looked sad again (for it was on that day that the lady
made her see the terrible picture of the sins of men and the
urgent necessity for expiation). When her ecstasy was over,
she repeated the word *"Pénitence"* three times. People hearing her repeated it from mouth to mouth.

Of that day Soeur Marie de l'Assomption wrote: "One
could see the rays of light which surrounded the Virgin
Mary reflected on her angelic face."

To whom, more clearly than to the great Mother of God,
would sin appear in all its hideousness? For as she stood at
the foot of the cross and watched His sufferings, she saw
that sin had crucified her Son. For this had she borne Him,
that He might redeem men from their sins. And yet on Calvary she knew that for many He died in vain. She saw men
who would prefer the slavery of their sins to the sweet yoke
of His liberty. As she was so closely linked with all her Son
loved, she was in a sense associated with Him in the redemption of the world. She knew how He loved and cherished

each soul, and she trembled for the eternal loss of any one. It was as if she foresaw the crowds of thousands and thousands from all over the world who would flock to Lourdes, some indeed to be cured of terrible physical ills, brought on in some cases by their sins, or by the sins of others; but more especially she saw those who came to be healed of the more penetrating ills of the soul.

Lourdes has constantly overflowed with sick souls, come to be healed of their wounds, to be saved from Hell. The idea of eternal punishment changes entirely when we realize that the lost perish by their own fault, by their own choice, whilst Eternal Love gazes on them, unwilling to intrude upon the freedom of their will, and yet longing for their salvation.

Bernadette, a child, so innocent and young, on that day began to learn the dreadfulness of sin. She learnt her first austere lesson from the lips of the *"petite demoiselle."*

And on the next day, Thursday, February the 25th, bending with solicitude over all these infirmities of mankind, the lady was to make them a royal gift for their healing. We have the testimony of a woman from Lourdes, a friend of the Estrades, Mlle. Elfrida Lacrampe, whose parents owned the Hôtel des Pyrénées.

Mlle. Lacrampe began by being a sceptic. She was a little irritated by the way Bernadette kept saying "Let me pass, let me pass" as she made her way to the grotto, and she watched critically as the child lifted her dress before she knelt down, in order to keep it clean. She had a place quite near the child the whole time. All of a sudden she saw her move, still on her knees, make her way up the slope which led to the inside of the grotto, and then come back in the same manner—all of which was a *tour de force*.

". . . I ought to have admired the dignity of the child's movements more, in such a position and on very sloping, uneven ground, sprinkled with stones, and falling away in very abrupt ledges. But at that moment I saw . . . only the ridiculous agitation in Bernadette's movements, because they seemed to be pointless."

This is Bernadette's own account of the whole thing. "The

lady said to me: 'Go and drink at the spring and wash yourself there.' Seeing no spring, I was going to drink in the Gave. She told me it was not there. She made a sign with her finger, showing me the place of the fountain. I went to it. I only saw a little dirty water; I put my hand in it. I could not drink it; I scratched, and the water came up, but it was muddy. Three times I threw it away: but the fourth time I was able to drink some.

Very deep in the earth was a remarkably pure and limpid spring unknown to men, which made its way underground towards the Gave, but that morning, at the touch of the child's hand, it sprang forth through the rock in a humanly inexplicable manner. The fountain of great healing first appeared on that morning. At Matins choirs of monks and nuns throughout the land were singing Psalm 76:

"The waters saw thee, O God, the waters saw thee: and they were afraid, and the depths were troubled. . . .

". . . Thy way is in the sea, and thy paths in many waters: and thy footsteps shall not be known."

At Lourdes on that day took place the miracle of the discovery of a spring which was already in existence, a discovery on the express designation made by the lady to Bernadette. But of course the crowds, who did not see or hear the lady, had no explanation for the child's mud-covered face, for her strange behaviour in drinking the muddy water. They all began to whisper, "She's mad!"

A certain Catherine Oustallet has written that when Bernadette got up from her knees again, she pulled up her petticoat and wiped her face. Catherine said to her: "Do you want my handkerchief?" She thought it most remarkable that the child's face became so clean after she wiped it.

Then Bernadette stretched her arm towards the top of the slope to pluck three little handfuls of a very short herb. (This herb is believed to have been saxifrage, though somebody said it was like clover and very green.) She put some of it into her mouth, then spat it out immediately. More cries from the crowd: "The poor child is going mad!" But the lady had said: "Eat the herb which you find there."

All this recalls the penitential herbs which the Jews ate

with lamb at the Passover. The Lourdes mystery is full of signs and symbols, as if God were trying to teach us to love invisible things by the use of the visible and tangible.[1]

Bernadette's Aunt Bernarde wrote: "When the ecstasy was finished we took her back again, as some people were making fun of her. On the way we went quickly to escape the crowd. They pursued us as if it were a show."

According to Mlle. Estrade, the critical Elfrida Lacrampe noticed that, after the ecstasy, Bernadette slipped her hand under the kerchief which covered her head, and scratched herself. Elfrida turned to Mlle. Estrade and said, "Do you expect me to believe that that girl sees the Blessed Virgin?" Amongst the onlookers who sneered was Mme. Jacomet who, we feel sure, would have plenty of amusing news to bring back to her husband.

[1] ". . . ut dum visibiliter Deum cognoscimus, per hunc in invisi-bilium amorem rapiamur." Preface for Christmas.

8.

BERNADETTE, HER CURÉ
AND THE POLICE

Friday, February the 26th, was again a day of grief for Bernadette, for she did not see her lady at the grotto. However, the crowds made no complaint. It was moving to see how united they were to the child in spirit. All said their prayers. She wept all the way home, leaning on her aunt's arm, and when she got to the *cachot* she wept more bitterly still.

But later in the morning some people from the town went to the grotto and were astonished to see a little ribbon of water bubbling from the hole which Bernadette had scratched the day before. Soon it became almost a stream, increasing in size at every moment.

Saturday, February the 27th, was bitterly cold, but that did not prevent the crowds from coming from a great distance. Some peasants left their homes soon after midnight in order to be at the grotto at three in the morning. A schoolmaster called M. Clarens, irritated because the clack of clogs on the cobbled streets prevented him from sleeping, finally rose himself at three o'clock and went to the grotto.

On the rocks, on the strip of land and even in the field opposite the Gave, was a compact mass of people. The crowds stayed there quietly till half-past six, when Bernadette appeared. Clarens noted how prayerful the people were. It was an inspiring thing to witness. Policeman Pierre Callet was impressed by the extraordinary silence of the crowd. He said it was "as if they were in church." Another inhabitant of Lourdes, Cyprine Gesta, has written: "During the ecstasy, there was a sort of ominous silence among the people. You felt frightened, but at the same time you wanted to stay on." Another very young girl has said: "While we were there we were happy; we should have liked to stay there forever." Catherine Oustallet said: "I wept at the sight of so many people on the rocks among the shrubs, along the edge of the rocks where there are now railings, and also on the boulders."

It was during this apparition that the lady said to Berna-dette, "Go and kiss the ground as a penance for sinners."

On the way home, Bernadette said to her Aunt Bernarde that the lady had commanded: "Go and tell the priests to build a chapel here."

"I suppose that means you will have to go to Abbé Peyra-male," said the aunt.

"Oh dear," said Bernadette, "I'm so frightened of him! He's so big and he shouts so when he talks. However, I'll have to go." Indeed, she always carried out the lady's be-hests immediately.

Abbé Marie-Dominique Peyramale was forty-seven that year. He had been Curé of Lourdes since 1854. (He had been nominated in the month when Pope Pius IX defined the dogma of the Immaculate Conception.) He was the son of a doctor of Momères, the same hamlet in which Berna-dette's godfather lived. An eighteen-year-old young lady of Nantes, in a private manuscript, has described him as being very tall, with a broad forehead, an imposing walk and fiery eyes. M. Estrade has said that he was a typical man of the mountains. He was curt of speech, and one was not at first drawn to him. "There were two men in him, one severe, the other kind, simple, and good; and you forgot the first when once you had met the second."

He was indeed a typical curé of the last century in France, authoritative and very jealous of his authority. If he lost his temper, his voice was like thunder. His clothes were very shabby indeed, the reason being that he could never turn away a poor person, and many of the people of Lourdes had their rent paid by him. He had a great, kind heart for the poor. (It is related that one day he had been given a present of a capon. The cook put it to boil and left the kitchen.

When she returned, the capon had gone: the curé had given
it to a poor man.) His curate Abbé Pène said he was very
good company, for he was witty and very well-read. He
could hold his own with the most cultivated people of the
town. He was very tolerant of unbelievers, but open disrespect for the Blessed Sacrament he would not allow. Once
he saw an onlooker at a procession wearing a hat and smok-
ing a cigar: he knocked both hat and cigar to the ground.

From the beginning of the apparitions, Abbé Peyramale
had forbidden his curates to go to the grotto. He did not
want the Church to be involved in this affair at all. Too
ready and uncontrolled a belief in the miraculous can so
easily bring discredit, not only on the clergy, but on the
Church itself. He knew that miracle-fakers were nearly
always women, and for that reason he mistrusted them.

As Jean Hellé said in his book on miracles: "Lying is feminine . . . when a man lies he is easily detected, because a
man does not know how to lie, but a child knows and so
does a woman."[1] A case in point is that of Rose Tamisier,
at this time of very recent memory. She had managed to
deceive her parish priest completely. He wholly believed in
her supernatural Communions. She said that she had seen
blood flowing from the wound in Christ's side in a picture
painted on the chapel wall. It was proved to be a trick: she
had obtained blood disgorged from leeches and daubed it
on when no one was looking. Quite soon investigators were
sure that she had perpetuated sacrilegious fraud and therefore deserved punishment. She fell into a trap set for her
and was arrested on February the 13th, 1851, and sent to
prison for twenty-one months. After she came out, she never
confessed to her frauds. "Her biographer informs us, on the
contrary, that she bombarded the clergy with letters de-
manding Communion, which was refused her on account of
her perseverance in error. During the last period of her
life, she was just a poor woman hanging around churches,
stoutly refusing to confess her fraud, abandoned by all, a
poor solitary wretch endlessly fumbling over the tale of her

[1] *Miracles,* trans. by Lancelot Sheppard (New York, McKay,
1952; London, Burns, 1953).

fantastic fabrication. She was her own victim and her own executioner. The sacred and terrifying role of God's chosen one cannot be played with impunity."[2]

St. John of the Cross, when he was told by one of his excited fellow friars that something miraculous was happening in the next street, refused to leave his prayers. Abbé Peyramale was just such a solid, incredulous, reliable pastor, one of those pastors who are the glory of the Catholic Church. As St. Gregory the Great said, "The incredulity of Thomas was more useful to our faith than the faith of the other disciples." And the incredulity of Abbé Peyramale greatly served the cause of the Blessed Virgin.

Earlier on, he had written a full account to his bishop, Mgr. Laurence, whose bishopric was at Tarbes. He wrote with irony and zest. Then, on Friday, February the 26th, he paid the bishop a personal visit. When he returned he told his curates: "I put before Monseigneur the fact that amongst us there are some who think they can, without harm, be present at the grotto, whilst there are others who are of the contrary opinion. I added: 'Monseigneur, may we be present, or should we remain in the background?' Monseigneur, after a moment of reflection, replied: 'Go there.' I objected, 'If we go there, Monseigneur, they will say it is we who are behind this girl and who make her go in for this play-acting.' 'Very well,' the bishop replied, 'do not go, then.' "

And then the rumour was circulated that the austere Mgr. Laurence was laughing at Bernadette and her visions, and if any priest seemed enthusiastic about it, such as Abbé Dézirat, his fellow priests smiled at him pityingly.

With her gift for mimicry, Bernadette had, in times past, imitated the gruff voice of her curé, but she was very far from feeling in a mood for mimicry when she went to deliver the lady's message to him. He lived in a one-storeyed house on the road from Tarbes to Argelès. (The house has only just been pulled down to make room for additions to the post office.) It was surrounded by a garden and a courtyard. In spite of the cold, the curé was reciting his breviary in the courtyard when he heard the sound of the street door

[2] Hellé, *op. cit.*

opening. He raised his eyes and saw Bernadette. He did not recognize her, but asked who she was and what she wanted.

"I am Bernadette Soubirous."

"Ah, it is you," he said haughtily. "They're telling strange stories about you, my poor Bernadette." Turning on his heel, he walked towards his house, while Bernadette followed him like a little lamb. Without looking round, he thundered: "Come in." He showed her into his sitting-room, and then, when he had sat down, he said: "Now, what do you want of me?"

Bernadette replied, quite simply, *"Monsieur le curé,* the lady of the grotto has charged me to tell the priests that she wants a chapel at Massabielle."

He replied in a tone which was far from accommodating: "Who is this lady?"

"It's a very beautiful lady all surrounded by light who appears to me at Massabielle."

"I don't understand at all. How has this lady shown herself to you?"

And then, with a sincerity which was unmistakable, she told him all that she had told the others. Tears started in the abbé's eyes, but he kept his face expressionless. "What is the lady's name?" he persisted.

"I don't know."

"Haven't you asked her?"

"Yes, but when I ask, she smiles without answering."

"And you maintain that she has charged you to tell me that she wants a chapel at Massabielle?"

"Yes."

"My dear child, are you out of your mind? A lady whom you do not know, a lady who is perhaps as crazy as you are, comes to tell you to invite us to build a chapel for her at the grotto! And you accept such messages; you suppose we are stupid enough to subscribe to this? Look here, my child, you are only a little play-actress. However, as you seem to believe in this lady, try to find out first of all who she is, and then if she thinks she has the right to a chapel, ask her from me to prove it by immediately making the grotto rosebush flower."

When the storm had passed, Bernadette rose timidly, cast

one unreproachful glance at her curé, dropped a curtsy, and left.

Sunday, February the 28th: rain had fallen during the early part of the night, and the cold was terrible. The crowds had been there for three or four hours before Bernadette appeared. Some were perched on the brink of the precipice, hanging on by the shrubs. It was miraculous that more of them did not fall into the Gave. The people trying to climb down the path were constantly slithering, falling, sinking into the mud. Somebody observed a very strange thing—no mud clung to Bernadette's clothes.

This time Bernadette went on with her penitential exercise, kissing the wet ground. The mud was all over her hands and her lips. Pierre Callet seems to have lost his head that morning. He turned to the crowds and shouted in a loud voice:

"All of you kiss the ground." And immediately all obeyed.

The rain continued to fall. Whenever some timorous person put up an umbrella, there were cries of "Put the umbrellas down!" The crowds were remarkable, for they must have heard the rumour of the miracle that had been exacted by *M. le curé,* and they all looked towards the rosebush. Yet, when it failed to flower, there were no sneers, no cries of disappointment.

When she returned, Bernadette went to *M. le curé* to tell him that she had given his message, but that the lady had done nothing but smile.

In the meantime, the judge of Lourdes, M. Ribes, seeing that his fellow officials, M. Dutour and M. Jacomet, had failed in their dealings with Bernadette, decided to try his hand with the young visionary. He would be brief, threatening and sarcastic. He wasn't going to be laughed at by the gentlemen drinking liqueurs in the Café Français. So on that Sunday, the 28th of February, Bernadette, as she left High Mass with the pupils of the Hospice, was asked by the roadmender, M. Latapie, to come along with him. He wrote his own fairly amusing and lively account of it all:

"I took her gently by the arm. 'Why are you taking her away?' asked a nun, starting to cry. 'I've got my orders,' I said. Bernadette said to me, 'What do you want of me?' I replied, 'You've got to come along with me, child.' She started to laugh and said, 'Hold on tight, otherwise I'll escape.' I was beside the child and the police superintendent was behind me. People looked on speechless with astonishment.

". . . When we came in, the judge said to Bernadette in the local dialect, 'So you're here, you young monkey.'

" 'Yes, sir, I'm here.'

" 'We're going to lock you up. What do you go looking for in the grotto? Why do you make so many people flock there like that? Somebody is behind you, egging you on to act like this. We're going to put you in prison.'

" 'All right, do. But make it solid and well-locked. Otherwise I will escape.'

"They were not amused. The judge said, 'You must stop going to the grotto.'

" 'I won't give up going there.'

" 'You'll be locked up.'

" 'If I'm not able to go, well then, I won't.'

" 'I'll make you die in prison.'

"At that moment the Sister Superior of the Hospice came in. She was in tears. She said, 'I beg you, gentlemen, leave the child to us. You'll be the death of her!' "

The upshot of all this was that Jacomet and Ribes spoke to Dutour and decided to write to their attorney-general at Pau. They told him about Bernadette Soubirous, who was becoming a center of interest. They foresaw that on Thursday next, the 4th of March, the last visit to the grotto would take place, and they knew that, as it was market day, there would be enormous crowds. Police precautions should be taken.

When Bernadette went back to the *cachot* at midday, she found her mother in tears again. She threw her arms around her neck and cried, "Don't cry, the Blessed Virgin will look after us."

But their lives were not uniformly anxious. Louise still had a genius for home life under difficult circumstances. Bernadette was always gay. Jean Barbet, the Bartrès schoolmaster, has given us a charming account of how Bernadette invited her little friends to the *cachot;* they brought flour, eggs, milk and butter, and Louise made that treat of the poor—fritters. Just as St. Francis of Assisi was very much attached to a certain kind of almond cake, so Bernadette had a weakness for fritters. M. Fourcade recalls that eating fritters with the Soubirous family ranked among the happiest memories of his childhood.

Their friends in the neighbouring slums, people with a natural antipathy for the police, were all on Bernadette's side. "You needn't be afraid of the police," they said. "We'll protect you. They have no right to talk to you like that. Everybody is free to pray where he likes." When the policeman who had behaved so rudely to Bernadette during her ecstasy came down with the cholera, everyone, including his wife, thought that it was a judgment on him. And when he recovered it was said that it was because Bernadette had forgiven him.

One thing is quite clear: her family completely believed in her. "What is the lady's voice like?" asked her mother. Bernadette replied with a smile, *"Fine, fine,"* "Light and fresh." (Which emphasizes that the lady was very young.) "But how do you hear her?" asked her mother. Bernadette replied, "I hear her with my ears"; then, putting her hand on her heart, she said, "and then I hear her here." (Alphonse de Ratisbonne, the famous convert from Judaism, said about this same lady: "She said nothing to me, but I understood everything.")

When some people expressed surprise to Bernadette that the lady should know the Lourdes dialect, she used to say with great simplicity: "Can't God teach all languages to His own?"

Monday, March the first, was the twelfth day, and François Soubirous, who had been anxious about the safety of his favourite child, decided to go to the grotto to protect her. On this morning a priest, who was not under Abbé Peyramale's jurisdiction, appeared for the first time at Massabielle: the Abbé Antoine Dézirat, aged twenty-seven, newly ordained. When he was staying with his old curé at Omex he had heard about the marvels at the grotto and was curious to see for himself. He left in a carriage in the small hours of the morning with some other inhabitants of Omex. Although it was very dark, he took a roundabout way to avoid crossing Lourdes, because the curé of Lourdes had forbidden his priests to go to the grotto. He arrived at Massabielle at daybreak, rather impressed with his own daring and wondering whether he might find the Evil One disguised as an angel of light. Mgr. Trochu said of him: "He was very gifted, had a tender heart and was very devout."

The police attempted to count the people as they returned from the grotto that morning, and there were about thirteen hundred according to Jacomet's report: there might have been as many more on the roads of the countryside. Peasants, workmen, men of the middle classes and several soldiers were at Massabielle awaiting Bernadette. When she arrived, an hour after daybreak, Abbé Dézirat saw that she was calm, free from any sign of exaltation or illness. All of a sudden somebody said, "Let this priest pass." A way was made for him and he found himself very near her.[3] He wrote: "You could tell from her attitude and from her expression that she was carried away. There was such peace and serenity and such an atmosphere of deep prayer about her. I couldn't possibly describe her smile, and the way she looked at the apparition was just as moving. I can't imagine any purer, sweeter or more tender sight.

"I had observed Bernadette minutely when she came to the grotto. What was the difference between what she was then, and what I saw her to be at the moment of the apparition? All the difference between matter and spirit.

"A thrill ran through the crowd: Bernadette alone saw the apparition; but everybody had, as it were, the sense of the lady's presence . . . Joy mingled with fear showed on every face. You can hardly imagine anything more impressive . . . I felt that it was good to be there, like being in the antechamber of heaven."

But again seized with scruples about the presence of a priest at the grotto, the abbé tore himself away from the place.

M. Estrade describes something strange that happened on this occasion. Bernadette knelt down, and she was about

[3] Quoted from Mgr. Trochu, who himself quotes from a "Relation autographe" by the abbé.

to begin her rosary when suddenly a look of anxiety came over her face. Then she held up her rosary. She lifted it as high as her little arm could reach. There was a moment of waiting, then she put the rosary into her pocket. Immediately she brought out another, shook it and lifted it as high as the first one. The look of anxiety disappeared and she smiled, bowed and began her prayer again. By a spontaneous movement, the people in the crowd took their rosaries, shook them, cried *"Vive Marie,"* and knelt down to pray with tears in their eyes.

The explanation was this. A poor sickly dressmaker called Pauline Sans, too ill to go down to Massabielle herself, had asked Bernadette, as a great favour, to use her rosary at the grotto. Bernadette told the Abbé Pène and his sister, Jacquette, afterwards, "I had promised to do this for her, and I did it. Towards the end of the apparition the lady asked me where I had put my own rosary. I answered her that I had it in my pocket. She said, 'Let us see it.' Then I put my hand in my pocket, took out the rosary and showed it to her, holding it up towards her. The lady said to me, 'Use that one,' which I did immediately." This was the little rosary which her mother had bought her for two sous.

On that day one of seven well-authenticated miracles took place at the grotto. Eight years previously, thirty-eight-year-old Catharine Latapie of Loubajac, six kilometres away, had seriously injured her hand by falling out of an oak-tree from which she was shaking acorns. The two last fingers of her right hand were twisted, and this prevented her from spinning, knitting and performing other domestic tasks. The doctor considered the condition incurable. On March the 1st, she went to the grotto with her children and several other persons. Praying fervently, she dipped her hand in the spring and it was instantly cured. All pain had gone and she could move her fingers as nimbly as before her injury. The shock was such that she was seized prematurely with the pangs of childbirth. She begged Our Lady for her further protection. The pains ceased, she walked back to Loubajac, and a quarter of an hour later she was happily delivered of a son.

François Soubirous' anxiety over Bernadette produced a fresh complication for the already precarious economic situation of his family: while he was at the grotto protecting his child he was unable to earn money. Very often there was no food in their home in the rue des Petits-Fossés—perhaps just a dry crust of bread and an onion or two, from which poor Louise would make soup. They were suffering acutely from hunger and cold. Jean-Marie looked fine-drawn and Bernadette was coughing.

One day, a knock came at the door. Some kindly peasants from the Béarnais, wishing to show their respect for the Soubirous family, had sent two baskets overflowing with good things, fruit and vegetables, a joint or two of meat and good crusty bread from their own ovens. Poor little Jean-Marie, now deprived of his snacks with Mlle. Estrade, how terribly tempted he must have felt! But they were a proud people, those Soubirous, as proud as Basques, and they were good Christians. They thanked the donors and refused the gifts absolutely. They could not be persuaded to accept a crumb. Shortly afterwards, a large supply of very good fresh bread was sent to them by a well-wisher who had ordered it from Maisongrosse, the baker who had accused François Soubirous of stealing two sacks of flour. This bread was refused and sent back untouched. One can imagine Maisongrosse saying to himself, *"Tiens, tiens, perhaps I was mistaken that day."*

Police spies and *agents provocateurs* came to the *cachot*, spoke pityingly of the Soubirous' poverty and offered them money. They refused it with horror. When this was reported to Jacomet it gave him furiously to think. And Madame Jacomet too.

On Tuesday, March the 2nd, the thirteenth apparition occurred—a brief one. An hour afterwards, the child was seen, accompanied by her aunts Basile and Bernarde, going towards the presbytery again. Unfortunately several people had got there before her and had given the curé a garbled account of what the lady had said. As a result, the aunts and Bernadette were ill-received, so ill-received that Bernadette lost her nerve and forgot to tell the second half of the message.

M. le curé shouted more loudly that day because he was hoarse. "Ah, you have gone on visiting Massabielle! What have you come back here for?"

"The lady has told me that she wants people to come in procession to the grotto."

"I repeat once again, what is this lady called?"

"I don't know, *Monsieur le curé*. She does not want to tell her name."

"Ah well, since she won't tell you her name, you're a liar. It's a scandal. Workmen leave their work to go and see a liar. You realize, I suppose, that they will talk about you and the grotto everywhere. The scandal you are giving will be known. You've behaved like an animal. Eating grass! A procession to the grotto! If the lady wants to come, it is not to me she must apply but to the bishop. Doesn't she know that? Liar, how should we make a procession for this lady? We'll do better than that. We will give you a torch and you can go and make the procession yourself. You have a fine following as it is. You don't need any priests."

Bernadette replied: "I don't speak to anyone or ask them to come with me."

Basile Castérot, who gives this vivid account, says that the curé kept striding up and down the room in a fury, saying: "What a trial that family is to us, turning the whole place upside down! What next: a lady, a procession!"

It was frightening to see and hear him. The poor child, "all huddled in her hood," just stood there, not daring to move. At length, all three left in a hurry.

Outside in the street Bernadette clicked her tongue with dismay. "Oh, I forgot the other half of the message about the chapel! I must go back. The lady wants me to go."

Aunt Basile said, with a sinking heart, "Heavens above! Not again!" (As she explains in her account of the incident: "To hear *Monsieur le curé* made us tremble. We shook in our shoes as we listened to him.") None of them felt equal to another such encounter.

However, before evening poor Bernadette met a good neighbour, Dominiquette Cazenave, aged thirty-six, a member of the Confraternity of the Children of Mary. She said to her, "Please will you take me to *Monsieur le curé*? Neither my mother nor my aunts want to come with me."

This kind woman went to the presbytery on Bernadette's behalf. She said to *M. le curé:* "The little girl who goes to the grotto has to speak to you and her parents don't want to come with her. When may I bring her to you?"

"Bring her this evening at seven."

"Please, *Monsieur le curé,* don't frighten her."

"No, of course not."

"I'm very sorry, *Monsieur le curé,* that you don't see this girl when she is in ecstasy."

And with that she withdrew, leaving him to his thoughts.

So in the evening Bernadette, clinging to Dominiquette's arm, appeared at the presbytery again, and this time *M. le curé* made them both sit down. Bernadette repeated her first message and added the part about the chapel. "Even if it were only a little one," she explained. But *M. le curé* was adamant. He said he must know the lady's name, otherwise no chapel would be built. When she came out again into the dark Dominiquette pressed Bernadette to ask the lady her name, and Bernadette replied: "Yes. If I remember."

Early on Wednesday, March the 3rd, Bernadette went to the grotto accompanied by her mother. About four thousand people had assembled there. Alas, the lady did not appear. Bernadette and her mother rose from their knees, sobbing, and the crowds, deathly silent, parted to let them go home. A waggoner, Jean-Marie Cazenave, who had seen the grief of Mère Soubirous and her daughter, remarked: "I said to myself, if the child were pretending, what would prevent her from saying that she had seen this morning just as well as other days?"

Anna Dupas, who called to see Bernadette, at her home, found her leaning against her bed, grieving, her face in her hands. "What have I done to her?" she kept asking. "Perhaps she is angry with me." Just before half past eight that morning, her cousin André Sajous, who had been to Massabielle and had watched the child crying, came to her and said, "If you want to go back, I will go with you." Bernadette again heard the call to return. To avoid the crowds, they took the road at the foot of the citadel.

In the town there was a whispered rumour going about:
"She will not see her again. People have been misbehaving
in the grotto." As to the misbehaviour, we have Our Lady's
word for it, although what form it took is not known. Afterwards Bernadette explained to her cousin Jeanne-Marie Védère that the lady said to her, "You did not see me this
morning because there were some people who wished to see
what you looked like in my presence, and they were un-
worthy of it. They had spent the night in the grotto and
they had dishonoured it."

That evening Bernadette again went to the curé and told
him that the lady had only smiled when she was asked to
make the rosebush flower. "But she wants the chapel," she
repeated.

"Have you got some money to build it?"

"No, *Monsieur le curé.*"

"And I haven't any either. Tell the lady to give you
some."

During Bernadette's absence at the presbytery, visitors
had arrived at the *cachot* from Momères, near Tarbes—
Bernadette's Aunt Thècle, Madame Védère, and her daughter, Jeanne-Marie. This cousin Jeanne-Marie Védère was to
be a most important and interesting witness. (We have already quoted her testimony.)

(François Soubirous' sister Thècle had married a baker of
Momères. Her son, Jean-Marie Védère, was Bernadette's
godfather. He was a soldier, an upright young man who
was not ashamed to practise his religion in the army. It is
reported that when he heard Bernadette howling at her
christening he said to François Soubirous: "She will be very
bad, that girl. She howls too much." It is said that the lady
warned Bernadette not to become too attached to her godfather, because he was going to die young, and indeed this
came to pass.)

Jeanne-Marie Védère, who was a village schoolteacher,
longed to become a Carmelite nun, but she could not obtain
her father's permission. She must have been an exquisite
contemplative soul, and she won Bernadette's complete
confidence.

(When, at long last, Bernadette had learned to read, she devoured the life of her patron, St. Bernard, and found out so much about the Cistercian Order that she was able to tell her cousin Jeanne-Marie Védère all about it. She prophesied that Jeanne-Marie would join an order where the nuns wore white habits and ate no meat. And in fact Jeanne-Marie did become Mère Marie Gertrude at the Cistercian Abbey of Blagnac in the Haute Garonne. She died there as Subprioress in the year 1899, leaving a reputation for great virtue.

Had Bernadette herself had sufficient health to join this austere order, in which the nuns rise at two o'clock in the morning, she would have done so. But since she was not strong enough for such austerity and wished to enter only an order where she could keep the rule in full, she joined the Cistercians by proxy, as it were, through her cousin. The reason for her attraction to this order lay in their great devotion to Our Lady. When, afterwards, Bernadette had entered religion, her novice mistress must have sensed this attraction, for she intercepted—as she had the right to do— two letters from Jeanne-Marie, written to Bernadette from Blagnac, fearing, no doubt, that they would only trouble her and give her doubts about her vocation.)

Jeanne-Marie and her mother stayed in the rue des Petits-Fossés. No doubt André Sajous put them up for the night on the first floor, with Bernadette. Anyway the whole family, the visiting relations included, had an evening meal together in the *cachot*.

When the two cousins were alone together, Jeanne-Marie questioned Bernadette about the visions, cautiously, so as to avoid endangering the child's humility. Bernadette told her about the lady's sash and rosary: "The sky was not so blue," she said, "and the beads of her rosary were more transparent than mother-of-pearl or crystal or the finest jewels."

They all said evening prayers together. Bernadette vigorously scolded Toinette because she showed little taste for prayer. Bernadette always led family prayers. She would not begin until they were all kneeling. Her bearing was most reverent; she prayed upright, never leaning on the furniture.

In the meantime the mayor and the police, foreseeing that there would be at least twenty-five thousand people coming to market on the morrow, took counsel together, as to how to prevent disorders among these hotheaded folk. Accidents could so very easily happen on the rock overhanging the turbulent river. In order to impress the crowds, M. d'Angla ordered the police to carry blunderbusses and loaded pistols, and to wear chinstraps and gloves. They were to pass inspection before they set out. The most level-headed members of the force were to be on duty, and all were to assemble at six o'clock the next morning at the Hôtel de la Mairie. That evening M. Jacomet and others went to inspect the grotto itself, as there had been some rumours of practical jokes and sabotage.

At five-thirty the next morning, three physicians from Bordeaux, brought by a lady of Lourdes, came to the Soubirous' door, interested in examining Bernadette. They were allowed to do so, and she patiently answered all their questions. (The three physicians came back at three o'clock that afternoon. Their judgment on her was that she was healthy, both physically and mentally, but they said to François Soubirous, "If you want to keep your children, you ought to leave this place. It is too damp and airless here. You will all catch diseases in this place.")

At six o'clock, Bernadette went to Mass, accompanied by her Lourdes aunts, and her aunt and cousin from Momères. She prayed a little apart from them.

In the meantime, the streets, the alleyways, the market place, the roads were completely blocked with mules and horses, carts and carriages. Some country people had walked all through the night. They kept repeating to one another: "The Blessed Virgin will appear and we shall all see her." Several witnesses have said that they prayed all the way and that sometimes whole villages turned out to join the moving crowds. With full hearts they recited the rosary, the litanies of the Blessed Virgin and the Magnificat. The night was calm, the stars shone.

There were about twenty thousand people in all. The environs of Lourdes were overflowing with them. All the paths, all the hillocks, all the fields from which one could get a glimpse of the mysterious grotto were literally black with people. It was like a vast sea. Children had climbed the aspens in the meadow. Policeman Male says that there was a crowd hanging above the grotto. "If one person had fallen, he would have brought down ten more with him. It was a miracle that no one was killed."

For some of these people to wait for hours was almost heroic. Here is the testimony of Mlle. Jeanne Adrian, a schoolteacher from Gavarnie, who had arrived at eleven o'clock the night before. She knelt on very sharp stones until nine o'clock the next morning without being able to stir a limb. "I felt absolutely no discomfort from this prolonged kneeling in the same position and did not notice any cold from the river. I felt only peace and a tremulous joy at the thought of seeing Bernadette for the first time."

In church, where she was hearing Mass, when the faithful had made their Communion, Bernadette felt the call to leave for the grotto. Without saying a word to her relations, she sped swiftly out alone.

Jeanne-Marie Védère, who had noticed this, ran out after her. She caught her up and said, "Why have you left us behind like that?" Bernadette replied smiling, "Something made me leave and I didn't think to tell you." When Jeanne-Marie saw the crowds, she said, "But, Bernadette, in the grotto we'll be separated."

"Don't worry, you will be near me."

From that moment onwards Bernadette never broke silence of her own accord.

Some quarrymen who belonged to the Confraternity of the Ascension had worked the night before to widen the steep path down to the grotto, and also to put strong posts on either side of a path, quite near the grotto itself, to protect Bernadette. When she reached Massabielle, Bernadette asked for her cousin Jeanne-Marie Védère, for she had indeed been separated from her by the crowd. Jacomet and a policeman then brought Jeanne-Marie to her.

The child knelt down and began her rosary, her eyes turned fixedly towards the niche above the rosebush. And then, quite soon, there was a marvellous change on her face, and everyone cried out, "Now she sees her!" They all knelt, even M. Jacomet. Jeanne-Marie Védère has written, "I can't tell you the joy and happiness I felt at that moment. You could feel the presence of something supernatural, but however hard I might look, I could see nothing."

In the meantime Lourdes was completely empty—an astonishing sight on a market day. It was like a deserted city, a city of the dead. Abbé Pène, who came out at that moment to say his Mass, was struck by the solitude and the silence of the Place du Marcadal, and he could not resist going to a grove of chestnut trees on a height on the north of the road to Pau which gave him a view of the grotto. He has written:

"I was there when the heavenly lady appeared to Bernadette. The sky was clear and the sun was beginning to touch the mountains and the valley. My mind was filled with all sorts of thoughts and emotions. I did not altogether believe in her but I very much wished that we had been allowed to study these happenings at close quarters, since they might conceivably reveal some important manifestation of God's will."

But to return to events at Massabielle: Jeanne-Marie Védère records that Bernadette now rose from her knees and went into the grotto. "She stayed there, her eyes fixed, as though two people were face to face looking at one another. . . . I felt frightened . . . and drew back a little when I saw Bernadette graciously bowing and smiling."

When Jeanne-Marie questioned her afterwards, Bernadette explained that the apparition had been so near that you could have touched her by raising your hand.

Although the hoped-for miracle did not take place, the extraordinary thing is that the crowds showed no anger. As Mgr. Trochu has pointed out, had there been in these events any element of the merely human, the disappointment of the crowd, which had been noticed by Jacomet, would have vented itself in anger. "Instead, the disappointment was made up for by a conviction of the working of grace, as many witnesses testified."

For example, the policeman Bernard Pays, after seeing Bernadette crossing the Pont Vieux, was so much impressed

that one evening a short time afterwards he went down in
civilian clothes to pray in the grotto with his wife. Pays said:
"Since that day no one wants to leave Lourdes without having seen Bernadette close to."

The quarryman Martin Tarbès has written, "The people
nearest to the house having managed to get into it, I went in
with Bernadette. We made her go up to the first floor, at the
Sajous', and people began to come into the room, in single
file. . . . I helped to keep them moving. They went in by one
side and came out by the other, after having shaken Bernadette's hand or kissed her. This lasted for two hours."

Jeanne Adrian records: "I followed her home, and I had
the pleasure of kissing her warmly. Everybody wanted Bernadette to touch their rosaries." When it came to Jeanne-
Marie Védère's turn, Bernadette said, "Come now, you too?
What do you want me to do about it? I'm not a priest." However, after a moment's reflection she added, "Give it to me.
I will make it touch mine. Keep it, not because I have
touched it, but because it has touched the rosary that I had
during the apparitions."

The crowd was asking for Bernadette outside, and she
was obliged to show herself at the window. She was very
tired that evening and said to a friend of hers, who enquired
about her fatigue, "It would have been bearable if it had
been only the embracings." The police had to be called in to
prevent the collectors of pious souvenirs from chopping off
pieces of wood from the door and chimney piece of the poor
little room. Then a rumour went through the crowds that
Bernadette's parents had made everybody who wanted to
see her pay fifteen centimes. So she was more closely
watched than ever. A policeman asked everybody who came
out of the door, "Have you given money to the child?"
Eventually M. d'Angla could testify that he had been unable
to discover either Bernadette or her parents ever accepting
any money.

The Jesuit Père Cros tells us a touching anecdote he heard
from Martin Tarbès. "After everyone had gone, there remained only one, an unknown lady. First she wanted to give
some money to Bernadette, who refused it. Then she wanted
to buy Bernadette's rosary, but she refused either to sell it

or give it. Then she offered her some oranges and Bernadette did not want them, and as this lady begged her very much not to refuse, Bernadette replied, '*Eh bien,* madame, yes, but on condition that you will eat them with us.' The lady accepted and I, Martin Tarbès, remained with them and we dined together."

Jeanne-Marie Védère had kept the fast day. Up till three o'clock, she had eaten nothing. When Bernadette heard of this she exclaimed, "Look at her! Her way to God is by fear instead of by love. You make Him a severe God, whereas He is a loving one. You would have given Him more pleasure by eating something."

Again that evening Bernadette went to see the curé to tell of her lack of success on questioning the lady with regard to her identity. He made it obvious that he thought the whole business was a delusion, and when she returned to the *cachot* the poor child cried.

9.
THE LADY DISCLOSES HER NAME

And now twenty days elapsed. As she felt no call to go to the grotto, Bernadette remained away. In fact during that time she was most unwell with asthma and a cough.

In the meantime, on March the 6th, at Tarbes, the local newspaper, *L'ère impériale,* had charged that the child was simply cataleptic. (The Shorter Oxford English Dictionary says that "catalepsy is a disease characterized by a seizure or trance, with suspension of sensation and consciousness.") In its March 16th issue, the *Memórial des Pyrénées* seems to have taken up her defence and describes her as a very well-behaved girl, guileless, devout, and above all very gay.

Now in spite of the apparent eclipse of Bernadette, people came to the grotto, and everyone drank at the miraculous fountain or took away some of its water. By Sunday March the 14th, the grotto was lit up by candles every day. On March the 16th religious emblems appeared at the back of the grotto. There were a crucifix and three engravings representing the Virgin, surrounded by branches of laurel and box. Already there were rumours of cures among the simple people.

In the midst of all this, the whole affair was reported to higher government spheres in Paris. From being a purely local incident, it was now on its way to becoming a national one. The mayor, the prefect, and the police of Lourdes were in a wretched state, wishing by all that was holy that they had been able to suppress the whole business from the very beginning.

In ecclesiastical circles, however, things were very different. Easter Day fell on April the 4th that year, and on March the 15th the curé wrote to his bishop to say that the whole population had been stirred to the heart by these happenings, and that he had never seen such crowds at the Sunday sermons. Then he dared to suggest to his Lordship, that in view of the circumstances, it was not really necessary to have a mission. What would it serve to have special sermons if sinners were already being brought back to God by the events at Massabielle? Then Easter Day drew near. The confessionals were crowded with people, some going to confession for the first time in years. The parish priests were overjoyed.

One day Dr. Dozous met a group of about twenty stone masons. Amongst them was Louis Bouriette, who twenty years before had lost the sight of his right eye after the explosion of a mine.

"Monsieur le docteur! Monsieur le docteur!" cried Bouriette. "I can see! I can see quite clearly now!"

"What are you talking about, my good fellow?" replied the doctor. "You know quite well your blindness is incurable. What is this all about?"

But almost before the man told him he knew.

"Monsieur le docteur, I told my daughter to bring me some of the water from the new spring at Massabielle. The water wasn't as clear then as it is now. I rubbed my eye with it and then . . . I saw! I saw quite clearly!"

The doctor confessed that he was shaken. He knew that much more than he could guess at would come of this.

The people were in a ferment. They all talked of strange new happenings in the town of Lourdes. For example, M. Dutour, returning to his house from a party with his family and servants at one o'clock in the morning, had found all the candles lighted in all the rooms! And then on that strange 4th of March, at eight in the evening, people leaving the market suddenly saw a very bright light, in the air, on the town and around the grotto. It became so light that you could pick out a pin two yards away, and this went on for two or three hours. And then there had been that strange first procession of thirty women from the district opposite

Massabielle. They came with their candles and their resin torches all alight, singing litanies, and the onlookers were amazed.

Somebody said to Bernadette, "You've heard the rumours about the healing powers of that spring? Can't you see to it that your poor father's eye is restored?" But she knew that her own family would never benefit materially.

In the meantime, among the sceptics at the Café Français, a strange story was circulating: "Quite easy to explain the presence of that beautiful lady in the grotto on the eleventh of February. Why, it was Madame X who had gone there for an assignation with her lover! You know, he's an officer. When she was surprised by Bernadette, she played this trick on her, and the child is so simple that she was taken in." This whole silly story was disproved by the fact that the Madame X in question had been in childbed on February the 8th.

On Tuesday, March the 23rd, at eight o'clock in the evening, M. Jacomet was irritated to find a procession of six hundred people assisting at an inauguration ceremony in the grotto. In a wire frame ornamented with moss and flowers they had placed a plaster statue of the Virgin. This frame had been put there by Pauline Bordeu's family, who used to lend it every year for the temporary altar of the Blessed Sacrament in the rue du Baous on the feast of Corpus Christi. Visits to the grotto went on sometimes far into the night, and several carriages were seen coming from Pau, bringing people who had come only to visit the grotto.

On the night of Wednesday, the 24th of March, the eve of the feast of the Annunciation, Bernadette woke from her first sleep and knew she was being called to the grotto. She told her parents. "We cannot deprive her of this happiness," said the two Soubirous, and gave their consent for her to go. The good people of Lourdes who were so devoted to the Virgin hoped that something would be revealed on this great feast day. Bernadette went at five o'clock, asking her Aunt Lucile to come with her to carry her candle.

When she knelt down in her accustomed place between the stream and the rock, she saw that her lady had preceded her, for the light was glowing in the niche above the rose-

bush. According to M. Estrade's account, this is how Bernadette described the apparition: "She was there, calm and
smiling, and she was looking at the crowd as an affectionate
mother looks at her children. When I had knelt before her,
I said I was sorry for arriving late. She was always kind to
me, and she made me a sign with her head that I did not
need to apologize. And then I told her how much I love and
reverence her, and how happy I was to see her again. After
speaking to her of whatever came into my heart, I took out
my rosary."

The sky was clear and the dawn was breaking on Lady
Day. Oh how Bernadette longed to know the name of this
strange lady!

At that instant the oval of light moved from above the
rosebush, drew nearer to the ground and stopped under the
vault of the grotto. Bernadette rose and went towards the
apparition. Holding her lighted candle in her hand, she remained standing; several of her relations and friends had
followed her and were surrounding her. The lady was standing in the opening of the niche, and from there she looked
smiling at the statue and the candles which surrounded her.
Although they did not know it, she was very near to some
of the people who knelt there. So Bernadette, plucking up
courage, said in a resonant voice: "Madame, would you be
so kind as to tell me who you are?" The result was just as it
had always been, a gracious inclination of the head, a smile.
Again the child said: "Oh, Madame, would you be so kind
as to tell me who you are." Again the same movement and
the smile. Just then in Lourdes the priests were probably
reading the Gospel for the day. "The angel said unto her,
Hail Mary full of grace, the Lord is with thee, blessed art
thou among women."

Bernadette explained afterwards that she now felt more
daring. She went on asking for the lady's name. And then,
the lovely thing happened. The apparition, which, until
then, had kept her pale hands joined together, now opened
her arms, and lowered them. Then she joined her hands
again, drew them closer to her breast, and lifting her eyes
to heaven she said:

"I AM THE IMMACULATE CONCEPTION."[1]

Then she smiled again. She spoke no more, but still smiling, disappeared.

When the ecstasy was over, Bernadette asked permission from her Aunt Lucile to leave her candle there. This was the first of many that were to be lit on that wondrous day. Bernadette said afterwards to her Aunt Lucile: "The lady asked me if I would leave the candle to burn in the grotto, and as it was yours I could not leave it there without asking you."

On the way home Bernadette looked radiant. A family friend took her into her arms and whispered in her ear, "Bernadette, have you been told anything?" The child began to laugh, her face aglow with joy. The friend persisted and said, "Why are you looking so happy?" Then she replied, "I am the Immaculate Conception."

All the way back, a school friend of hers, Jeanne-Marie Tourré, walked with her, and she kept hearing Bernadette say the same words over and over again. "What are you saying Bernadette?" she asked her. "Oh, I'm repeating the name which the lady has just told me, because I'm frightened of forgetting it."

Instantly she went to the curé, accompanied by her Aunt Basile.

"We were not very well received," the aunt recorded. "The sudden arrival of the child, who was trying to remember the message and did not even greet him, annoyed him. He said 'What do you want today?' But without saying either *Bonjour* or *Bonsoir*, she kept repeating, 'I am the Immaculate Conception.'

" 'What are you saying, you conceited little thing?' cried *Monsieur le curé*.

" 'I am the Immaculate Conception,' she repeated. And then she explained: 'It's the lady who has just said these words to me.'

" 'Good! Good!' replied the priest, whose feelings were beginning to be stirred. However, he continued, 'Do you know what that means?'

---

[1] "Qué soy ér' Immaculado Councepciou."

" 'No, *Monsieur le curé.*'

" 'You see, it's your imagination again. How can you say things that you don't understand?'

" 'All the way from the grotto I have been saying "I am the Immaculate Conception" over and over again.'

" 'That will do,' said *Monsieur le curé.*" Then, adding that he would consider what was to be done, he dismissed them.

Afterwards he told Mme. Ribettes, who kept a grocer's shop, that he was so dumbfounded on hearing this, that he felt as though he were reeling and would fall.

As M. Estrade has said in his book, "One can tell lies with the words one knows, but not with words one does not understand." And indeed, on the evening of that very day, M. Estrade and his sister Emmanuélite invited Bernadette to come and see them. Bernadette asked them quite ingenuously: "What does it mean, *Immaculado Councepciou?*" She never could pronounce this last word correctly. (And when she described all this much later to Mme. Ribettes and to Marie Ida, her daughter, she imitated the Lady with a voice, expression and gestures which drew tears from their eyes.) M. Estrade has written, "Towards the end of her account the child was very much moved. She stopped a moment, then with tears in her eyes and her voice trembling, she repeated to us with a heavenly expression the Virgin's unforgettable answer."

Very soon Mary's name was known to all the crowds returning to their hamlets from the grotto. "We know who *she* is! We had already guessed!"

M. Estrade has written: "The feast of Easter, Sunday April the 4th, followed closely. Happy and proud because the Queen of Heaven had taken for herself the freedom of the city, the inhabitants of Lourdes went joyfully to Communion; apart from a few sceptics, the enthusiasm was general."

To the Pope who proclaimed the dogma of the Immaculate Conception, Bernadette wrote at the end of her life: "How good the Virgin is! She had come to confirm the words of our Holy Father."

10.

THE DOCTORS, THE BISHOP AND SATAN'S REVENGE

*"Misery me!" sighed Louise Soubirous, as she heard knock-*ing at the door. "When will I ever be able to do any tidying up here?"

Three doctors were at the door, Drs. Balencie, Peyrus and Lacrampe, sent by M. Lacadé, the mayor, on the advice of Baron Massy, the prefect. They had come to examine Bernadette to see if she shouldn't be locked up in the lunatic asylum!

When the girl was presented to them, these solemn gentlemen in black passed their hands over her skull to see whether she had any of the bumps of madness. (Gall's theories were fashionable then.) In their report they said: "She is in good health, has never had headaches or nervous attacks, drinks, eats and sleeps perfectly well. However, young Bernadette's health is not so good as one might suppose. She is quite obviously asthmatic, her breathing is slightly irregular and wheezy . . ." And then, trying to explain how she could have seen these apparitions, they go on to say: "This child is of an impressionable nature. She may have been the victim of an hallucination. A reflection of light has no doubt caught her attention on the side of the grotto." Extraordinary that they speak of "reflection of light" on a grey rock facing north, which deceived a child, not only at midday, but at five o'clock on a dark winter morning, and say that this should be sufficient to plunge her into a "state of pure ecstasy."

One of the first results of hallucination on human character is that the victim starts going downhill morally. The con-

nection between hysterical religious exaltation in a woman
and her lack of self-control, her idleness, her jealousy, her
pride amounting to megalomania, her vindictiveness, her
cruelty, all coming to a grand climax in attempted suicide,
has often been observed.

Now it strikes one forcibly that Bernadette was always
completely mistress of herself. Throughout, she showed
complete good sense, like St. Joan of Arc during her trial.
In fact the robust answers of the two girls are very much
alike. Between the apparitions, Bernadette continued hum-
bly to work at her catechism, and her French, which, since
it was never used at home, she found extremely hard, and
to do her duty in the house by her mother and her brothers.
Even the school nuns, most critically observant, noticed that
she had changed and had become more prayerful.

Benedict XIV, speaking of the discernment of apparitions
in his *Treatise on the Canonization of Saints,* wrote: "The
subject must not have prayed for graces of that kind. She
must have spoken of them to the competent authorities, and
while receiving them she must have kept her peace and
freedom of soul. She must have been eminent in humility
and mortification."

Mgr. Trochu quotes the psychiatrist, Dr. de Grandmai-
son de Bruno, who wrote in June 1913: "Bernadette's visions were not subjective but objective. They went far beyond her intellectual capacities. They were not connected
with her habitual occupations. They were reasonable, clear
and precise." And from this he concludes that she showed
no trace of hallucination.

Twenty years after examining Bernadette, in 1878, Dr.
Balencie gives us reason to suspect that he had qualms of
conscience about the day he saw Bernadette, for he writes,
alas twenty years too late: "It was impossible to suspect
Bernadette of fraud, and we were thus disconcerted as we
considered not a single vision, but a whole series of them.
What made the hypothesis of hallucination seem improbable
was the variety and yet the unity of the phenomena occur-
ring in the various apparitions. Moreover, we could not
understand why the same person in the same place, in the

same circumstances, had twice been unable to see what she had seen so many other times."

After their examination in March 1858, the doctors turned to poor weary Louise and said: "The child is simply suffering from quite understandable fatigue. She should not be sent to a home. When she has gone back to her ordinary life, she will cease to think of the grotto." And bowing low, they left.

On April the 2nd, M. Dutour wrote to M. Falconnet, the attorney-general: "It is not now in Bernadette's footsteps that the crowd has returned [to the grotto].

"Attention is concentrated more and more on the grotto."

At this juncture Baron Massy turned to the Bishop of Tarbes and Lourdes, Mgr. Bertrand-Sévère Laurence.

Monseigneur Laurence was then aged sixty-seven, having been born eight years before the French Revolution. His photograph shows a fine head, a resolute mouth, a face marked by austerity and hard work, a hard, reserved, prudent look, a shrewd eye and a firm chin. As he was making the tour of his diocese at the time, he had been absent from Tarbes, his episcopal town, for six weeks during February and March. He was a man providentially well fitted to fulfil a very delicate role in the whole affair. How fatal for the cause of Lourdes would have been one of those sceptical bishops of the eighteenth century, or an exalted enthusiast, or an aristocrat of the *ancien régime* who took no notice of *les petites gens*—the humble folk—or a prelate to whom the Mother of God meant nothing! He was the youngest of the eleven children of a peasant family of Oroix, who had become extremely poor after the destruction of their house by fire. When his mother was asked how she could feed so many children, she replied, "By loving the last one very much." In his boyhood he kept his parents' flocks, and did not learn to read till his late teens. Even then he was largely self-taught, in the intervals of being a barber's assistant to the neighbouring farmers. He was a very austere young boy with a delicate conscience, who showed a marked taste for the things of God. (As a childish prank he had once stolen a goose and stuffed it into a fox's lair. Afterwards, he con-

fessed his crime to the owner and offered to pay for the
goose.)

Eventually he was trained for the priesthood at Bétharram, near Lourdes. His lifelong love for the Virgin Mary
was thus nurtured in one of her oldest sanctuaries. He had
the good fortune to come into contact with some of those
splendid, rock-like priests of the early nineteenth century,
priests whose courage had been forged in the post-revolu-
tionary years. He became Superior of the Seminary of
Saint-Pé, where he distinguished himself by encouraging
outdoor sports, himself playing ball with the pupils and
singing local songs. He was austere in the advice he gave to
young priests, advocating plain hair styles and the giving up
of coffee-drinking! His sermons all showed his ardent devotion to the Virgin Mary. When he spoke of her, he was
visibly moved, and that, with him, was rare. He looked
upon her as the dispenser of the treasures of Divine Love.
But there was an austere note in his sermons on her, as if
long beforehand he were in sympathy with the lesson of
Lourdes which speaks so much of penance. He says no one
can count on the intercession of Mary who does not practise Christian obedience. It is recorded that he was often to
be found in his study, lost in prayer before his favourite
picture of Our Lady.

From 1835 onwards he started to restore the very ancient
sanctuary of Notre Dame de Garaison. It was there that in
the early sixteenth century, a shepherdess, Angleze, had had
a vision of Our Lady. Angleze eventually entered a Cistercian abbey, where she was notable for her obedience, profound humility, sweetness of character and discretion. Mgr.
Laurence wished to restore the whole diocese to the patron-
age of the Virgin Mary. There were so many ancient sanctuaries in Bigorre. As Gaëtan Bernoville said: "His stern
look did not frighten the good people who saw how like
one of themselves he was. All the men of Bigorre seem to
be hewn from the rocky ridges of their own mountains, and
he like the rest of them." With his compatriots he appreciated the *grain de malice* which gives a special flavour to the
local dialect. Once, when he was visiting his native parish of

Oroix, he said to a peasant woman: "Do you remember the time when we kept cows together?" To which she replied: "Oh yes, *Monseigneur*, but you have quite a different goad now." He was very simple in his ways, calling unannounced on country friends, arriving across the fields at the back door, and bringing joyful embarrassment to the whole household. Even before the encyclicals of Pope Leo XIII which did so much for the cause of social justice and the living wage, Mgr. Laurence loved the poor, and was haunted by the horror of slums. Those sick poor whom he visited in their hovels, how much he wanted them to enjoy the pure air of the Pyrenees and the cures at the nearby watering places! So in 1849, when he had already become bishop, he opened a home for them at Barèges.

In his administration, he was economical and down-to-earth, very observant, nothing escaping him. For robust and quiet balance, he had no equal among the bishops.

And then came the apparitions of 1858: soon his whole diocese was in a turmoil. But, for a long time, he knew how to keep silence. Now when the prefect wrote to him and sent him the medical report on Bernadette, he was obliged to emerge from this discreet silence. In his reply, he admits the possibility, the extreme possibility and even the likelihood, of hallucination as a result of cerebral lesion, but then he adds something of the utmost importance: "Only, I would have you observe that I do not rule out the supernatural."

For the first time, all these good Christians—the Massys, the Dutours, the Jacomets—were being made to consider the possibility of the supernatural in the whole affair.

In the meantime on Easter Day, the church of Lourdes was packed with people. There were 3,625 visitors to the grotto. The total for Easter Monday was over nine thousand. On Easter Tuesday evening, Bernadette experienced the same irresistible call to go to Massabielle. She was there on the Wednesday morning at six o'clock, surrounded by twelve thousand people.

Her ecstasy on that occasion lasted three quarters of an hour and was noteworthy for what is known as the "miracle of the candle."[1] This was observed and recorded by Bernadette's childhood friend, Julie Garros, who was later to become a nun at her convent. It was also witnessed by Madame Foch, the mother of the great field marshal.

Julie observed that the candle in Bernadette's grasp was slipping down, little by little; at last the flame itself was enclosed within the child's hand. A cry arose from the neighbours who surrounded her: "Oh God, she's burning!" But Dr. Dozous said, *"Laissez faire!"* The flame licked her hand for several minutes, but she remained utterly still. Then came the end of her ecstasy, and the candle slid to the ground. There was an immense sigh of relief from the spectators.

Dr. Dozous took the child's hand, rubbed it with his elbow —for it must have been blackened by smoke—and cried out in a loud voice: "It's all right!" These words were rapidly passed round to the very edge of the crowd. The enthusiasm was delirious.

The doctor went on with his experiment. Taking the candle, he put the flame under Bernadette's hand. Instantly she snatched it away, crying, "You're burning me!"

Insensibility during ecstasy is well known to mystical writers. P. Joyau, in his life of St. Thomas Aquinas, has given a remarkable example of it (quoted by Mgr. Trochu):

"One night when he [St. Thomas Aquinas] was dictating in his cell a passage on the Holy Trinity, he needed to have recourse to prayer to obtain understanding of a very obscure text. He knelt down, took a candle, and said to his secretary, 'Whatever you may see happening, don't call me.' Then he entered into contemplation. At the end of an hour, the candle was almost entirely consumed. Our saint had not felt the flame, which had reached his fingers."

After this, Bernadette remained away from the grotto for some time, and devoted herself exclusively to learning her catechism[2] in preparation for her first Communion, which was to take place on June the 3rd.

---

[1] This was the second occurrence. The first was on February the 23rd.

[2] The copy of her catechism is still treasured by the nuns at the Hospice: the part about Holy Communion is well-thumbed. In

And now occurred something very like those Pyrenean storms which spring up suddenly, blotting out the sky and hiding the mountain peaks, fraught with fearful thunder-claps and terrifying lightning flashes which leap from the growling clouds like demons from their lair, prowling men-acingly round the valleys as if loath to abandon them be-fore they have carried off their prey, and then just as sud-denly disappearing, leaving the sky serene once more and the air purer and more limpid than ever.

In Lourdes the devil himself seemed to be let loose with all his train of ugly followers. The sweetness and candour which was Bernadette's very atmosphere was for a time ob-scured in the eyes of her observers by a series of repulsive incidents, all the more distasteful for the contrast they made with those they aped, yet in some respects bearing the stamp of the supernatural—that supernatural, however, which is the province of Satan, and which thus tended to bring Ber-nadette's visions within their own evil orbit.

Their author seemed to be lashed to fury. To quote the Apocalypse: "The dragon was angry against the woman"—"the woman clothed with the sun" who was so resolutely crushing his head, as the Book of Genesis says in a passage applied by the Saviour to the Mother of the Saviour. No way of discrediting the simple child she had chosen was too loathsome, no class of person to be unwittingly employed as his dupe, too young and too innocent—or, on the con-trary, too deeply steeped in sin—to be used for his own vile ends.

And so false visionaries pullulated in the town or in the country round about, casting a tenuous veil of doubt over men's minds and subtly antagonizing them.

Perhaps charity is the first and greatest commandment; a woman with a venomous tongue concealed under an out-ward show of piety was amongst the first victims of Satan's

this "Catéchisme de Monseigneur Laurence," she learnt that "without humility, you cannot be saved." The passage about con-trition is marked with a cross. She learnt that "the happiness of Heaven consists in seeing God, loving and praising Him, and be-ing free from all sorts of afflictions," and that "avarice is an un-controlled love of this world's goods."

wiles. She was a wine-merchant's servant, an elderly woman, and at the grotto she suddenly started to cry out that she had seen *Aquéro*. The good women with her, over-gullible, took her back with the greatest respect to her master's house, where the supposed visionary fell into a dead faint. After this all the *dévotes* of Lourdes flocked round her in admiration. Must we believe in a direct intervention of the devil? Certainly not. But habits of sin lay souls open to temptation and diminish their resistance to it, and we shall see that at this moment the Father of Lies was, in fact, very active and making use of every sort of device for his own purposes.

On the 19th of April the police superintendent had written a report to the prefect about another case, and this time we are brought up with a jolt by the unseemly choice made of the instruments involved—on the one hand, a member of the local Confraternity of the Children of Mary, Claire-Marie Cazenave, aged twenty-two, a genuinely good girl, virtuous and religious but a little too impressionable, and on the other, a couple of really bad women, Madeleine Cazaux, a drunkard, and Honorine Lacroix, a hardened prostitute of over forty. With two other unnamed women the little group of five set off for the grotto, and, borrowing a ladder from the farm of the Espélugues and impelled by what motives, good or evil, we know not, but showing a complete lack of decency and respect for the place, climbed through a hole in the vault of the grotto. Finding themselves in a steep corridor, they wormed their way along on their stomachs, slithering down it like lizards for several yards until they reached a sort of crypt just large enough to hold them. The Cazenave girl, whose intentions were, presumably, good, seems to have begun to regret her escapade —as who would not in this dark, tomblike, claustrophobic place?—but she kept her head. "Since Our Lady deigned to leave Heaven for this spot, we were not worthy to set our feet in it, but as we have come, let us at least pray," she called out to her companions. By now they were in a state of panic and wanted to return, saying that they would pray down below in the grotto. Claire-Marie then said that she would stay behind by herself, but the others did not want to

leave her and so, perforce, found themselves kneeling on
the slimy stones saying the rosary by the flickering light of
a candle. All of a sudden they were startled by the appearance at the other end of the gallery of a form of medium
height which disappeared—and this is significant—as soon
as the blessed candle was raised in its direction, coming back
when the candle was moved away. The evidence of those
who saw it seems rather confused; Honorine Lacroix said
it was a child of four or five with curly hair falling on her
shoulders, blue eyes and a pale face with a touch of colour
on the cheeks. Another woman said it was a girl of about
ten, and a third was unable to see it at all, and was much
distressed thereby, crying out, "What have I done to be deprived of seeing what my companions see?" The others
appear to have taken it for granted that it was the Virgin
and exclaimed, "Holy Virgin, how pretty you are! What
beautiful hair you have!"

All this seems simple enough to explain: the figment of
overexcited minds. But, once again, it was exactly the sort
of thing that would repel right-thinking folk and make Bernadette appear to be just one more false visionary—and
what could be more in line with the striving of the powers
of darkness against the holiness of the Mother of Christ?

And the darkness was preparing to invade even more
deeply this spot which had so recently been the scene of
such sweetness that the most sceptical spectators had felt
themselves enveloped in the mysterious charm emanating
from the little girl kneeling there, unconscious of everything
but the vision of light and beauty so lovely that its radiance,
made almost visible on the upturned face of the child,
seemed to flow over the crowd in waves of peace and grace.

The ludicrous, the grotesque and the farcical were now to
add their tale of profanity, as though, despairing of piercing
the good sense of the people of Lourdes, the demon of deceit
wished, in a last angry gesture, to sting their pride and slur
their honour by the mockery of a horrible buffoon.

Three persons appeared to one pseudo-visionary: a man
with a beard, a young woman and a child—suggesting, of
course, the holy family of Nazareth, in whom we cannot
imagine the slightest vulgarity or imperfection; and yet we

find, to our horror, the man in this vision described as curling his moustache like the villain of any penny dreadful, and all three of them behaving in an unsuitable way. The profanation is comparable to that which a visitor to St. Petersburg after the Revolution saw in a church where one of the aisles had been converted into a skittle alley, and where a young man was painting a moustache on to the face of Our Lord in a beautiful old fresco. Merely to disfigure a poster in this way is a vulgarity, but what of the disfigurement of a sacred image?

A fifteen-year-old girl, Joséphine Albario, on April the 17th, began to claim that she also had seen the Immaculate Conception. She too wept, she too made strange movements, but she went one better than Bernadette, for, according to her, the Virgin was carrying a child and beside her stood a man with a long beard. Joséphine had clambered up the rock of the grotto and had to be brought down, carried home and put to bed; but that was not the end of her visions. M. Estrade and two colleagues saw her there again a few days later, taking up a pose intended, presumably, to convey the sorrow of a Mater Dolorosa. Her play-acting must have been convincing, however, for M. Estrade believed for a moment that he was once more in the presence of a genuine ecstatic. And yet something was missing that warned him of a possible fraud. He remembered how, seeing Bernadette's raptures, he had been completely carried away, whereas Joséphine's only left him surprised. A friend of hers says that she writhed and shrieked and wailed, and if this was all part of the pose she was adopting as interpreter of a sorrowful vision of the Mother of the dead Christ, then the horror is added to a hundredfold. From her subsequent admission that although she had indeed seen some mysterious personages she had felt that they were not genuine, it would seem that she was really a dupe of the Evil One and not merely suffering from delusions, induced or otherwise, or deliberately trying to deceive.

We have not, unfortunately, even yet exhausted the records of false visionaries and foul visions. On Ascension Day a young boy started shouting in front of the grotto. Dressed all in white—why does that seem so indecent?—with headgear which he had pushed into the shape of a top hat, he proclaimed that he was a prophet sent by God and the Blessed Virgin Mary to chastise humanity. Later on he was found in an inn, where the countryfolk were shocked by his outrageous behaviour, and he was arrested by the police.

Fortunately, the inhabitants of Lourdes seem to have been very shrewd and clearheaded about all this, and their sense of humour came to the rescue. One day when a boy appeared at the grotto commanding everyone to recite the rosary, and announcing that God was going to say it with them, a good woman protested: "But there's the world topsy-turvy, if God is going to pray to the Blessed Virgin!" Lucile Nicolau treated the business as a laughing matter, although she felt infuriated. Perhaps that is the best way to treat the grotesque, for certainly, otherwise, we should feel the sacrilege too deeply. There was the spinning youth described by M. Estrade, a peasant lad—was he merely a little simple?—who turned round and round, stared into the air and pursued some imaginary object with his hands; and the little girl who let out forced half laughs as she knelt gazing at something, until all of a sudden she turned over and rolled down the slope towards the river, being prevented from falling in only just in time. There was Minimo, the seventeen-year-old boy of Lourdes, who saw someone going from tree to tree having sometimes the appearance of the Virgin, sometimes a man's face. Horror and fear used to seize him, and during his trances, observed frequently by Madame Prat, he shouted and looked so frightful that she had to turn away.

Perhaps because *corruptio optimi pessima*, "the corruption of the best is the worst," the incidents which shock us most are those which involve children. We who have read the story or seen the play by Henry James, "The Turn of the Screw," know the particular horror which is attached to evil done by innocent-seeming and beautiful young children, by those "blue-eyed angels" whom one instinctively trusts, but who lie and deceive. Two priests were horrified one day to see a young lad in the grotto going through all Bernadette's motions of saying the rosary, holding a candle, bowing towards the niche, clambering towards the rock on his knees, but . . . looking entirely hideous, with shrivelled, repulsive features. Other children who aped Bernadette became loathsome to look at too, and some behaved like little animals.

Antoine Nicolau, miller of Savy, the man who had tried to bring Bernadette back from the second apparition, stupidly thought to give pleasure to his little nephew, or, perhaps, to persuade the Virgin to reveal herself to the child, by lifting him up to the niche, saying, "Look at the Virgin." The little fellow was frightened and asked to be taken down, but later on his uncle put him in again, and this time the boy said he saw something, and became frenzied, gnashing his teeth, grimacing and showing all the signs of possession by the devil. Another child, Alexandre Réau, the son of a Lourdes hairdresser who lived next door to the Estrades, saw at the grotto a sight which seems to be a deliberate mockery, and therefore of diabolic inspiration. Instead of the simplicity and purity of the *petite demoiselle* seen by Bernadette, we have a lady richly adorned after the manner of the times in furbelows, all golden, partly hidden by a lurid cloud, as though in a storm. She had large black eyes which frightened the little boy, who thought she was "going to eat him up." This child was perhaps a particularly innocent young soul, for he appears to pierce the pretence and divine beneath it what he called "the ugly one." But he was trembling all over and his eyes were starting out of his head and it was long before he could be calmed down. It was Mademoiselle Estrade, particularly good with children, who was asked to come and see what she could do to restore the child to normality.

Brother Léobard, the Lourdes schoolmaster, like many others, had grave doubts on the subject of Bernadette's visions when he found children from his own school suffering from a collective delusion, indulging in what he considered play-acting, and affirming that they too had seen Our Lady.

Is it not a double sacrilege to find the innocence of youth or childhood itself profaned by the profaning of holy things?

Sometimes the vexations were of a different kind and not always at Lourdes. Voices would be heard suggesting in some way that Lourdes was unholy or that people should not go there.

For example, Madeleine Lacaze, on her way to the grotto, heard a voice saying, "Woman, go away. The Blessed Virgin does not want you to go further." As far away as the Gironde district someone heard these words, "Leave Lourdes where only bodies are cured, here is the Lourdes of souls." It looked as if the Evil One had a special hatred for the people of Lourdes, and one day a woman from Omex who was present when some pseudo-visionary children were there heard in a mincing voice like that of an affected child these words coming from the grotto, "In the Valley of Batsurguère, and especially at Ossen, there are many respectable people. At Lourdes there is only the riff-raff." We shall hear an echo of this same diabolical voice, in a more subtle form, later on when Bernadette has gone to Nevers and finds herself amongst people, socially her superiors, who wonder why the Virgin should have chosen this peasant girl when there were so many apparently more refined souls who might have responded in a more elevated way, more nobly, without all the vulgar publicity, to the visit of the Immaculate.

The Prince of Darkness had had his hour—a long hour indeed, covering the period from April 1858 to February 1859; the powers of evil had been let loose and their influence had been brought to bear on those little ones of whom Our Lord had said that, rather than scandalize one of them, it were better to have a millstone hung about one's neck and to be drowned in the depth of the sea. The forms that the scandal took were various, as we have seen, extending from downright parody and burlesque of sacred things to such little acts of irreverence as throwing away the flowers from the altar at the grotto.

As Père Duboé has written, "Satan wanted to arouse suspicion against Bernadette's pure and splendid visions, but nobody who saw these things was deceived for long. The sight of them provided a triumphant proof in favour of the ecstasies which they were intended to dishonour." And so, at last, the rumblings of doubt were stilled, the clouds of conflict lifted, the dark mists of suspicion cleared from the valley. The immovable truth of Bernadette's message stood up magnificently against the storm-purified sky of her innocence like the rock of Massabielle itself.

11.

THE YEARS OF WAITING

Nothing makes one see more clearly the importance of great changes, either in a human situation or in the topography of a town, than to skip a few years and then observe them in a new perspective. Eight years went by before Bernadette left Lourdes for Nevers. It would be so easy to dwell for a long time with Bernadette at Lourdes during her last years there, before she became a nun at Nevers. But then one would go beyond the bounds of a single volume and slip into three!

By June, 1866, Bernadette had greatly changed in appearance. The photographs show her with a special beauty of her own as a little girl, and when she was a nun, at the end of her life, she was exquisitely beautiful. In her coffin, she was celestially lovely. But in that in-between stage, at twenty-two, the photographs are very unflattering. She looks awkward in her thick, unbecoming clothes; she has all the heaviness of ill-health, and she looks like just an ordinary peasant girl. So much for outward appearance. But she was no longer the little ignoramus of eight years ago. She could speak French, she could read; her spelling was never very good, but her handwriting had greatly improved, and was eventually to become quite pleasing. She had even acquired a charming style in letter writing. Always humble, Bernadette thought she was good for nothing, but she was a wonderful needlewoman, an adept at housework, and she had a special gift for looking after the sick poor. She had known all the horrors of poverty, and her heart had gone out particularly to one afflicted woman dying slowly of cancer, and to another unfortunate creature who had drunk too much and had fallen into the fire. Bernadette nursed her like a mother, and when she was about to leave the Hospice, she said to her laughingly, "Now you will have to give up '*imbibing*,' won't you!" Bernadette, more than anyone else, knew how the poor, with their empty stomachs and their attacks of exhaustion, were tempted to rely on just a drop more of the fiery liquor which gave one that fictitious, momentary energy, that feeling of release.

Learning to read had been so difficult. She had been obliged to learn her catechism orally, laboriously, syllable by syllable. A lady in the town had helped her in the evenings. Julie Garros, her junior by five years, the *enfant terrible* of the class, had been deputed to teach her in recreation time. Julie didn't like this in the least, and used to leave her to go and play hop-scotch with her friends. "Bernadette," she would exclaim, "how dense you are! You'll never learn." In despair, Bernadette had gone down to the grotto to wash her eyes with the spring water, hoping that it would help her to learn to read! And then, at last, had come a delightful nun called Soeur Elizabeth Rigal, sweet and kind with an angelic smile, who at length taught her how to read, and who declared that she "never had any trouble in teaching this charming child."

Bernadette would never forget the difficulties of that April of 1858. There was one day when she and her mother had appeared before M. Dutour. He had been comfortably installed in a chair. Bernadette and her mother had been made to stand for three hours. At length, kindly Madame Dutour, passing through the room, said: "There is a chair. Wouldn't you like to take it?" Bernadette, who was by then very much out of temper, replied sharply, "Oh no, we'd only make it dirty." She had not minded for herself, but she had felt for her poor mother. Bernadette finished up by sitting on the floor, cross-legged like a tailor. This well-deserved snub had infuriated M. Dutour and he had spoken of arresting them and sending them to prison. Poor Louise Soubirous, who had heard the word "prison" once too often, went home in floods of tears. Bernadette said to her, "Why are you crying, Mama? We haven't hurt anybody."

Bernadette herself, too, that April, had endured enough.

She coughed and coughed, and there were great rings under her eyes. *M. le curé* had been very kind; he had spoken about her ill health to the bishop and it had been agreed that she should be sent to Cauterets to take the baths. But even there she had been watched by the police.

M. Lacadé, the mayor of Lourdes, who had thought of bringing wealth to the town by making it a new watering place, had the spring analyzed by M. Latour of Trie, who concluded that "it could be classed among those waters which contribute to the mineral riches of this region." Fortunately, on the 3rd of June, a second opinion was asked for. M. Filhol of Toulouse analyzed the water again and showed that it was not a mineral water but completely ordinary, though of very pure quality. That water became the cause of several intrigues. The chemist, M. Pailhasson, the father of the horrid little girl who had smacked Bernadette's face at school, declared that the water was very bad. (He afterwards confessed that he had not analyzed it, and it became obvious that he had feared the town people of Lourdes would stop buying his eye lotions!) Then on June the 8th, 1858, the mayor of Lourdes announced that it was forbidden to go and fetch water from the spring, and equally forbidden to go to Massabielle. Much use this order was. The barriers which had been built were broken down four times, and women were constantly being fined for trespassing. Throughout, Bernadette remained calm and kept silence.

And then had come the great day, the Feast of Corpus Christi, Thursday June 3rd, when she made her First Communion in the little chapel of the Hospice. Like all the other girls, she wore a white dress, a white veil on her head and a white cape over her shoulders. (Only the cape is preserved at the Hospice as a relic. It has silk ribbons which no doubt were meant to fasten under her chin.) All the girls carried lighted candles. M. Estrade records that when Bernadette went back to her place, she "simply showed great happiness." On the evening of this wonderful day, Mlle. Estrade asked the child: "Tell me, Bernadette, which made you the happier—to receive our Lord or to talk to Our Lady in the grotto?" Bernadette hesitated for a moment and then replied, "I don't know. They go together and can't be compared. All I know is that I was very happy both times."

And on that afternoon, a wonderful cure occurred at the grotto. Six thousand strangers had come to visit Massabielle, with three or four hundred sick. In fact, an unbelieving magistrate of Lourdes was to complain of these crowds of limping, ulcerous invalids who flooded the town and filled him with such disgust. A poor jobbing workman of the countryside, accompanied by his wife, carried to the spring his little five-year-old boy suffering from paralysis of the spine. Dr. Dozous helped to hold him under the pipes of the spring for five or six minutes. Then, no sooner had the child been dressed and put down on the ground, than he got up again and walked with the greatest of ease to his parents. They burst into tears of joy and covered him with kisses.

On June the 4th at Tarbes, the prefect made up his mind that Bernadette must be got rid of at all costs, particularly as she seemed to have set an example to all those other mad visionaries in the district. They maintained that the report of the three doctors indicated that she should be locked up in the lunatic asylum. M. Lacadé, the mayor, went to discuss this with the curé. But if he thought he would find an ally in the gruff priest, he was much mistaken. There was a tradition in Lourdes that the curé had one night kept three mountain wolves at bay with his walking stick, and on this occasion, when the pastor saw his most innocent, his whitest lamb in danger, he rose up in his wrath and confronted the mayor. From having served in the lunatic asylum of Tarbes he knew its horrors. In a menacing voice he made a speech which concluded: "Tell the prefect that his policemen will have to cross over my dead body before they touch a hair of that child's head." This message was conveyed to the prefect at Tarbes, and that was the end of the matter.

After the last vision, on Wednesday April the 7th, Bernadette had not gone to the grotto for some time. There was the notice forbidding entry, anyway. Fortunately, Bernadette did not know at first that this notice was attached to the plank which her father was supposed to have stolen. Found lying in some outhouse of the mayor's, it had been

used, quite without malicious intention, by some workman.
But another workman told a newspaper, and a horrid article
about it appeared in September in the *Lavedan,* in which her
poor father was slandered. The curé tried to make François
Soubirous sue the newspaper for libel, but he was as calm
and quiet as ever, and refused to do so.

Some young girls had gone up to the simple little room
which Bernadette was given by her cousin Sajous on the
first floor and decorated a tiny shrine of the Virgin. It was
up there, after her day's hard work, that Bernadette loved
to sit and think of her Lady. Would she ever seen her again?
And then came a blessed day, Friday the 16th of July, the
Feast of Our Lady of Mount Carmel. There was an altar
dedicated to her in the parish church, and the day was also
the feast of the Slate Workers' Confraternity. Bernadette
went to Communion in the morning, and then in the evening, when she went back to church to pray, she heard the
call to return to the grotto. She rose and went to fetch her
Aunt Lucile, and together they went to the Ribère meadow
opposite the grotto, which was half hidden by planks.

It was eight o'clock in the evening and the sun was setting.
Bernadette took out her rosary and knelt down. Several
women who had been praying there joined the newcomers
who had followed Bernadette as she walked through the
town. They too took out their rosaries and prayed. A few
Aves, a movement of joyful surprise and then. . . . Bernadette joined her hands and raised them towards the marvellous vision. She cried: "Yes, yes, there she is! She is greeting us and smiling at us above the barriers!"

She said afterwards, "She appeared to me in the normal
place without saying anything to me. I had never seen her
look so beautiful."

One of her friends asked her: "How could you see her
from the meadow of the Ribère? The Gave is so wide at that
spot and the planks of the barrier were so high." Bernadette
replied, "At that moment, I saw neither the Gave nor the
planks. It seemed to me that between the Lady and myself
there was no more distance than at other times. I only saw
her."

This was the eighteenth and last apparition. "Since then,"

Bernadette testified, "I have never seen her again." (In passing, we must mention, as Abbé Laurentin has pointed out, that the main visions took place on Thursdays, on which day the Church especially commemorates the Blessed Sacrament. This emphasizes the Eucharistic nature of Lourdes' message. Many of the sick are healed when the Blessed Sacrament, carried by the priest, passes near their stretchers.)

Oh how tiring were the crowds flocking into the house, asking Bernadette to repeat, over and over again, the story of the apparitions! And how hard on her parents, who were thus hindered from going out to earn their living! To those who argued with her and doubted the veracity of her story, she would always reply very calmly, "I am not charged with making you believe it. I am charged only with telling you about it."

There had been an atheist, the Comte de Bruissard, on holiday at Cauterets, who, hearing that Bernadette had again seen Our Lady on the 16th of July, came over to Lourdes hoping to catch her out in a lie. One day Bernadette was sitting on her door-step, mending her stockings. She applied herself to this small task as if it were a great work of art. She looked up and there he was, the Comte, the man who denied God. She answered all his questions on the apparitions, because she knew it was her mission to answer. And then he said something surprising. "And how did she smile, that beautiful lady?" She looked up at him with astonishment, and then, after a moment of silence she said: "Oh, monsieur, you would have to be from Heaven to smile that smile again."

"Could you show me how she smiled? I am an unbeliever and I don't believe in your apparitions."

Her face clouded over and she said, "Then, monsieur, you think I am a liar? However," she added, "as you are a sinner, I will try to show you how Our Lady smiled." And she did so, looking upwards.

The man was so deeply touched that he went to the grotto and was converted. Afterwards he wrote: "Since then, I can't forget that heavenly memory. I have lost my wife and my two daughters, but it seems to me that I am not alone in the world. I live with the memory of the Virgin's smile."

On Wednesday, July the 28th, Bernadette was called to
the presbytery to meet a very important visitor—the gov-
erness of the Prince Imperial, the wife of Admiral Bruat;
she was accompanied by her three daughters and a Bon
Secours nun. This nun recorded afterwards, "When she
saw me, Bernadette threw herself into my arms and showed
great affection for me. . . . She had a heavenly expression in
her eyes which I have never forgotten.

"I begged her to go with us to the grotto. 'No, no,' she
replied, 'I am forbidden to, I can't.' But then she added
that she would show us the way as far as the bridge, which
indeed she did. And during the journey she walked by my
side, passing her arm through mine and holding my hand.

"When she was leaving us, she kissed me several times
and showed us the path to the grotto. . . ."

The rural policeman, Jean Callet, on duty at the grotto,
picked some branches of the rosebush for these new visitors. They were praying at the grotto inside the barrier when
they were joined by the great Catholic journalist, M. Louis
Veuillot. And then, supreme blunder, the policeman took
out his notebook and wrote down their names. They would
all have to pay a fine for disobeying the mayor's orders! But
this turned out to be a great blessing, because it provided
the incentive for Louis Veuillot, who had come to Lourdes
especially to study the case of the apparitions, to write
about them in the Catholic newspaper *L'Univers*. And as
for Admiral Bruat's wife, she told the Empress Eugénie all
about it.

Only July the 28th, Monseigneur Laurence ordered the
formation of a commission charged "to inquire into the
authenticity and the nature of the happenings of the last
six months." This commission was composed of eminent
ecclesiastics, geologists, physicists, chemists and physicians.

In the following month of September, the Emperor and
Empress were at Biarritz. They had heard from Madame
Bruat about the grotto being closed and had asked for a
revocation of the order. As a result, on Tuesday October the
5th, towards three o'clock in the afternoon, the rural policeman beat his drum and read the mayor's proclamation to
the people of Lourdes, that from this day onwards, access

to the grotto would be unhindered. Before night fell, all the inhabitants of Lourdes came to drink at the miraculous spring.

The Soubirous, a short time after the apparitions, had moved from the *cachot* to a house close to the church. There is an old tradition that Our Lady had once appeared to Bernadette in the *cachot:* the child must have found it difficult to say good-bye to this place, although she knew, of course, that life would be much easier for her mother if she had more room.

On Wednesday, November the 17th, Abbé Peyramele, accompanied by other priests, went down to the grotto for the first time. He found it very hard to hide his feelings. They had a good look round and then summoned Bernadette. (When there were important visitors, he would make her come to the presbytery, but he tried to keep her humble. He would say, "Here is the little girl you wish to see. The Blessed Virgin has given her graces which she doesn't deserve. Many of her companions would have been more deserving.")

The family did not stay long in the house near the church, but at last, helped by the curé and the bishop, they rented the Moulin Gras, on the Lapaca stream, and once more François Soubirous became a miller. Bernadette had her own little room. From her window she could see the great trees of the Ribère in front of the grotto.

In April 1859 an Englishman called Mr. Standen came to call, and as he showed some interest in the workings of the mill, Bernadette called her little brother Jean-Marie to open the sluice gates, and then she explained the way the whole mechanism worked in a very intelligent fashion. When he left her, Standen was convinced that he had been speaking to a very amiable little girl, superior, for her age and her social position, both in manners and in education.

The curé ordered some wonderful bell-ringing on the Feast of the Immaculate Conception 1858. He had set all the bells ringing as if the bishop himself were coming into the town. And this good parish priest who had asked for the miracle, that the rosebush should flower in midwinter, again asked God for a sign that Bernadette had not been deceived.

The sign was granted to him one Sunday during Mass. He noticed somebody kneeling before the altar with a luminous halo around her head. He was very much struck by this. He gave her Communion without looking at her face or realizing who she was. Then he looked at her as she went back to her place and, when she turned round to kneel, he realized it was Bernadette. At that moment his anxiety ceased and he no longer had any doubts about the apparitions.

Quite soon, Bernadette was allowed to increase her Communions from once to twice a month. Abbé Pomian, her confessor, realized that her visions had given her understanding beyond her years of the mysteries of the faith. When she prayed, the sisters could not help noticing in her eyes an expression which was not in the other children's.

In the spring of 1859 Bernadette went to Cauterets and again in October. It was the visitors to the Moulin Gras who were so exhausting, with their foolish, prying questions, and their offers of gold pieces. Jean-Marie got into serious trouble with Bernadette on this score. At their request, he had once carried some water from the spring to some visitors to Lourdes, and they had given him two francs—a fortune in those days to poor people! He brought these two francs home in triumph. "Didn't I tell you never to accept anything?" Bernadette cried. She was furious. She gave him a sharp slap and ordered him to return the two francs immediately. He obeyed, and when he came back, Bernadette searched him thoroughly to make quite sure he had not hidden them on his person.

Bernadette was still mischievous in the classroom. Just before her Confirmation on February the 5th 1860, during a nun's catechism class, there had been whisperings and stifled gigglings in the schoolroom. The nun stopped and said:

"I am sure that the Holy Spirit will not come down on those children. They're too frivolous." She pointed to Bernadette's place. A little confused, Bernadette rose and said:

"It was all my fault, Sister."

"Do you mean to say that a child who has had the favour of seeing Our Lady can upset the class like that?"

"*Ma soeur*, I have to take snuff for my asthma. I offered

a pinch to my neighbours. They refused it, but they pretended to sneeze all together, and that's what made them laugh. You see, Sister, it wasn't their fault."

The sister punished no one. She found it very hard to keep a straight face.

Bernadette shared another good joke at the Hospice with Julie Garros, during the strawberry season. Some deliciously fragrant red strawberries were ripening, under their leaves, near the windows of a room where a town dressmaker gave dressmaking lessons to some of the pupils. Bernadette was there, and next to her the restless *enfant terrible*, Julie Garros. "It was hot, the windows were open. We were looking with greedy eyes at the strawberries." At the time of the short recreation, during which they all stayed in the room, Julie confessed that she really must have some of them. Bernadette said, "I will throw my shoe into the garden. You go and fetch it and bring back some strawberries." And so she did.

In mid-July 1860, in order to safeguard her privacy and her humility, the curé and the mayor arranged that Bernadette should become a boarder with the nuns at the Hospice. She was then sixteen and a half. It was hard to leave her mother and father, particularly as in the September of the previous year, Louise had had another little boy and Bernadette was his godmother. But she was assured by the nuns that she could go home nearly every day, and her poor, harassed parents would be freed from this continual flow of relentless visitors. *M. le curé* arranged that if ever Bernadette was interviewed by anybody at the Hospice, it should be in the presence of a nun—this might make them more considerate and discreet.

When she went to live with the nuns, Bernadette did not know for certain that she was going to join them eventually, though she knew that she would one day be a nun somewhere. And then, she had said of Our Lady: "When you have once seen her, you can never love the earth again." The nuns gave her a cheerful, well-ventilated room of her own, and very good food, and never accepted a sou in payment. This charming house with its long pillared colonnade still stands, and the "Sisters of Charity and of Christian In-

struction" still run a hospital there. No doubt, one of the
devoted sisters attended to Bernadette's head, so that those
importunate little visitors which attacked even St. Margaret
Mary as a child were annihilated with antiseptic lotions!
This child of the poor was naturally neat and tidy, fulfilling
St. Thomas Aquinas's dictum that peace is the tranquillity
of order.

The nuns held free classes on the ground floor, but on the
first floor, two paying classes—one at five francs a month,
the other, which was Bernadette's, at two francs. This was
frequented by the daughters of artisans who were not poor,
and the daughters of business people. Her schoolroom
looked westward. Through a big window Bernadette could
see the valley of the Gave and the poplars of the Ribère, the
poplars she loved so much and was always to remember.

Bernadette's besetting sin was obstinacy. One Sunday
after Vespers, the nuns told her to take off her new Sunday
dress, and she refused point-blank. And then there was the
day when she wanted to go down to her parents' mill, against
the nuns' wishes. She felt a sudden, overwhelming need to
see her new little brother and argued about it for two hours.
And what about the stirrings of feminine vanity? There was
the day when Sister Victorine caught her spreading out her
skirt to make it look like a crinoline, and the day when she
put a kind of busk into her corset. But this "fever" didn't
last long.

We have a charming story recounted by brown-skinned
Bernarde Vignette. She used to go into Lourdes with her
donkey from the nearby countryside. One fine day she met
Bernardette a little below the cemetery, going to Massabielle. She herself was going to Omès, which lay in the same
direction. Bernadette asked her in patois, "Will you take me
on your ass?" ("*Boulé mé pourta sus én asou?*") Bernarde
Vignette replied, "Climb on." ("*Pouyets.*") Bernadette
twined her rosary round her arm and mounted, helped by
her little friend. Bernarde held the bridle. It took a quarter
of an hour to get to Massabielle. Bernadette said how
frightened she was of meeting *M. le curé*. When she dis-
mounted she asked with a laugh, "How much do I owe

you?" Bernarde answered, "Pray for me." (*"Qué prégaras per you."*) She asked if Bernadette often went to the grotto. Bernadette replied, "Every day. If it's not in the morning, it's in the evening."

M. Estrade tells us that during her little pilgrimages to Massabielle, Bernadette would begin by kissing the ground, go on to drink some of the miraculous water, and then, so as not to attract attention, she would kneel in the shadow of the grotto, where she would devoutly recite her rosary.

At the thought that one day she would be removed from this place, never to see the grotto again, Bernadette's heart would stand still. Why, it was her Heaven on earth! But wherever she was, she would in spirit make a daily pilgrimage to that beloved grotto.

Protected though she had been by the nuns at the Hospice, all her lessons had been interrupted by the constant flow of visitors. In the classroom, the nuns had put her desk near the door so that she could leave without disturbing the others. Over and over and over again, she had to tell her story, reproduce the Lady's gestures, answer the same questions. But, as has been said: "The objectivity of the apparitions comes out all the more clearly for being reaffirmed in unchanging terms over a period of twenty years."

And then there were the silly women who wanted to have locks of her hair, as if they were relics. She simply refused to give them. All she would do was to write on a little holy picture "p p Bernadette," which meant *"priez pour Bernadette."* And then her schoolfellows would tease her and call her "Pé-Pé-Bernadette," which always made her laugh.

During one of those parlour sessions Bernadette, though usually calm and collected, lost her temper with the curé of a neighbouring parish. He had asked her for the twentieth time, "Was the Blessed Virgin very pretty?" and she replied: "Oh yes, *Monsieur le curé,* much prettier than you."

Somebody asked her once: "Would you recognize her in Paradise?" and Bernadette replied, *"Bien sûr,* provided she hasn't altered."

Then there was a day when a Dominican priest (who afterwards left the Church) said to her sneeringly: "The

Virgin Mary might have taught you to speak correct French while she was about it." And Bernadette replied, "She certainly never taught me to make fun of humble folk."

A certain important lady said to her, "You said that the Virgin Mary has confided secrets to you." Bernadette replied, "Yes, Madame." The lady said, "You shall tell them to me." At these words Bernadette changed entirely. She rose from her chair, put her hand on her chest, and looking at this great lady without a trace of shyness, she replied resolutely: "Madame, I keep my secrets to myself." And right after her interview with this important personage, she chattered with a friend of hers, Romaine Mingelatte, about the nut harvest: she had not been in the least impressed by the conversation with the society woman.

Mgr. Laurence wished to preside in person at the final session of the Court of Enquiry which took place in the church sacristy. Bernadette was summoned. She appeared, wearing her white cloak and her sabots. When, on their demand, Bernadette showed the gesture of the Lady as she said: "I am the Immaculate Conception," the old bishop thrilled from top to toe, and two great tears rolled down his cheeks. When Bernadette had gone, he cried out to the others: "But did you see that child!"

At last he made his proclamation, on Saturday, January the 18th, 1862: "We are convinced that the apparition is supernatural and divine." He said that he judged the tree by its fruits, for the apparition was divine because the cures bore a divine stamp. Then the old bishop broke out:

"Rejoice, inhabitants of the town of Lourdes! The Queen of Heaven has deigned to bend her merciful gaze on you . . . A new era of grace begins for you."

Ah yes, on that day Bernadette really felt she had fulfilled her mission towards her Lady. And now soon they would build a chapel and they would go in procession, as she had asked.

In the spring after the proclamation, she had been very ill with pneumonia and had been cured by drinking a drop of Lourdes water. In October she went to the Nevers Sisters, at Bagnères-de-Bigorre. When she was questioned about the apparitions, she who was usually so gay and mischievous would become grave and serious. Other orders longed to possess this rare pearl. They were even stupid enough to come and make her try on their habits to tempt her. The Sisters of St. Vincent de Paul came to Lourdes and put their immense white starched coif on her head. Then the Sisters of the Cross tried their long cornet on her head, and she exclaimed: "I don't want that tunnel." A Carmelite friar came and said she ought to become a Carmelite, and Bernadette replied:

"I love Carmel, but if I embrace religious life, I want to enter a congregation where I can keep the rule."

He said: "But my child, the superiors can always give dispensations." She replied, "I don't want dispensations, Father. I want to follow the rule without any exceptions."

The Sisters of the Hospice rather frowned on her seeing her cousin, Jeanne-Marie Vèdère. Perhaps they were afraid she might influence Bernadette to join the Cistercians. But when the curé heard of their disapproval, he said that Jeanne-Marie was to be allowed free access to Bernadette. The Sisters of Lourdes, according to Julie Garros, were forbidden to speak to Bernadette of her entry into any religious order. In fact the Nevers Superiors really rather dreaded the responsibility of taking her into their midst, because of the numerous visitors who would flock after her, to the great disturbance of conventual peace. They shivered when they recalled the turmoil brought by Mélanie, the visionary of La Salette, to all the convents where she had gone.

In 1862, Mère Ursule Fardes, the Lourdes superior, was replaced by Mère Alexandrine Roques.

In the meantime the chaos of Massabielle was being transformed into order. When the grotto was cleared, the curé wrote to the bishop to say that the lowering of the ground level had given it a most grandiose appearance. The architect of the new chapel wished the grotto to remain as it had been during the apparitions, open to the sky and to the murmur of the Gave.

On Tuesday October the 14th, 1862, they started to build the foundations of the future chapel, and Bernadette was glad to see her father going to work there. Soon the hills around were echoing with the blasting of the rocks, and the curé said enthusiastically: "Detonations make the earth tremble, and no doubt, they make Heaven thrill!"

In the afternoon of Thursday the 17th of September, 1863, the curé appeared at the Hospice with M. Joseph Fabisch, professor of Sculpture at the Lyons School of Art. He had already done a sculpture for Notre Dame de la Salette and had been commissioned by two demoiselles de Lacour to make a statue of the Virgin in white marble and place it in the niche of the apparitions. He had not wished to start work without gleaning some information from Bernadette. He asked her to reproduce the attitude and gestures of the Virgin when she said, "I am the Immaculate Conception":

"The girl rose with great simplicity. She joined her hands and lifted her eyes to heaven. . . .

"But neither Angelico of Fiesole nor Perugino nor Raphael has ever achieved anything as sweet and at the same time as deep as the glance of that young girl.

"No, I shall never forget as long as I live that expression of rapture. I have seen in Italy and elsewhere the masterpieces of great artists, of all those who excelled in depicting the transports of divine love and ecstasy: in none of these have I found so much sweetness."

In 1864 the feast of the Annunciation was celebrated on the 4th of April: this was the day chosen for the blessing of the statue. But neither the curé nor Bernadette was able to assist, as they were both ill. The streets of Lourdes were garlanded with ivy and box, and with star-sprinkled draperies. Twenty thousand people followed Mgr. Laurence in procession from the church to the grotto. When he arrived at the place beneath the rosebush, the bishop unveiled the statue. He blessed it and incensed it. The crowd remained utterly silent. The curé of Sainte Geneviève in Paris preached on a text from the Song of Songs: "Arise my love, my beautiful one, and come. My dove in the clefts of the rock, in the hollow places of the wall, show me thy face, let thy voice sound in my ears, for thy voice is sweet and thy face comely."

The sculptor, who was among the crowd, was most unhappy. He confessed afterwards, "I must mention one of the greatest sorrows that, as an artist, I have experienced in my whole life. It is the disappointment I felt when I saw my statue in place, lit up by reflected light coming from below, which completely changed its expression. Ah! I understood at that moment that the coloured sculptures of the ancients and of the Middle Ages had their *raison d'être*."

When Bernadette saw the statue, she said: "Ah, it's very beautiful but it is not she." And later she said: "Oh no, it is the whole difference between earth and heaven." Fabisch had failed in one important point: the Lady's extreme youth.

On Friday September the 25th, 1863, the Lourdes Hospice had a very important visitor, Mgr. Forcade. As a young missionary priest, he had been imprisoned by the Japanese. Now, at forty-seven, he was Bishop of Nevers. He had a handsome profile and kind eyes, and was very gay in private conversation. Bernadette had been told to ring the bell to announce his coming, and he found her clinging to the cord. *"Prou-prou-prou!"* he said, which in the patois means "Enough, enough, enough!" Bernadette was inclined to trust a bishop who spoke her native dialect, and when she went back to the kitchen to scrape the vegetables she was laughing merrily.

When he was taken on a tour of inspection of the house by the Superior, he noticed Bernadette again, cleaning carrots by a corner of the kitchen, and during the meal she helped his servant to serve him at table. Then he saw her alone. After she had told him about the apparitions, the following conversation took place. (It is recounted in a pamphlet Mgr. Forcade wrote after he became Archbishop of Aix.)

"Well, my dear child, and what are you going to do with yourself?"

After a moment's hesitation: "Nothing special."

"How nothing? One must always do something in this world."

"Oh well, I am with the kind sisters."

"No doubt. But you are only here, and can only remain here, temporarily."

"I'd like to stay here always."

"That's easy to say but hard to accomplish."

"Why is that?"

"Because you are not a nun and it is essential to be one to be admitted into a community of sisters. . . . Here you are nothing, and on that footing it is not possible to achieve anything durable anywhere."

There was a long silence, and then he continued: "And now you are no longer a child. Perhaps you would be quite pleased to make a suitable marriage?"

The reply was very spirited: "Good gracious, no! I have no desire for that!"

"But then, why shouldn't you become a sister? Have you ever thought about it?"

"It is impossible, Monseigneur. You know very well that I'm poor. I haven't got the necessary dowry."

"But, my child, they sometimes accept poor people as nuns without a dowry, when they have a real vocation."

"But, Monseigneur, the young ladies whom you take without dowries are clever and capable, and will make it worth your while. But I don't know anything and I'm good for nothing."

"Oh, so you're good for nothing? But I saw you not so long ago in the kitchen, and I realized then that you could always do something. In religion they would know how to use you. Besides, in a novitiate they would complete your education."

He concluded by advising her to pray to the Blessed Virgin Mary for light.

When the bishop went to Toulouse, he met the Superior General, Mère Louise Ferrand, from St. Gildard's Convent at Nevers, who was there with her secretary (the next Superior General), tall, beautiful Mère Joséphine Imbert. Mère Ferrand explained that she hesitated to take Bernadette because of her health. She said, "She will only turn into a pillar of the infirmary, by her continual presence there."

However, at the conclusion of the interview she said, "We will receive her if she asks to be admitted."

By the feast of the Assumption, 1864, Bernadette had decided. She said to the Lourdes Superior: "My dear Mother, I have decided to become a nun, and if your Reverend

Mother General will accept me, I should be happy to enter your Congregation."

From then on Mère Alexandrine Roques admitted Bernadette to all the community exercises. She went on with her embroidery, and when given the task, she proved herself to be an excellent infirmarian.

The crowds continued to come as usual, particularly on feast days. They simply exhausted her. She complained to a priest, "I am always going up or down stairs. . . . I am tired of seeing so many people. Pray for me—that God will either take me or that He will soon allow me to consecrate myself to Him."

Mère Joséphine Imbert, who was now Superior General, seemed to show no great anxiety to receive her. Towards the end of 1864 she told the bishop, again at Toulouse, "We will receive her directly her health is stronger."

After a winter of ill health Bernadette was admitted, at the end of 1865, as a postulant at Lourdes. She had by then joined the class paying five francs a month, frequented by the young ladies from the richer families of Lourdes. A very sentimental photograph has been preserved of all the young ladies in crinolines, holding each other's hands, and sprightly, elfish Bernadette in the midst of them with an amused and rather subtle smile on her lips. All the other girls look very affected. Bernadette alone, dressed in her Pyrenean peasant's dress, seems completely natural.

Occasionally she was asked to mind a class in the sister's absence. She knew how to keep them in order, for she loved children. Once she said to them:

"Mes mignonnes, you have behaved yourselves very nicely. I am going to give you a reward. We shall say a Hail Mary together."

1866. The decisive year. Very soon after Easter, which fell on April 1st that year, Bernadette, on the advice of her Superior, wrote directly to the Nevers novice mistress, Mère Marie-Thérèse Vauzou, at that moment taking the place of the Superior General, who was ill. Bernadette told her of her great desire to give herself to God wearing the veil of the Sisters of Nevers.

The letter so delighted the novice mistress that she read it aloud to her novices. Then she said:

"You understand what a grace and what a favour it is for us to receive the privileged child of Mary, and how grateful we ought to be. For me, it will be one of the greatest joys of my life to see the eyes which have seen the Blessed Virgin."

And then she sent such a motherly and affectionate letter to Bernadette, that she was delighted, and she wrote in her turn to her old Superior, Mère Ursule, saying that the noviatiate must be a real heaven on earth.

On April the 15th, 1866, trains had started running from Bordeaux to Lourdes. A special train appeared on Whit Monday, the 21st of May, for the inauguration of the sanctuary by the bishop. The train was crowded, and even so, it had to leave thousands of people behind at stations all along the line. The rocks which used to lie scattered in front of the grotto had been taken away, the ground had been levelled and drained and a large granite barrier had been put along the Gave. The course of the Savy stream had been diverted. An inscription had been put near the miraculous spring:

"Go and drink at the fountain, and wash there."

It was all so greatly changed that Bernadette hardly recognized it, though when a priest asked her, she was still able to point to the place where she used to kneel.

Bernadette took part in the procession to the grotto with other Children of Mary. According to her cousin, Jeanne-Marie Védère, she was as lovely as an angel in her white dress and veil. The crowds kept crying out, "Oh, what a pretty saint, *la jolie vierge!* . . . How lucky she is." She was almost smothered, and pieces were snipped off her veil. The nuns had to form a bodyguard around her, or else her clothes would have been torn to bits. And all Bernadette could say was *"Mais qu'ils sont imbéciles!"*

In the evening, the crowds besieged the Hospice, some even climbing the walls in order to see Bernadette. A few of the soldiers convalescing in hospital had quickly to don their uniforms in order to defend the place. In the end, to satisfy everybody, Mère Ursule Court made her walk up and down under the gallery. Poor Bernadette complained, "You are showing me off just like an animal at a show."

On the first of February, 1865, little Justin, then ten years old, died in his mother's arms. And then, at the beginning of 1866, Louise Soubirous had her ninth and last child, a little girl, who only survived long enough to be baptized. After this final blow—five children now lost—Louise Soubirous knew that her health had gone and that her days were numbered. When Bernadette had left them for Nevers, it would be the Soubirous' sixth child gone. They would be left with Toinette and the two boys. But generously they did not oppose her vocation, though Louise had grown increasingly to feel that she could not live without her Bernadette.

Bernadette went to Bartrès, it is said to bid good-bye to her foster mother. Some of her conversations there are reported by Abbé Zéphyrin Vergez.

One can picture her last walk up the hill to Bartrès, in late June. At the end of an hour's walking, the spire of the little church came into sight. She paused for a moment and glanced up at the hillock on the right, to the hut where she had herded her flock on wet days. A bark, a scuffle, and here was her old sheep dog, Pigou. She bent down to caress him. A flood of memories assailed her. Could she ever get used to the indoor life at Nevers? Oh! never to keep lambs, never to be alone again, when she had grown so to love solitude and silence. She would always remember those long hours, surrounded by her familiar snow-capped mountains. Then she recalled the words of her Lady:

"I do not promise to make you happy in this world, but in the next."

Just then, a kindly village woman, who had often given her food for her basket, appeared at a turning in the road. When she saw Bernadette she embraced her heartily. She had always thought there was something mysterious about the child since the day, during a storm, when a torrent had divided to let her pass with her lambs. She was a reliable woman, and she had told this story to one Louis Courtade, who passed it on, on his deathbed, to the parish priest, M. l'Abbé Vergez. Bernadette steadfastly denied all these miracles, and reliable authors have scarcely touched on them:

yet . . . it is strange that these charming legends had passed into the traditional folklore of the countryside.

However, this Bartrès woman knew Bernadette's matter-of-fact nature too well to remind her of these things at such a time. "Pray for us all here, Bernadette, when you go away," she said.

More neighbours appeared at their doors to greet her, and ducks and hens and piglets joined in the general commotion. Bernadette was, in a sense, the private property of Bartrès, for the villagers had dandled her as a baby. Bartrès was one of those many obscure hamlets of France which, by the native goodness of its inhabitants, had won a blessing and deserved to shelter a saint: no one was ever seen intoxicated, a sacristan had devoted his evenings to teaching the villagers to read and write, and they all knelt in the fields when the church bell tolled the hours of prayer. How one would love to unearth parish records, like those of the seventeenth-century villagers on the Loire, who, all assembled in their church one day, were privileged, collectively, to see a vision of Christ in glory!

As Bernadette neared the Lagües dwelling, Justine, the fourteen-year-old daughter of her foster mother, whom she had once looked after, ran to meet her. Flinging her arms around her neck, she cried: "Oh, I wish I could come with you!"

At the farmhouse, they were all in tears, all of them. Bernadette alone was tearless. She is reported to have said: "Come now, let us be brave. The little time we have to pass on earth must be well employed. I am glad to be going."

And then she walked back to Lourdes for the last time.

What a different journey from the one in January, eight years ago, when hunger for Christ in Holy Communion had driven her back to the *cachot!* . . .

As Michel Carrouges has said, in *Fêtes et Saisons* for October-November 1956: ". . . the apparitions were one thing and the destiny of a saint would remain quite another matter . . .

"But the girl could go nowhere without being surrounded by admiration. It was a very great danger.

"She has passed unscathed through a hard childhood and

the period of conflicts about the apparitions. But now . . .
she has matured, she has learnt a great deal, she has been
the centre of attraction of a crowd of people; will she be able
to remain untouched by it? Will that simplicity of hers give
place to the arduous humility of the saints who face life
clear-sightedly?"

"She is no good at anything,[1] says the Mother-General;
and the bishop quite agrees. . . . It is not the same thing to
say so oneself and to hear it being said to one. It is one thing
to say it and quite another to base one's life on such a dictum. Bernadette has received the glory of the saints at the
beginning of her life, and she must strip herself of it. To
find the road of sanctity, she must behave as if this glory did
not exist. All she has received from the Virgin, she must
give back to her in silence and sacrifice, to find it again in
the only glory which does not fade, that of God's kingdom."

She would be leaving for Nevers on Wednesday, July the
4th. On Tuesday, the eve of departure, in company with
several nuns, Bernadette went to the grotto to say good-bye.
She knew she would be leaving Lourdes for ever. She knelt
below the statue and prayed with her eyes fixed on it. Then
she sighed and started to sob. "Oh, my Mother, my Mother,
how will I ever be able to leave you?" She rose to press her
lips to the rock under the rosebush.

The Superior said gently: "Now we must go."

Bernadette implored: "Oh, just one more minute, it's the
last time."

She wiped her eyes, gave one last long look at the statue,
then, without looking back again, she returned to the town.

Mère Alexandrine said: "Bernadette, why are you grieving in this way? Don't you know that the Virgin Mary will
be your Mother everywhere you are?"

"Oh yes, I know; but the grotto—oh, it was my Heaven!"

She spent the last evening with her family at her father's
mill, now called "La Maison Paternelle," which still belongs
to the descendants of the Soubirous family.

The following morning, very early, the whole family

---

[1] *"bonne à rien."*

came to say good-bye. They were all in tears. She alone was dry-eyed. Trying to smile, she said, "You are very kind to cry, but I cannot stay here always."

A benefactress had insisted on her accepting a light-blue dress with dark-blue stripes. She carried for the journey a large and rather pathetic French umbrella and a cloth bag for her immediate necessities. The kind nuns had packed her trunk, taking care to put in it all sorts of good things, such as chocolate and snuff and the dark handkerchiefs which were necessitated by snuff-taking, and flannel under-wear. With her went Mère Alexandrine, the Superior of Lourdes, Mère Ursule, the Superior of Bagnères, and two other postulants.

The grotto can be seen from the train on its way to Tarbes. One last anguished look, and then . . . no more.

And now, to Nevers, to be trained in sanctity. Eventually, it was not the visionary of Massabielle whom the Church canonized: it was the nun of Nevers. And she was raised to the altars of the Church because she had practised virtue to an heroic degree.

BOOK TWO: THE NUN

❋

12

THE NUNS OF NEVERS

*Nevers is a quiet cathedral town, in whose dark, twist-*ing streets are found charming old houses and Norman churches. The convent of the nuns of Nevers, St. Gildard's, founded in 1856, is a short distance beyond the park, almost on the western outskirts of the town. Built on a hillock, it is a vast white building with an imposing façade and two wings. The name St. Gildard's is derived from that of the priory on whose site the convent was built. In Bernadette's time the landscape was completely rural, but today the fields, once so green and peaceful, are covered with houses. The air is healthy up there, and there is no record of any epidemic ever touching St. Gildard's.

It was a hot day in early July. Doves could be heard coo-ing in the distance, and the summer breeze was heavy with the scent of lilies and roses. In the cloisters, the black-habited nuns were walking slowly towards the gardens, their hands in their sleeves, as the rule demanded. The folds of their skirts were heavily pleated, their faces were framed in spotless white caps with two flaps coming down in front, called *bavolets*. Over the white wimples, the professed nuns wore a black veil. The postulants had a charming little black tulle bonnet, frilly-edged and tied under the chin with a bow.

The private studies of the Superior and the novice mis-tress adjoined on the ground floor of the convent, opening out on to the cloisters, but they had two sets of doors for greater privacy. From the novice mistress's room a smiling novice now emerged. Half an hour ago, when she had gone in, she had been in tears, but now she was fully at peace.

"Oh," she said to herself, "how good our Mother is! A real mother."

In the novice mistress's room, from which the novice had just emerged, Mère Marie-Thérèse Vauzou now sat alone, at her desk between the window and the fireplace, her eyes fixed on a statue of Our Lady of Sorrows. She was a striking, almost a distinguished-looking woman of forty-one, with an air about her of having a strong personality. The firmness of her mouth, with its rather thin lips, was contradicted by a melancholy, almost pathetic look in her deep-set, heavily-lidded eyes, under plaintive brows. She had a long, intelligent, finely modelled French nose.

Mère Vauzou had been in office now for the last five years, responsible for so many young souls. Eventually she was to be elected to the highest posts in the order, in which she was respected and loved for many years. She lived only for the order.

The daughter of a Corrèze notary, Laure-Guillaumette Vauzou had a "lively, ardent nature." Even in her school days she had liked to rule over her fellow students. After a careful education in various good schools, she thought that she was called to the vocation of marriage, but when she was seventeen years old, on the feast of All Saints, 1842, came the day which she called "the day of her conversion," and she had decided to leave the world. She had entered the novitiate of the Nevers Sisters in 1844, the year of Bernadette's birth.

She had soon been given teaching posts. Her pupils came to her quite freely, as they would to a mother. She had been Superior of the boarding school of Blaye, and she was still remembered for her assiduous and tender care especially of the sick, and all this in spite of living a very austere life herself. One day, one of her nuns accidentally discovered that all the time she was hurrying up and down the stairs with trays for her sick nuns, she wore a hair shirt and iron chains, and at night she used to take the discipline.

When she went to be Superior at Montpellier, a nun said that her community was a little Paradise. It has been said of her that "never did she leave a grief unconsoled, a distress without succour." In spite of her severity, her novices loved and trusted her. When they looked in her eyes and saw that glance so gentle, so deep, they knew that her heart was filled with kindness and supernatural love for them. And when they left her room after a talk about their difficulties, they were ready for all the sacrifices of a nun's life. They longed to be more generous, they wanted to conform to her ambitions for them and be more virile in God's service.

In her own interior life of prayer, she had two great attractions: firstly, devotion to Our Lady of Sorrows; secondly, nocturnal adoration of the Blessed Sacrament, for she loved to keep the Holy Hour on Thursday nights, like St. Margaret Mary.

God had given her a very refined, sensitive and impressionable nature. She loved her novices, but she wanted also to be loved by them in return. She could only help them if they were completely open with her. She did not want them to have any superficial attainment: she wanted them to dig their foundations deeply. She gave her instructions in a striking manner. With a word, she could sketch an abuse, a fault, and pitilessly unveil all the lower, human side of a novice, the side which the novice hardly dared look at herself. Her words and phrases had a certain piquant charm, a savour all their own:

"Each one of you must become a little violet and not a sunflower. Look at this flower, it is very dazzling, but where is its perfume? As for you, you must give all your perfume to Our Lord. However, if you insist on being sunflowers, I allow it, but only on condition that the Sun to which you ceaselessly turn shall be Jesus.

"You have often seen the horns of snails, haven't you? Well, directly you touch the horns, he draws them into his shell. Now, when you see the horns of self-love, lock yourself up in the shell of humility.

"In the community be . . . like sugar in water . . . that is to say, so lost in the midst of your companions, that you will be indistinguishable. Crush that little self underfoot."

She was so much adored that once, when she was away, a novice was caught drawing a picture of herself as a dove flying after some other dove—Mère Vauzou—and on it she had written, "Come back to us quickly, dear mother."

Mère Vauzou loved humility very dearly, and she felt that this great virtue could be acquired by humiliations. On New Year's Eve of 1862, she had spoken of this to her novices. "In the world, they wish each other prosperity and happiness. I wish two things for you, humiliations and mortifications." If there was any novice in her flock who was gifted and cultivated, she must learn the spirit of humility and self-effacement.

On that July afternoon of 1866, shortly before Bernadette's entrance into the convent, she picked up the instructions concerning novices written by the founder, Dom de Laveyne, and read: "The sister charged with leading the novices will take great care, during the time of their probation, to notice if their disposition is fervently inclined to obey and to endure snubs and shamings. She will make them practise all that is most hard and mortifying in a nun's state; she will put them to the test by trials, by humiliations, by making them embarrassed and confused . . . ; for your life, my dear sisters, is nothing but a life of abjection, humility, of crosses and curbings. 'Do not,' says St. John, 'believe in all spirits, but put them to the test to see if they be of God.' "

She closed the book and was lost in thought. Yes, she would have to apply these wise rules to this new postulant, of world-wide renown, Bernadette Soubirous. For the good of her soul, the girl would have to learn to be ignored. She took a key from her voluminous nun's pocket and unlocked a drawer in her immense desk. She drew out from it the manuscript of the Life of Marcelline Pauper, the illustrious daughter whom Dom de Laveyne had trained.[1] Here was a nun who had lived for years seeing Christ in vision, and who tried to respond to such extraordinary favours by a life of almost formidable austerity. In the novitiate her novice mistress had subjected her to a series of humiliations and harsh treatments. She thought that would be the decisive test as to whether the novice were deceived or not. Although Marcelline had been unused to manual labour, she now

[1] This was not printed till 1871. Its revolutionary preface censured all those overcautious superiors who were frightened of visions and ecstasies.

made the fire for the bakery oven, baked bread, milked cows, cleaned stables and carried dung.

No one knew better than Mère Vauzou how important it was to protect the intense young novice from the perils of her own imaginings and from the temptations of the Evil One, who would whisper in her ear that she was really something unusual, if he saw her enjoying sweetness in prayer. She, the novice mistress, would only be doing her duty by her novice if she protected her strenuously against this. Mère Vauzou had heard how Bernadette at Lourdes had been treated as a saint—the crowds calling out, "Oh, the pretty little saint!" At Pau, she had been mobbed by crowds and had to be protected by the police. Her visions had received full ecclesiastical approval at the end of a long and careful investigation. And now hundreds of pilgrims were coming to bathe in the stream, to pray in the grotto, and some were cured of their ills. The child was no doubt surrounded by perils, ever leaning towards a temptation to spiritual pride. It was the duty of the Sisters of Nevers to protect her from this or she would lose her immortal soul.

Then Mère Vauzou started thinking of another child ecstatic, Mélanie Calvat, who also had seen Our Lady, in the mountains of La Salette, who also had sought admittance to the cloister, and who had done nothing but cause scandal by her wanderings from one convent to another, and by her pride and spirit of independence. For eight years, the saintly Curé of Ars had had doubts about these apparitions, and as for Mgr. Dupanloup of Orléans, he had had a longstanding antipathy for Maximin, Mélanie's fellow visionary. He used to say: "Sometimes the ancient serpent lodges in hands joined in prayer."

But no, there could be no doubt about the authenticity of Bernadette's visions: they were marked with the seal of ecclesiastical approval. Still Mère Vauzou often had a nagging, uncomfortable little doubt: the rosebush had not flowered. Abbé Peyramale had told Bernadette to ask the lady to make the rosebush flower in midwinter, and nothing had come of it.

And, to return to this Mélanie—such a worry. In 1854 the bishop had harshly refused to admit her to profession at the

Providence of Corenc, because she clung obstinately to her
own interpretation of certain things. She was lacking in
humility and Christian simplicity. In May 1854 she had
changed to the Sisters of Charity—and there she had *bitten*
her Superior! She had not been venerated there as in her
first convent. Far from it: it had been made clear to her
that she must reform entirely if she were to stay, and she
had remained only three weeks. They said of her that she
was "headstrong and full of herself."

Then Mgr. Newsham had taken her to England to the
Carmelites of Darlington, and there for her Clothing ceremony she had been dressed like a bride, weighed down with
jewels. The ceremony was attended by the élite of English
society. At this convent she had adopted mystical attitudes
and invented all sorts of stories. Nevertheless, for three or
four years, all seemed to be going well. Then she began to
get restless again. After six years she was throwing letters
over the wall to the postman. Eventually she returned to
France.

Thereafter she oscillated between Carmel and the Sisters
of the Compassion. She was forbidden to speak about her
visions or to reveal herself. But alas, she spoke of them to a
curé of Marseilles, who then spread the news. As a result,
she was not kept in the order. "Heaven knows what will
happen to her now," thought Mère Vauzou.

Yes, all the trouble started in the first order, where Mélanie had been surrounded with an atmosphere of quasi-
veneration. Seeing Visions did not make one a saint, only
the practice of virtue. St. Thomas Aquinas said that these
gratuitous graces are not sanctifying in themselves. There
is no connection between them and the merit of the re-
cipient.

And now Bernadette must be protected, not only from
the crowds, but from herself. Here she had been called by
God to a retired spot, and God would speak to her heart.
Pope Benedict XIV said: "Give me a religious who perfectly
and perseveringly keeps his rule in its letter and spirit, and
I will not hesitate to place him on the altars of the Church."

And then Mère Vauzou's mind went back to what Christ
had said to her own patroness, St. Teresa of Avila, in a vis-

ion: "I prefer one nun who will serve Me with attentive
generosity to a thousand others who fulfil their duties towards Me with tepidity and negligence."

Indeed, she thought, there were some flowers which could
not bear the sun's rays. If they are to be deliciously per-
fumed, they must be kept in the shade.

She thought: what a privilege for the order to receive
Bernadette! And what a great privilege it was for her, Mère
Vauzou, to be responsible for training her. Perhaps, after
all, the Lord had looked with approval upon her own long
years of austerity and fidelity to the rule, and had ordained
in His providence, that none other than she should be the
guide of so precious a soul, a soul who had been favoured
with the sight of His own mother. Perhaps also it was a
reward to her for her own great devotion to the Mother of
God, a devotion she had sought to inculcate in her novices.

She rose, locked up the books, smoothed her habit and
adjusted her veil. Then she went into the room which was
the office of the Superior General, Mère Joséphine Imbert.

Mère Imbert and Mère Vauzou were great friends. Owing
to the chest complaint from which Mère Imbert suffered,
she had often to rely on Mère Vauzou to do her work for
her, when she herself was coughing away in the infirmary.
She trusted Mère Vauzou implicitly, and in fact her reliance
on her stemmed from deeper causes than her own ill health;
she was rather timid, and thus perhaps the more inclined to
take her friend's views on a situation involving personal
relations. Mère Imbert was of stately height and bearing
and had been nicknamed, for this reason, "the Empress."
Her portrait in oils, still in the community room, shows her
actually to be rather commonplace. There is even a hint of
unkindness in her face. But we are told by all the chronicles
that she had a man's intellect and a woman's heart. You
could see, as she swept along the corridors of the cloister,
that she was really somebody, a person of importance.

In those days the nuns of the order were called "Les
Dames de Nevers"—quite a contrast to the Sisters of St.
Vincent de Paul and the Little Sisters of the Poor. Most of
them had been to convent boarding schools where they had
learnt good manners, and a certain refinement. They knew

how to express themselves elegantly and politely, and how to begin and terminate letters with all the usual elaborate French courtesies. Their manners had a certain polish and distinction. For each one of her daughters, Mère Imbert had the gift of just the right tactful phrase, which would help her in her difficulties. Her kindness kept them in thrall. Each one of her nuns would leave her presence, persuaded that she herself was the object of her especial kindliness. The warmth of her heart was proverbial.

This day, when Mère Vauzou came to see her, she was looking rather pale, despite the hectic flushes in her cheeks, and she had a handkerchief clutched nervously in her hand. She greeted her friend with a smile. "Come and sit down," she said. "I suppose you have been thinking of Bernadette, just as I have, and praying for wisdom to guide her aright. I think she will be easy to manage. Our Lourdes nuns have often told me that she is a warmhearted, spontaneous little creature."

Mère Vauzou said nothing, but she felt pleased. "Ah," she thought to herself, "I have always been a little frightened of mystics. If she is a real mystic, she'll probably reconcile me to these strange, extraordinary happenings at Lourdes. If only she would trust me and open her heart to me!"

As Bernadette was coming without a dowry, the question of spending a few francs on her religious habit was discussed. Yes, her trousseau would be incomplete, they were quite sure. She was to be provided with snuff. Apparently she was to take snuff under doctor's orders. "I've been talking with Monseigneur about the question of visitors," said Mère Imbert. "He and I are completely in agreement, that she must be protected from the importunities of the outside world. Very, very occasionally, he says, he might allow a bishop to come and speak to her, but she must not be allowed to think that she is a personage of any importance. The life of the convent must go on as smoothly as before. We can't have flocks of callers at the guest parlour, and the extern sisters at the porter's lodge are to be told to admit no one."

Mère Vauzou said, "I suppose the posts will bring quantities of letters to her. I hope I shall have the time to read everything, though I daresay I shall not be able to answer them all. Our Lourdes nuns have told me that she has a cousin called Jeanne-Marie Védère who is going to become a Cistercian nun at Blagnac some time this autumn. She used to come and see her at the Lourdes Hospice. The nuns weren't too anxious to have her at first. When *Monsieur le Curé* heard about this, he insisted that she was to be allowed to see her as often as she liked. I suppose if she writes to Bernadette, it would be more prudent not to let her see the letters. She might suddenly begin to pine for the white habit of the Cistercians. We don't want to lose such a treasure: that is my one fear. I want the order to have the honour of keeping her."

Mère Imbert smiled. "Don't talk about honour, my dear Mère Marie-Thérèse. It is more in the nature of a very humbling responsibility than an honour. I've just been rereading our Dom de Laveyne's instructions to Superiors. He says that the Superior must deal gently with weak and imperfect nuns. I conclude from this, that if the Superior sees she's dealing with a holy nun, she can be quite severe. My first instinct when I think of this little Bernadette, so highly favoured by Heaven, is to run to her, to fold her in my arms, and to treat her with reverence and affection. I must resist that temptation for her soul's good."

Mère Vauzou said: "Yes, we must both resist the temptation. Oh Mother, what a consolation for both of us to look into the eyes which have seen Our Lady!"

13.

THE NOVICE

Having left Lourdes on Wednesday, July the 4th, and passed by Bordeaux and Périgueux, Bernadette and her little group arrived at the station at Nevers at half-past ten on the evening of Saturday, July the 7th. They were all very tired. The convent carriage was there waiting for them—that large closed carriage which Bernadette got to know so well. They crossed the leafy park, deserted at that hour, and at last drove under the convent porch. All the lights were out, for it was long past the nuns' bedtime. The Superior herself, who had just been seriously ill, had not been able to wait up for them. Also it was the time of the great silence, so there were no unnecessary words. They were given refreshment, and then Bernadette was led to the large dormitory with its four rows of beds swathed with long, white, beautifully pleated curtains. Her bed was at the far end, near a statue of the Virgin, which she could dimly see by the night-light.

Completely exhausted and very near to tears with homesickness, she undressed and slipped into bed. Alas, she did not sleep much, but cried a great deal. She kept thinking of her poor mother's face, already touched by the Angel of Death. She would never see her again. Nor her father whom she loved so dearly, who had come to see her every day when she had been at Bartrès. And her grotto—oh her grotto which had been her Heaven on earth . . . What a sacrifice! How could she ever live without it?

In the morning her eyes were very red. As they all washed their hands and faces in a central lavabo, the other novices looked at her with avid curiosity. To their astonishment, they found that she was not in any way different from any of the other postulants, except that she was much more timid. She looked very neat.

(Bernadette's exquisite cleanliness, her love of order and her care for all her possessions, was noted by more than one contemporary. She had been trained to this in a hard school by her mother, and in all the squalor of the *cachot* where six human beings, some of them rather disorderly, had had to keep clean in so small a space.)

A nun left a record of how she helped Bernadette to unpack the trunk she had brought from Lourdes. The Lourdes sisters had slipped chocolate in among the linens. Bernadette said, "They'll think me very greedy when I bring these provisions to our Mistress." The sisters had provided flannel shifts because of her asthma. Bernadette remarked that they had put in too much linen, she would not live long enough to use it all. She knew that her life would be short.

Just then Mère Vauzou appeared at the door. She looked at Bernadette, dressed in her new blue Pyrenean frock with its dark-blue stripes, and her little striped head-scarf, tied at the side. How tiny she was, almost insignificant! Bernadette looked up at her and smiled timidly, and then Mère Vauzou saw her eyes for the first time—those wonderful eyes. As one nun said, they seemed as if they had been created on purpose for seeing Our Lady. They looked as if the great visions of Massabielle were still reflected in them: great, dark, limpid, glowing eyes, suggesting untold depths. They had a completely otherworldly expression. And, like the eyes of the great St. Catherine of Genoa, they were fringed with long dark lashes. Mère Vauzou forgot all her good resolutions and opened her arms like a mother: "Welcome, my very dear child."

Bernadette hesitated for a moment, then cast herself into those arms and was lost in a large motherly embrace. A tear trickled down Mère Vauzou's face. She wiped it away hastily and then, controlling her voice, she said, "Now, my dear child, for the first week I am going to put you in the care of a Sister from your own district, Soeur Emilienne Duboé. She was with our nuns at Bagnères-de-Bigorre, near

Lourdes. She will be your guardian angel and show you round the house and garden. She will tell you our timetable and the rule and what is expected of postulants. Here she is."

Now Soeur Emilienne was twenty-five, and it was a good idea to put her in charge of Bernadette during those first trying days, for she could speak to her in her own patois. First of all she told her the timetable:

Five to five, rise.

Five thirty, morning prayer and meditation.

Six fifteen, Holy Mass.

Seven ten, breakfast.

Eleven fifteen, examination of conscience.

Half-past eleven, midday meal.

Twelve o'clock to one o'clock, recreation, followed by chapter meeting and then the reading of *The Imitation of Christ*, or recitation of the rosary.

Three o'clock, visit to the Blessed Sacrament, or some spiritual reading or the Stations of the Cross.

Five thirty, spiritual reading in community.

Six o'clock, meditation, and perhaps benediction of the Blessed Sacrament.

Six thirty, supper.

Seven to eight, recreation.

Eight thirty, evening prayer and reading aloud of a point for meditation on the next day.

Go to bed.

The rest of the postulants' time was occupied by housework, by helping in the infirmary or the kitchen, by teaching. In fact they were kept very busy.

Bernadette came to love the novitiate and the house. She spoke of the place as a "devout and holy shelter," a "dear and holy shelter," a "house of God." It seemed to her that the novitiate was a paradise on earth.

All the north wing of the convent belonged to the novices, and beyond that wing was a shaded terrace, gay with flowers, and overlooking large vegetable beds. The novitiate garden, into which Soeur Emilienne now led Bernadette, was a charming retreat with its lawns, flower beds and shrubberies. In the centre was a statue of Our Lady of Victories, called "Notre Dame de Force" by the nuns.

"We have recreation here," said Soeur Emilienne, "and our dear Mother Mistress comes to share it with us three times a week."

"Do you have skipping-rope?" asked Bernadette timidly.

"Oh yes, quite often, and hide-and-seek."

"I'm so glad. I love holding the rope for other people to skip." (She had never been able to skip herself, because of her difficulty in breathing.) "I'm glad our Mother Mistress will come to recreation."

"Oh yes, she's very kind to us, even though she may seem strict. Why, the other day she caught one of her novices trying to miss breakfast because she wasn't hungry. She has eyes at the back of her head, I think. She sent for her to her room and she said, *'Ma petite,* you will take your breakfast on your knees in front of the whole community for the next eight days. That will make you remember that one must always ask for permission.' "

"What is that little statue?"

"Oh, that one? Saint Teresa of Avila, our Mother Mistress's patron saint. On her feast day we act little plays in her honour. For example, I think next time we shall have the scene where the seraphim pierced her heart with a burning arrow. I'll have to make some paper wings. Oh, but I'm forgetting my duties. Mother Mistress told me she wanted me to talk to you a little about our founders and the aims of our Order. Come, we will sit on this terrace and admire the view. It overlooks the vines."

"Our Mother Mistress has seen the manuscript of Marcelline Pauper's autobiography," Soeur Emilienne said, when they were seated. "It would be a good thing if people who imagine that young girls only come into convents because of lovesick hearts could read it. Marcelline Pauper was one of the first and most illustrious nuns of our congregation, you know. She says that when she was seventeen, although she did not want to marry the young men who came to court her, she loved to talk with them because she appreciated their fine qualities and their intellects. There was a certain young man who loved her passionately. One day when she was enjoying listening to his pleadings, she says that 'Our Lord made His presence felt within me, and I felt His reproaches keenly. Grace was hemming me in.' She says herself that to realize the presence of God was as easy to her as breathing. And then one day, when she had become a nun and was leading a very austere life, Our Lord said to her, 'My daughter, love makes lovers equal. Do you want to resemble Me in My sufferings?' After that she lived in great austerity. She felt so very much drawn to praying for the conversion of sinners, that she would offer all her mortifications for them and try to make reparation for their crimes."

At these words Bernadette's eyes looked far, far away: she was recalling the day when Our Lady had said to her: *"Pénitence! Pénitence! Pénitence!"* What tenderness had been in her eyes as she gazed down on the sinners praying at the grotto in the dawn!

Soeur Emilienne continued: "Do you remember the picture of the Benedictine monk which hangs in the novices' room? (By the way, that's called St. Gertrude's—you know, the room with the desks and the china ink pots.) Well, it is Dom de Laveyne, our founder, and in 1680, in the reign of Louis XIV, he lived quite near here, at Saint-Saulge. Dom Jean Baptiste de Laveyne. He had become the titular prior of a dilapidated abbey. In fact he was the only inhabitant. To start with, he was far from saintly. He was passionately fond of playing tennis—a very worldly sport in 1680!"[1]

"And how was he converted?" asked Bernadette.

"A priest coming to see him found his room so neat and so charmingly arranged that he said: 'St. Benedict was not so comfortable at Subiaco.' He changed from that day. I'm afraid the picture of him in the novitiate hall gives no idea of what he was like. Apparently he was very tall. He had brown skin, black hair, and aristocratic manners. But it was his eyes which showed his true character. They were large and childlike, just like the eyes of your patron St. Bernard. And after the rebuke he'd received from that priest, he changed his ways and wore the severe Benedictine habit. But he didn't become too serious. For instance, he liked joking and amused himself by telling riddles. He locked his

---

[1] *Jeu de paume,* of course.

door when he wanted to pray and refused to answer knocks, for he wouldn't be disturbed during his prayer-time. At night he prayed in a room very near the church, so that when all was quiet, he could rise from his bed and continue his prayers. He loved that peaceful time.

"He noticed that there was no hospital or doctor in the village, so he began to train young girls to be nurses. He would tell them to imitate both Mary and Martha—Martha the busy housewife in their active life and Mary, who sat listening at Our Lord's feet, in their contemplative life. Little by little a small religious order was formed, and the nuns were eventually called 'Seours de la Charité et de l'Instruction Chrétienne.' They were dispersed at the Revolution.

"Dom de Laveyne had founded forty houses all over France. When the Revolution was over, Napoleon gave us the old Visitation Convent here in Nevers. You will see the lovely chapel in the town some day. But then we began to grow and grow, so we had to build this place. We've only been here ten years. Do you know that last year, the novitiate had one hundred and thirty-two novices and thirty postulants? Twenty-one new ones came this May." She did not add that she felt so many had been attracted to Nevers because of Bernadette.

"I hope I'll be allowed to look after the sick," said Bernadette. "I love the sick poor. And the more wretched they are, the better I love them."

"H'm," said Soeur Emilienne, "you'll have to become a little sturdier for that, I can tell you. Are you feeling chilly? I think we'd better take a little walk now."

She led her down to a very remote corner of the garden, where there was a niche in which stood a statue of Notre Dame des Eaux. St. Albert the Great, the teacher of St. Thomas Aquinas, wrote a large volume about "The Cult of Mary as Sovereign of Waters," and the Archbishop of Genoa, the author of the Golden Legend, preached ten sermons on "The Good and Powerful Lady of the Waters." It is touching to think that she who had opened the spring of healing at Lourdes should be so honoured in this spot at Nevers.

When Bernadette saw the statue with its delightful smile, and its hands outstretched in a welcoming, motherly gesture, she started crying again.

"That's right, cry away," said Soeur Emilienne. "It's the sign of a good vocation."

(During the trying days which were to follow, Bernadette often slipped away to Notre Dame des Eaux to cry her eyes out, and to seek consolation at the foot of the statue, which somehow reminded her of her Lady. When she wrote to the nuns at Lourdes, she said, "The two of us certainly shed floods of tears on that Sunday."

When she spoke about "our dear novice mistress," she said, "Every word from her lips goes straight to one's heart." And then she begs them to go to "my dear grotto. You will find me there in spirit, at the foot of that rock which I love so much. . . . I will not forget you either before the statue of Notre Dame des Eeaux, at the bottom of the garden, in a kind of grotto. I went there often during my first days here to unburden my heart. And since then our dear Mistress has allowed us to go there every evening.")

Just then Mère Vauzou appeared from nowhere, as she was in the habit of doing.

"Ah, here you are, my dear child. Now I want to tell you something of the utmost importance. You have come here to be forgotten by the world. You want some respite, I know, from all the importunities and questionings which you had to put up with at Lourdes. I have told our novices that you will, once and for all, tell them the story of the apparitions of Our Lady to you, and then they are forbidden, completely forbidden, ever to mention it to you again. And you of course will never speak to them about it."

And so it was that red-eyed little Bernadette, in her blue dress, was taken to the large community room, and there, in front of the whole community of nuns and novices, assembled in dead silence, she was obliged to speak of what she held most dear. The trial was almost too much for her shyness. She spoke in brief, clipped, almost dry sentences.

"Poor little thing," whispered one of the postulants. "She still looks tired from the journey."

She had always had to be prompted by her Lourdes Superior, and now Mère Vauzou did the same. In fact, Bernadette really only gave an account by answering questions.

"What was the Lady like?" asked Mère Vauzou.

Bernadette described her. "Beautiful beyond anything you can imagine, all dressed in white. She had a rose on each foot and her hands were joined."

And then Mère Vauzou presumed to touch on the question of the three secrets. And here Bernadette closed up inside herself, as it were, almost froze. The impression was unmistakable that she was completely outside Mère Vauzou's reach, that this all-powerful novice mistress would never be able to break into her inner citadel. Our Lady, who was Bernadette's novice mistress, had charge of this soul, not Mère Vauzou.

From that moment, Mère Vauzou began to feel thwarted. Until then, she had had free access to and full command over all her novices' souls. But over this one—no.

Bernadette went on, speaking only of the things of which she was allowed by Our Lady to speak.

When she got to the part about drinking at the spring, and how she had hesitated to drink the muddy water, the Lourdes Superior whispered in Mère Imbert's ear, with a twinkle, "You can tell from that how immortified she is." Bernadette heard, and replied affectionately, "But then, the water was so dirty."

Finally, she had to reproduce the words and the gestures of the Lady when she called herself the Immaculate Conception. And everyone witnessed the complete transformation of this simple peasant girl—the grace of her gestures, her beautiful smile, more of Heaven than of earth, the radiance in her eyes, lovely beyond description. And after she had said the immortal words, "I am the Immaculate Conception," there was a long and impressive silence in the assembly room.

The clothing of the postulants took place on July the 29th. Bernadette, like all the others, came into the chapel wearing a white muslin dress and veil. Then they were clothed with the habit. It had been left to Mère Vauzou to choose her new name, and as she explained it to the novices, she said, "It is only right that I should give her the name of the Virgin Mary, whose child she is in a special way. On the other hand, I wish to keep for her the name of her patron, of which Bernadette is the diminutive. And so now we must call her Soeur Marie Bernard."

Alas, Bernadette's health soon began to trouble her again. She confessed in a letter to a nun that she suffered every day from her head and her stomach. And all the time, though she treated her exactly like the others, Mère Vauzou knew that Soeur Marie Bernard was no ordinary novice and could not be trained exactly like her other charges.

In early September, after a long attack of coughing, Bernadette had a haemorrhage of the lung. She was sent to the infirmary, which was looked after by Soeur Marthe. Magnetic Mère Vauzou came to see her each day, looking very kindly. She would give her instruction on spiritual things and explain the rule and customs to her. Bernadette received her instructions most gratefully. It was not until the day when she turned to her and said: "And now, my dear child, what about the state of your soul?" that the novice mistress was aware of a slight shrinking away.

Bernadette quite simply told her what she had done, the books she had read, the prayers she had said. Mère Vauzou advised her to offer her sufferings to God, and Bernadette replied, "Yes, all this can be turned to account for Heaven." This is all she had to say.

When she left the infirmary, Mère Vauzou began to wonder if Bernadette were confiding in Soeur Léontine, from Bernadette's district, who was now assisting in the infirmary, so she gave orders that Soeur Léontine was not to go there again. When Bernadette heard this, her face clouded over. It was indeed a deprivation. But she did not complain.

By mid-October, she was so ill that Mère Vauzou ordered the novices to pray for her, and candles burnt day and night for her recovery. "We are not worthy to have her," sighed Mère Vauzou. On Thursday October the 25th, Bernadette looked as if she were going to die. She had already confided to her director, Père Douce, that she wanted to die as a member of the order. At seven o'clock in the evening, when the doctor had said she would not live through the night, the Superior, her assistants and Mère Vauzou held a hurried meeting, and the bishop was summoned in all haste. He found Bernadette panting, with the death rattle in her throat. She had just had another haemorrhage and the nuns had not had time to empty the basin of blood by her bedside. She whispered in a dying voice,

". . . not the strength to pronounce my vows."

The bishop said that he would pronounce them for her. "It will do if you reply 'Amen,'" he said. And this "Amen" she pronounced, according to the community chronicle, "with the fervour of an angel." Mère Joséphine Imbert put the black muslin veil on Bernadette's head, Mère Vauzou slipped her profession crucifix between her fingers and then put her rosary and book of rules on her bed. The bishop left, feeling sure that he had seen the last of Bernadette. When he had gone, Mère Vauzou offered to spend the night with her, but Bernadette said with a smile, "I am not going to die tonight."

When she heard these words, Mère Imbert scolded, half laughingly: "What! You knew that you were not going to die tonight and you didn't say so? And you're the cause of bringing Monseigneur along at this untimely hour and setting everybody at sixes and sevens on your account. You *are* a little goose (*une petite sotte*)! I declare that if you're not dead by tomorrow morning, I'll take away your profession veil which we've just given you, and I will send you back to the novitiate with your simple novice's veil."

Towards four in the morning Bernadette said to Soeur Emilie, "God didn't want me. I had got to the door and He said to me: 'Go away, it's too soon.'"

The next day, the nuns came to see her, and one of them said smilingly, as she looked at her crucifix and profession veil, "Oh you thief!" Bernadette replied, "Thief I may be, but in the meantime they belong to me. I'm going to keep them. I belong to the Congregation and they won't be able to send me away."

14.

A MARTYRDOM OF THE HEART

When Bernadette came to Nevers she had only one function-
ing lung. She stayed in that infirmary from September 1866
until early February 1867. On December 8th, 1866, she had
a great cross to bear. Her poor mother, worn out by hunger,
childbearing, suckling her babies and hard work, and pining
for her Bernadette, died on the feast of the Immaculate Conception. When Bernadette heard that she had died on the
feast she exclaimed, "Ah, she is in Heaven!"

It is always very sad for a nun to be absent from her
mother's deathbed. As with all daughters who dearly loved
their mothers, Bernadette remembered many things which
she regretted, how, for instance, she had once complained
about poor Louise's onion soup, and said that she had had
enough of it. She did not realize that her mother would have
died much sooner, had it not been for her and her constant
help. Bernadette must, too, have been tortured by the
thought of her father, now left alone with the three children.

There was a very disagreeable sister in the kitchen who
turns up three times in Bernadette's story. She was eventually sent away, but it is good to know that she repented
in the end. One day, Bernadette's infirmarian complained
about the food and asked if something more appetising
could be sent up to her. This lay sister answered gruffly,
"H'm, did her mother give her chicken every day, then?"

When this was unwisely repeated to Bernadette, she said,
"No, but what she gave me, she gave me so lovingly."

Bernadette had a very affectionate nature. There was a
real danger, according to some, that she might become too

much attached to her superiors and thus stumble on the path of holiness, which demands perfect detachment. Mère Vauzou had the gift for making herself very much beloved. Either she was very much loved or very much feared: one could not be indifferent to her. There is no doubt at all that Bernadette loved her very much indeed, and not only at the beginning but throughout her years at Nevers. Mère Vazou still came to the infirmary every day, and when she did so, we are told that Bernadette's face became radiant. But she was so inarticulate. She was not like the secretary-nun who knew how to manage the novice mistress and who, when she saw a dark mood looming, would just fling her arms around her neck. No, timid, simple Bernadette had not been born into the class of society which acts with that kind of insouciant spontaneity. She was a proud, poor peasant from the Pyrenees. This timidity, and the pride which was a form of integrity, were not understood by Mère Vauzou. She took Bernadette's reserve for indifference and for a certain lack of tact. From having been very enthusiastic about her famous novice, she gradually changed her attitude. As there was no fundamental sympathy between them, she began to see above all Bernadette's faults, and she exaggerated them. The gulf between their upbringings and backgrounds seemed to widen every day. Now if Mère Vauzou had been an aristocrat born and bred, instead of a notary's daughter, she would never have been afflicted by this deplorable class-consciousness. It is always true, and particularly in France, that the nobility have much more in common with the peasants than with the middle classes.

Mère Vauzou began to wonder why the Virgin Mary had revealed herself to somebody who was, after all, only a poor peasant girl. Why, in her own novitiate she could name several of her novices who would have been most suitable recipients of supernatural favours. They were so well-brought-up, so refined, so well-educated, so fastidious. There was her assistant, Soeur Graffeuil, a mystic indeed if ever there was one, who lived in a continual state of union with Our Lord in the garden of Gethsemane, and who had been granted the gift of tears. And there were other nuns before whom Mère Vauzou was prepared to kneel in veneration,

rather than before Bernadette. Mère Vauzou, true, was kind
to those who pleased her, but unfortunately she wanted to
be loved in return; she imagined that Bernadette did not appreciate or love her and she felt wounded, then offended
and finally angry. The finishing touch came when Mère
Eléonore Cassagnes was seen talking to Bernadette for a
long time by her bedside. She seemed to have won her entire
love and confidence.

It had probably been on a day when Mère Vauzou, on
one of her visits to the infirmary, had purposely passed by
Bernadette's bed without a word. Poor Bernadette was much
upset and Mère Cassagnes came to console her.

Mère Cassagnes was one of the most attractive of all these
charming nuns. Born in 1824 at the manor of Brengues in
the Quercy region, she had from early childhood loved giving alms to the many beggars who came to the manor. She
had much preferred studying in an attic to housekeeping,
and she had passionately adored the beauties of nature. Although much in the company of the young men whom her
brothers brought to the manor, she remained detached from
them all. "Not one of them has touched my heart," she once
said. "I don't want any of them."

When she became a nun, she showed herself full of understanding for the sufferings of others; no one knew better
than she how to encourage and console other nuns in trouble. The infirmary gave her compassionate nature full scope;
she called it "this antechamber of heaven." She led a very
austere life, slept on a board, wore iron chains and took the
discipline. Later in her life she made a vow of doing always
what she believed to be the most perfect thing. On her
deathbed, she looked like a queen lying in state.

Mère Eléonore Cassagnes was wholly suited to appreciate
a saint, and for twelve years she was Bernadette's confidante
and friend. Mère Joséphine Forestier recalled that she was
always doing little kindnesses for Bernadette, and comforted
her in the midst of the trials which she had to bear from her
novice mistress.

As we have already observed, from her youth up, Mère
Vauzou had shown an iron will and a desire to rule over her
companions. She once said to a newcomer to the boarding

school under her charge: "If you want my protection, you will have to do as I wish." She said later that she had learned quite early what persuasion would do to a young girl. And here was this little peasant girl who, unlike herself, knew nothing of severe voluntary mortification, who had been called to see Our Lady without having done a thing to merit it. In her notebook of private opinions, which every novice mistress was supposed to prepare before the profession day of her novices, Mère Vauzou had written, concerning Soeur Marie Bernard, "Caractère raide, très susceptible; modeste, pieuse, devouée; elle a de l'ordre"—which could be translated: "Of a stiff (or inflexible) character, very touchy, unassuming, pious, devoted; she is tidy." The stiffness, or inflexibility, could really be explained as being very much in the character of people born in the mountains of the Hautes-Pyrénées. For "touchy," one really ought to put "very sensitive." Mère Vauzou had been used to attracting young novices like a magnet, and here was this young thing who had come without a dowry, apparently refusing to be attracted.

And then, *au fond,* unlike Mère Eléanore, Mère Vauzou was not a mystic; mysticism was wholly alien to her temperament, and she had no comprehension of it. She was in fact an anti-mystic, and like all anti-mystics she showed a suspicious dislike for people who had received extraordinary favours. She resented ecstasies and visions because they excluded her as a novice mistress, and she could not interfere in these unknown regions. They were beyond her province and jurisdiction. She preferred a postulant whom she could humble and humiliate, whom she could teach and direct. She had a sharp tongue and could bring out all the ridiculous and foolish side of a shivering novice. Her photograph shows her to be a tough, solidly built woman with the appearance of iron health, and indeed she lived to extreme old age and was hardly ever ill. Her hands are coarse and ugly. No doubt she could not sympathize with the fragility of Bernadette and her terrible ill health.

As early as 1867 Bernadette started to have that tumour of the knee which eventually was complicated by a deep abscess. This, combined with her terrible attacks of asthma, her lung haemorrhages, earache, toothache, headaches, all crucified her flesh. It is distressing to realize that Mère Vauzou had no pity on this poor child, enduring such a physical martyrdom. No. She simply added to it a martyrdom of the heart.

It began when Bernadette emerged from the infirmary soon after Candlemas, 1867. Public rebuffs and rebukes Bernadette could have endured, but what was so terribly puzzling and so very difficult to bear was the sudden change to indifference on the part of Mère Vauzou. She now treated Bernadette as if she did not exist. She never looked up when she came into the room, she never smiled at her. She simply ignored her. Throughout, Mère Vauzou excused herself on the grounds that she did it to keep her humble. Oh, what sins nuns, because of their feminine psychology, commit for the best of reasons, as they say! One cannot imagine a monk doing such a thing—with the possible exception of "the thundering abbot," de Rancé, founder of the Trappists.

Mère Vauzou also made it quite clear to her novices that they would not please her if they displayed such enthusiasm for Bernadette. "She is quite ordinary," she used to mutter, "quite ordinary."

Very often Our Lord seems jealous of those who are directing His great saints: for example, He guided Saint Margaret Mary Himself, and only allowed Blessed Claude La Colombière to come into her life for a short while when absolutely necessary. Mère Vauzou would not allow that anybody but herself could direct Soeur Marie Bernard, not even the Blessed Virgin in person. As she judged the progress of her daughters' souls according to their confidences to her, and as Soeur Marie Bernard never made such confidences, Mère Vauzou concluded that her interior life was something very ordinary indeed. She started to disparage her in public.

There was the day in the novitiate room when Soeur Marie Bernard was seated on the footboard of Mère Vauzou's desk, mending her clothes. Mère Vauzou snapped at Soeur Bernard Dalias, "Why are you looking at Soeur Marie Bernard like that?" She replied, "I was thinking that you must be very happy to have Bernadette close to you." "But," replied Mère Vauzou, "I would have been just as happy to have any of you close to me. Bernadette is in the ordinary way (*la voie ordinaire*)." The phrase *la voie ordinaire* became a sort of cliché of the mistress of novices, and she kept repeating it to all and sundry.

In June of that year Pius IX canonized the little shepherdess Germaine Cousin. All the novices took part in a lottery for her statuette. When it was won by Soeur Marie Bernard, Mère Vauzou said in an ironic tone, "A shepherdess could only fall into the hands of a shepherdess." (Indeed, as a priest said many years later, Mère Marie-Thérèse Vauzou would have found Joan of Arc "badly brought-up.") Now remarks of that sort might have stung the pride of a self-important little middle-class novice, but Bernadette, who was a saint, was puzzled and hurt. She had her own proper pride, the native pride of a Pyrenean who had never let poverty get the better of her, who always wore clean and properly darned clothes, and who, in the depths of misery, had never accepted a sou from anyone. But spiritually, she was very humble indeed.

Very shortly after her return to the novitiate, the novice mistress said to Soeur Marie Bernard, "Now we can really pitch into you (*maintenant nous pouvons taper sur vous*)." And she was annoyed when Bernadette replied meekly, "I hope you will do it gently." And then there was a day—much later—when the whole novitiate went to greet the Mothers in the community room, and although Bernadette was ill, she thought it was her duty to come too. In the cloister Mère Vauzou met her and had something sharp to say to her. Bernadette exclaimed, "Oh, Mother Mistress!" in a tone which suggested, "Oh, she's always after me!" Then the mistress of novices said triumphantly, "Ah, so we have touched that little self-esteem of yours!"

Mère Vauzou herself said later that she never met Soeur Marie Bernard without saying something sharp to her. One would like more records of what these acid words were. It is strange that the novice mistress did not comment on faults which others noticed—the obstinacy which was characteristic of Bigorre folk, the quick temper (just as quickly repented of)—but only on faults which, presumably, were galling to herself. Bernadette had a fiery temperament, and only learnt self-mastery with great effort. She had a downright, abrupt way of saying things which shocked some of the other sisters. For example, when an older nun came into the infirmary one day and said to them all: "You've made your head infirmarian ill." Bernadette only commented: "It was her duty to look after us, we were ill."

One day at recreation, Mère Vauzou overheard a nun accusing Soeur Marie Bernard of self-esteem. They were in the garden at that time. Bernadette made a circle in the sand with the fingers of one hand and quickly put the index finger of the other hand into the circle, saying, "Let the one who has no self-esteem put his finger there." Mère Vauzou had heard and seen, and many years later, on the basis of this anecdote alone, she told Mère Henri Fabre that Bernadette suffered from self-esteem!

Every day the postman brought letters of praise from marquesses and counts, asking for Bernadette's prayers and thanking her for the benefits of her intercession. How Mère Vauzou must have sniffed! Mère Joséphine Forestier has said: "I wonder whether, considering Mother Marie-Thérèse's nature, the presence of Bernadette, whose fame was so great, did not give umbrage to her in some way"—*ne lui portait pas quelque ombrage*.

Now if Bernadette had not cared for Mère Vauzou or had been in robust health, these things would not have hurt her and she would have been detached about it all: outwardly polite but inwardly a little amused. She would have seen that her idol had feet of clay, and acted accordingly. But Bernadette, whose friendship once given was never taken back, never ceased to love her. She never really saw through her. Perhaps she was sometimes a little disillusioned, but she did not really know what Mère Vauzou was like. There was a day when Mère Vauzou, returning from a journey, was met by all her novices in the cloister. Bernadette, the smallest of the group, dashed up to her as a loving daughter to her mother, and flung her arms around her neck—most unlike Bernadette. Somebody reproved her afterwards, saying, *"Ma soeur* Marie Bernard, what a demonstration!"* Perhaps she did that in one last attempt to bridge the gulf between them by a show of affection, but it was no good. Once Mère Vauzou had made up her mind about somebody, she would never change it. Her resentments lasted a lifetime, as some of the other nuns had very good reason to know. Even if somebody proved to her that she was in the wrong in her estimate of a certain character, she would not change her mind.

And then the more she heard of the wanderings of Mélanie, the little visionary of La Salette, the more she was on her guard against this new devotion to Our Lady of Lourdes, and the more suspicious she became, lest Bernadette should be deceiving the public. Bernadette often cried about it all, but would never complain.

Supposing it had all been quite different. Supposing there had been an intense and deep sympathy between the two. Our Lady's prophecy to Bernadette, that she would not make her happy in this world but in the next, would not have come true, and Bernadette's sanctity would perhaps not have been achieved. In the Cause of her beatification, the authorities recognized that Bernadette's difficulties with Mère Vauzou contributed not a little to her final sanctity. Mère Vauzou was the stone against which Bernadette sharpened the arrow of her holiness. The vice-postulator of the Cause of her beatification, Chanoine Lemaître, declared that nothing established the heroism of Bernadette's virtue so much as the difficulties with her mother mistress. Soeur Stéphanie Vareillaud wrote to Mère Bordenave in 1908, when they were beginning research on the Cause:

"In order to become a saint, the little sister had only to let herself be fashioned, first by the Virgin Mary, then by her mistress, and then finally to humble herself."

Bernadette possessed so many virtues that the mistress of novices could have appreciated: a profound love of suffering, simplicity, innocence, union with God, abandonment to God's will. Had Mère Vauzou realized this, she would have loved Bernadette very deeply and could never have treated her so cruelly. And then Nevers would have become a Paradise on earth! How would she then have become a saint! How could she have been the lover of Jesus Christ crucified, detached from all earthly affection? As it is, she was beloved by most of her companions who, even in her lifetime, venerated her as a saint.

The sad thing about the whole story was that the Superior, Mère Imbert, was ill during nearly the whole of Bernadette's time at Nevers, and Mère Vauzou took up the reins of leadership in her place. So even when she left the novitiate, Bernadette was still under Mère Vauzou.

However, St. Paul has said in the eighth chapter of his Epistle to the Romans—"And we know that to them that love God all things work together unto good, to such as according to His purpose are called to be saints."

And so in that first February, Bernadette arose from her sick-bed and went down again to the novitiate. She almost ran to the door of St. Gertrude's room, so anxious was she to see her beloved mistress again. And there this new trial awaited her. One can imagine Mère Vauzou, not even looking up from her desk, simply behaving as if poor Bernadette did not exist, exhibiting a glacial indifference which cut the poor ailing child to the heart. Not only ailing but motherless now. (Bernadette twice said that Our Lady had made it clear to her that she must love her only, and she would replace the mother she had lost.) So many of the nuns who witnessed these things testified during the process for beatification. Sometimes there were acts of injustice and Bernadette was reprimanded for things she had never done. She was spoken to in an ironic voice, she was never encouraged. Mère Vauzou loved to thwart her more than the others. In fact, a nun recalling all this said: "As quite a young novice, seeing her humiliated, I used to say to myself in my lack of fervour, 'How lucky not to be Bernadette!'" Oh yes, Mère Vauzou might have excused herself on the grounds that she was only doing her duty to keep Bernadette humble, but a very shrewd sister, Soeur Joseph Garnier, asked herself if Mère Vauzou didn't act in this way "for duty on the one hand and by natural temperament on the other."

And the Superior, Mère Imbert, though she particularly loved Bernadette, showed her no outward affection. In fact, one day meeting her in the cloisters, she said to her, "You're good for nothing."

One day in 1870, on returning from a journey to Rome,

Mère Imbert met all the novices in the cloisters, and had a
kind word for each of them when she embraced them. When
she got to Bernadette she embraced her and never said a
word.

Some years later, Bernadette said to Mère Henri Fabre
at recreation, hiding behind an umbrella which she was
mending. "Mère Joséphine—oh, I'm terribly frightened of
her!" And one must remember that all these things happened to a young girl whose early years had been spent in
terrible physical privation and whose consequent physical
delicacy had made her ultra-sensitive. Bernadette was far
from apathetic. Two or three times she speaks about *"ma
nature bouillante,"* and she said to Soeur Marthe du Rais,
"It's all boiling up inside and they don't see what's happening there."

The other novices used to see her turn pale, but they
never saw her give a sign of displeasure or ever heard a
word of complaint. Once charming Mère Eléonore Cassagnes found her in tears near St. Joseph's chapel in the
garden. She exclaimed, "Oh my poor child, tell me what is
the matter," but Bernadette would not reply. Bernadette
wrote in her private notebook: "I resolve never to see the
creature but always to consider God in her." To a fellow
novice in trouble she said, "Poor dear, you must learn how
to go on reminding yourself that creatures pass, whereas
God alone remains and is enough for us."

This is the sort of thing that would happen. A lecture
was about to start in the novitiate room. When Bernadette
appeared, Mère Vauzou exclaimed, thinking, no doubt, that
a snub would be salutary, "Go away, Soeur Marie Bernard."
Bernadette said beseechingly: "Oh Mother!" Mère Vauzou
repeated, "Go away." And she had to go. There were rare
occasions, however, when the novice mistress softened just
a little. There was a day when somebody was reading aloud
in the novitiate the story of the apparitions at Lourdes.
Bernadette of course was not there, she was helping the
infirmarian. All of a sudden, in the middle of this thrilling
narrative, the door opened and the tiny figure of Bernadette
appeared. The reader stopped at once. Mère Vauzou turned

to Bernadette and said in a dry voice, "Soeur Marie Bernard, this is not the moment for you to come here. Your place is in the infirmary. Kiss the ground and go away."

When Bernadette had kissed the ground, Mère Vauzou said to her: *"Ma soeur* Marie Bernard, come here." Bernadette went to kneel at her feet, as was customary with novices, and then Mère Vauzou asked her what she wanted. Bernadette had a permission to ask for one of the patients. When she had granted it Mère Vauzou put her hand on Bernadette's head, which with her was the gesture of tenderness and protection, and added: "Now run away, my daughter." And Bernadette went away smiling at all of them.

But this was really the exception. Mère Bordenave, who loved and understood Bernadette, said, ". . . for her trust in God not to have been shaken, she needed almost heroic hope."

Indeed, when Bernadette died, the nuns at Lourdes all sighed with relief, for they felt that she really could not have endured this testing by Mère Vauzou much longer. The virtue of hope had been strained to breaking point.

On Wednesday October the 30th, after a seven days' retreat, the novices all made their first vows. Afterwards it was the custom for the bishop and the Superior General to meet and to tell them where they were being posted to. As this often demanded heroic resignation in young novices posted to disagreeable places, far away from their friends and parents, it was customary for the Superiors to create an atmosphere of affectionate teasing to help them to be cheerfully resigned. Now, according to Monseigneur Forcade and some nuns who were present, this is what happened.

"On the profession day, when the moment for the obediences came, there was none for Bernadette. And here she was on her knees before the bishop. The bishop turned and said to Mère Imbert: "Soeur Marie Bernard, what are you going to do with her?' Mère Imbert smiled a little and replied, 'That child is good for nothing. She would only be a burden to the house we'd send her to.' There was a short silence. The bishop looked at Bernadette and then he said something most inspired. 'The occupation I give you is to

pray.' And then he added, 'So you're good for nothing?'
Bernadette replied, 'Mother General never makes a mistake. It's quite true.'

" 'But then, my poor child, what are we going to do with
you and what was the use of your coming into the congregation?'

" 'That is just what I said to you at Lourdes and you told
me that it wouldn't matter.'

Monseigneur Forcade was not prepared for this unexpected reply, so he said, 'Are you capable of carrying bowls of
tisane or of peeling vegetables?'

" 'I will try,' she replied."

(Some other nun reported in the process of beatification
that Mère Imbert said "We will use her for blowing the
bellows.")

Without letting it show, Bernadette felt this humiliation
very deeply. She confessed to this later, but at the recreation
that followed, that day, she was particularly gay with her
companions, looking as if she had not felt it at all.

They gave her the post of assistant infirmarian to Soeur
Marthe Forès, a gentle creature who was to die several
years later of consumption. It is extraordinary how the doctor could have allowed the chief infirmarian to spread this
kind of infection everywhere. From what one gleans about
him, he can't have been a very good doctor, and poor Bernadette, when she was in great pain, used to cry out against
him and say, "Don't let him come near me."

15.

THE ASSISTANT
INFIRMARIAN

An earthquake occurred once at the Grande Chartreuse whilst the white-cowled Carthusian monks were solemnly singing midnight Office. They did not interrupt one syllable. They were true to their motto, *"Stat crux dum volvitur orbis"* (the cross remains while the earth spins round), and so it was at St. Gildard's throughout Bernadette's early years. During that time, it must be remembered, the Franco-Prussian War broke out. The Germans came so close to Nevers that the wounded soldiers being nursed by the sisters fled the town rather than fall into their hands. The nuns had taken on all the expenses of heating, lighting and medicines; they had also been obliged, when the Germans appeared, to house some of their horses in their stables. But all this was temporal: the only thing of importance is that the sick girl Bernadette was being trained to be a saint.

Two bereavements occurred which made her cross more heavy to carry. In February 1870, Monseigneur Laurence died in Rome, and on March 4th of 1871, just when the war was over, her father died at Lourdes, praying to the last. He had once been found praying before a picture of his girl, as if she were already a saint. Bernadette felt this loss very keenly and was found sobbing in the infirmary, leaning against the fireplace. She said she was glad that she always prayed to the heart of Jesus in agony for those about to die, for she had prayed thus on the day of her father's death. She was ill for some time after his death, and some people thought that she was enduring his purgatorial pains for him.

It is a good thing to picture the saints, as far as we can,

against their background. We are helped by contemporary descriptions as well as by portraits or photographs. One nun, coming into the infirmary, saw Bernadette, in her little white bed, with the carefully pleated white curtains on either side, as a beautiful and rather pathetic symphony in white. Bernadette was wearing her pointed white lawn bonnet tied under the chin, a frame for her pale face with its great dark eyes. She had a white shawl on her shoulders.

Many, many are the testimonies to the neatness, order and cleanliness of Bernadette's person and her surroundings. They speak of her love of neatness in all things. And she loved order and correctness in other people. If any young novice had not put on her coif and veil properly, Bernadette used to take her aside gently, begin all over again and then say, surveying her handiwork, "Now you are a real Nevers Sister." Around her and on her everything was tidy, well-cared-for and clean. She loved the white curtains round her bed and used to call her bed her "little white chapel." Perhaps it reminded her of the white hood she had worn during the apparitions.

As we have already observed, in the stage between the radiant beauty of her face in early childhood and during the apparitions, and the time when she became a nun, Bernadette had looked almost plain and the photographs are very disappointing. But when she began to acquire a fine-drawn look, when she got so thin with illness, and when she was being chiselled to holiness by her sufferings, she became more and more beautiful. And of course the apotheosis of that beauty is the photograph of her, rose-crowned, on her deathbed. Chanoine Guynot, who has gone up and down France collecting the testimonies of her contemporaries, says that a Soeur Philomène had described Bernadette in this way:

"Bernadette had a matt complexion, a mouth on the large side, a gently tapering nose, and very beautiful, gentle deep eyes under arched eyebrows, eyes which were not absolutely black, as people keep saying, but of a dark brown with a slight suggestion of grey blue which I cannot describe.

"Their brilliancy was what you noticed first, but what

struck you most was their extraordinary depth. You got the impression that her gaze barely touched the earth, as if it were mysteriously beckoned on by something undefined and far away, something beautiful which she longed for, and which gave to her eyes as well as to her lovely smile, a touch of melancholy which only added to their charm.

"Often I watched her in her bed looking at the pictures hung on her white curtains. They almost always illustrated Eucharistic subjects. For example, a monstrance on an altar, with a priest and a choir boy ('I am not pleased with that little choir boy,' she would say, 'he never rings the bell.') She would glance first at one picture, then at another, but then she would get a far-away look and . . . one divined regret, nostalgia for a beauty gazed at long ago which had long since disappeared, but which she hoped for, waited for.

"Her smile was modest and reserved. . . .

"Her manners were simple and gentle, and like her language and bearing, characterized by a *je ne sais quoi* which I should willingly call distinction, taking this word in a rather special sense. If she had not the culture and the manners, I would almost say the training, of high society, still less was she the little vulgar peasant girl one might imagine.

"I was struck with her good sense and that intellectual honesty which always found the right expression."

Soeur Philomène also speaks about the light touch of playfulness she gave to her speech, and which was peculiar to her.

Soeur Bernard Dalias also described her to Chanoine Guynot: "She was so tiny and so young, so much of a child, so full of life and spontaneity; she was very simple, and she seemed convinced of her littleness, or even, one might almost say, of her nothingness." Another nun who saw her in the infirmary said she was small and dainty—*mignonne*—with tiny hands. Another talks of her beautiful brown eyes and long lashes. Yet another speaks of the mischievous look they held hidden in their depths. The testimonies about the beauty of her eyes are endless: a Mère Valentine says that one could not forget her eyes once one had seen them. "Neither photography nor painting could fully portray them.

Only a heavenly artist could do that." Finally, Soeur Athanase speaks about those eyes filled with such mystery and
shining with such light and beauty that she picked her out
at once, among all the others, although she had not been
told which was Bernadette. She was struck with their youth
—they were the great beautiful eyes of a child—and then
by their extraordinary look of contemplation, as if the vision
of long ago were still imprisoned within them, as if Bernadette's soul had remained clinging to that beauty.

A fellow patient of hers in the infirmary, Soeur Marcelline, had noticed that on the days on which Bernadette received Communion, one could not fail to see the love that
she had for Our Lord. Her eyelids were lowered, her face
was pale, transformed, and completely celestial.

It is not surprising that when Bernadette was about again,
and took up her duties as infirmarian, she was looked on as
the angel of charity. Mère Bordenave remembers how she
put new heart into her patients by her gentle strength for
. . . "She could not see anyone suffer without being moved
to compassion."

She used to urge her sick patients to be brave: "Accept
your crosses as so many marks of Our Lord's love for you."

All this would perhaps make one imagine that she was
some ethereal, stained-glass image of a saint. Not at all. She
was practical, businesslike, she knew how to keep both
young and old patients in order, and to be firm when necessary. There is nothing like being nursed by someone who
has known severe illness herself. She always knew what to
do, how the patient felt. Here is an example of her strictness.

Soeur Julienne Capmartin was coughing away in the novitiate when Mère Vauzou said: "I am tired of hearing
Soeur Julienne cough," and she sent her up to the infirmary.

"Bernadette took me to the dormitory and ordered me to
get into bed. Then she brought me a hot drink and I buried
myself in the blankets. She tucked me up, closed the curtains and ordered me to keep warm. Then she went out."
Her patient goes on to describe how she gradually forgot
her orders until she was sitting up reading her Office, and
how Bernadette, returning, removed the book with these

words: "Fine fervour, that, stitched with disobedience!" A few days later, back in the novitiate, the novice asked Bernadette for her Office book. What was her consternation to get this reply, "You will have to go and ask your mother mistress for it!" As you can well imagine, she preferred to do without it.

The novices and postulants had to clean the four infirmary rooms, and they were under Bernadette's orders. She gave a salutary lesson in humility to a certain Soeur Justine, who in her old age told Chanoine Guynot: "I was still a postulant. They'd given me some job in the infirmary. Well, one day during a big turning-out, I had dusted, scrubbed, polished all the morning. The bell having rung, I was just going, when Bernadette said to me, 'The work is not finished. There is still this and that, but you haven't got time. You will have to do it some other day.'

"And then I was stupid enough to say to her, with a certain satisfaction, 'I have polished the copper knobs with scouring-powder!' These were the balls on the iron beds. Bernadette replied 'Yes, they are shining all right. You have rubbed them hard, you've looked after them very well. You've done all that work because it could be seen.' She served this up to me so nicely that I wasn't hurt, but I felt all the same this little lancet stroke to my pride, and I went away having learnt my lesson and saying to myself: 'Do you understand? You looked after the knobs because they can be seen, but the work that cannot be seen, the work that remains hidden and which the Bon Dieu alone sees, have you done that so well?' I have always remembered those copper knobs."

It is during infirmary recreations that Bernadette was at her best. She was full of charm and gaiety and used to sing patois songs from the Pyrenees, and laugh when the others couldn't understand them. Here is one which has been gleaned from the village of Bartrès itself:

> "U moutou éstélat
> De blanc e négre barragat
> Soy fatigat dou cérca
> E l'abéret troubat?

> Lou moutou qui cerqui
> Qu'ey plâ encournat,
> Bestit de lâ blanque
> E l'oelh de négre pingourlat."[1]

And this would lead to agreeable reminiscences, when the little shepherdess would tell them about the characteristic sheep of the Pyrenees, whose ears peeped through the whorl of twisted horn. At the thought of those far-away mountains, her eyes would look dreamy, and then she would sing again. (She had no illusions about her singing voice, she would make them laugh by telling them that when she sang everybody ran away.) She might sing "Aqueres Montagnes":

> "Oh those mountains which are so high,
>   They prevent me from seeing where my loves are.
> If I knew how to see them or to meet them,
> I would cross the water without fear of drowning.
> How high they are, but they will bow down,
> And my loves will draw near."

They all knew they were forbidden to talk about the apparitions at Lourdes, but they were not forbidden to think of them. The visions were reflected in the far-away gaze of the little assistant infirmarian.

"Bravo, bravo, Soeur Marie Bernard," some sister would exclaim, "now sing for us again—'Charmante Pastouréte.' "

"All right, sister, if you like," Bernadette would reply, and then she would sing:

> "How much do you want to earn, charming shepherdess,
>   How much do you want to earn for keeping the sheep?
> A pair of clogs and an apron,
> And a hundred crowns I need, monsieur,
> And I need a hundred crowns, monsieur.

[1] "A lamb with a star
      Mottled in black and white
      I'm tired of looking for him
      Have you found him?
      The lamb that I'm looking for,
      Has got good horns,
      Cloaked with white wool,
      And his eyes spotted with black."

"You want to earn too much, charming shepherdess
You want to earn too much for keeping the sheep.
If that is too much, if that is too much.
I will do with a pair of clogs,
I will do with a pair of clogs."

But Bernadette's specialty at recreation was mimicking the community physician, Dr. Saint-Cyr, who had certain little habits and ways all of his own. And Bernadette had a gift for mimicry. How she made them laugh! (Once she herself laughed so heartily that she coughed blood and had to go to bed.)

"Oh dear, oh dear," gasped Bernadette one day, holding her sides as she shook with laughter. A novice said: "I'm sure if Mère Vauzou were here, she'd say we'd all go to Purgatory for a long time."

"How's that?" asked the others.

"The other day, when she saw me rocking with laughter, she said: 'My poor little sister, you'll have a long Purgatory, you're not serious enough.' "

Just then Bernadette took a pinch of snuff. "Ah-ha," said a sister, "you'll never be canonized!"

"Why not?" asked Bernadette.

"Because you take snuff. They nearly didn't canonize Saint Vincent de Paul just because of that."

"Well," said Bernadette, calmly taking more snuff, "does that mean because you don't take snuff you'll be canonized?"

One of Bernadette's great charms was that she always had a ready answer. And she had her own original way of saying things. If she wanted to say that she longed to hide herself, because of an attack of shyness, she would say: "I wished I were a mouse curled up in its hole"; or, about a sister agitated because she couldn't go to Mass: "She is wriggling like a cut worm." Or about a very boring old sister who used to come in from outside and talk endlessly, even when you were ill: "I prefer her heels to her nose. When you are in pain you want to be alone."

Bernadette's special turn of phrase was characteristic of the people of Bigorre. She had been given a roasted bird to eat, and after the meal, she cried: "Quickly, quickly, fetch me a basin. My little bird is flying away."

One day in the infirmary the milk was boiling over. A nun ran to it and cried out, "Here's my milk running away." Bernadette from her bed said, "Go quickly and fetch a policeman!"

And then, when they applied leeches to her back, she said, "You can pull hard, my dear, I'm as difficult to kill off as a cat."

Bernadette had been told that the flashy young women in the park were not all innocent: she pitied the victims of vice with all her heart. One day, she was dandling a doll which one of the nuns had dressed for the doorkeeper's little girl, and she said: "Oh my poor little doll, you look like those unfortunate girls in the park."

Anyway, whether by mimicry or by turn of phrase, like all saints she enlivened recreation for her sisters, and they would go away refreshed.

"Well now," said one of the sisters one day at recreation, "don't make our dear Sister Marie Bernard talk any more. She's terribly out of breath. I'm afraid she will have an attack of asthma if you're so heartless." Just then the bell rang for the end of recreation. Bernadette rose quietly and smilingly left the room. Nothing, nothing would make her speak during silence time: if she met her childhood friend Julie, who had become Soeur Vincent Garros, she fled as from the plague.

Her kindness was not restricted to the sisters, but was also poured out on the servants of the house. There was a young kitchen maid called Jeanne Jardet who came to the convent at seventeen. She caught a severe chill through going out in the cool of the evening after being in the hot kitchens all day. And though that was not her province, and it must have taxed her strength, Bernadette used to climb up the stairs to the maids' dormitory under the eaves, right up to the highest floor of the house, to see her. Jeanne always knew she was coming, because she heard her humming a little. She would say to herself, "Ah, here she is," and feel happy at once. Perhaps Bernadette broke the rule by humming to avoid taking the little servant by surprise.

How like her to respect somebody else's privacy! The minute she came in, Bernadette would greet the statue of the Virgin Mary which was in front of the door. She was always rather out of breath and she wheezed as she breathed. Then she would say to Jeanne, *"Eh bien,* my child, here I am. How are you today?" She would plump up her pillow, put her coverlet in order and tend her as a real sister or mother would. Then she would say, "When we get to heaven, we'll be happy, but here . . ." And she would make a gesture as if to say, "Don't count on this life."

But there is always some fly in the ointment in community life. For example, there was that disagreeable kitchen sister. On the testimony of a Soeur Anastasie Carrière, we see how Bernadette managed her.

"A sick sister had asked her [Bernadette] to go and fetch some hot water from the kitchen. She would have asked permission, but nobody was there, so she took some water from the tap. Just as she was doing so, the kitchen sister, who was rather inflexible, arrived and said to her,

" 'What are you doing here?'

" 'I came to fetch some hot water for a sister who needs it. As nobody was about I took the liberty of helping myself with the intention of asking for permission afterwards.'

" *'Ah ça,* you should have asked for permission. Put that water back where you took it from.'

"She was rather at a loss, she told us, not knowing how to put it back. At that moment the mother assistant arrived in the kitchen and asked what it was all about, and the kitchen sister said, 'You see that little sister? She has come to take water without permission.' And then Soeur Marie Bernard explained herself and the mother assistant said, giving her a little tap on the shoulder, 'All right. Take the water to your patient.' And as she went out, Soeur Marie Bernard could not help laughing. The kitchen sister noticed it and said to the mother assistant, 'You see that little bit of a sister, she is laughing. A bigger one would snivel.' "

Another time, Soeur Marie Bernard went to the kitchen to fetch the matches she had forgotten. The bell had just summoned her to the novitiate. The kitchen sister said, "What time is it, sister?" and Soeur Marie Bernard replied,

"Five minutes past four." "At what time are the novices supposed to come and fetch the matches?" said the kitchen sister. "At half past three," replied Soeur Bernard. "Another time try to come at the right hour," said the kitchen sister, and she added, "Open that cupboard and take the box," which Soeur Marie Bernard did and went off with it. The kitchen sister, noticing this, said, "And what about the rest of us if you take the lot? Take what's necessary and put the box back in its place."

All these little annoyances used to amuse Bernadette, where they might have irritated anybody else, and she used to imitate that sister at recreation and make the others smile about the whole story.

It is not surprising that one sister prayed for an illness so that she might go to the infirmary and be nursed by Bernadette. And her prayer was granted. One day, Bernadette noticed a nun with bleeding chilblains and said to her, "You make me ashamed of hands like yours. You must come to the infirmary for me to put honey on them."

And then there was the nun whose eyes were troubling her. She was rather tall, and as Bernadette was the tiniest of them all, she had to climb on a chair to put drops in her eyes. And as the drops made her eyes run, Bernadette used to joke and say, "I give her a few drops and she gives me hundreds." Then there was one poor nun who had a lot of teeth out—without, of course, any morphia or gas. When the dentist had left the infirmary, she was holding her face, writhing with pain and groaning: "Oh, how it hurts!" Bernadette came up to her and said to her gently, "Don't you want to suffer for God?"

16.

THE TESTIMONY OF
A CHILDHOOD FRIEND

As we read through the testimonies of Bernadette's various companions taken under oath, we get the impression that her fellow novices were aiming at a high standard of perfection and, moreover, were a very delightful set into the bargain. But even more precious and interesting is the witness of a nun from Lourdes, of one who had known her since childhood and who had been present at three of the apparitions—Julie Garros, who became Soeur Vincent at Nevers. What an imperfect, indeed, what a dreadful, little postulant! Her behaviour is that of a bad twelve-year-old schoolgirl. She had a great many faults and she was not even particularly devout. And yet the pictures she conjures up are full of life.

We must remember that at Lourdes, she was such an *enfant terrible* at school, that the nuns had had to put her next to Bernadette in the hope that she would improve. It was Julie who was supposed to teach Bernadette to read at recreation but used to slip away to play instead. She was very particular about her clothes and refused to wear the same kind of dress as Bernadette at her confirmation. One day, she set fire to the spinning wheel of the girl next to her.

We remember how Bernadette had been caught by a Lourdes sister, trying to make her skirt stick out like a crinoline. It is Soeur Vincent who tells us that Abbé Peyramale had forbidden the Children of Mary to wear crinolines. And so, in spite of her childish attempts at modishness, Bernadette dutifully exclaimed: "The crinoline . . . it is a work of the devil." Poor, feminine little Bernadette! It is only a little touch, but it shows how human she was.

One begins to wonder what Mère Vauzou thought of Soeur Vincent. She would probably lift her shoulders with disdain and say, "Oh well, what can you expect of a little peasant?" When she appeared as a postulant at St. Gildard's, Bernadette, delighted, opened her arms and cried, "Here you are at last, you bad lot (*mauvais sujet*)! So you've given in at last?" Afterwards Soeur Vincent exclaimed with feeling, "She was a real friend to me! She loved me supernaturally, otherwise she would not have put up with me in the way she did." And Soeur Vincent needed her friendship during those difficult early days, for she was always in trouble.

One day, during a Corpus Christi procession to the Nevers hospital, Soeur Vincent, in order to see the way, had made a hole in her veil with a big pin. (The nuns lower their veils in the presence of the Blessed Sacrament.) When Bernadette heard about this, she was dreadfully shocked and trounced her soundly. She said, "I'm horrified! You've shown disrespect to the Blessed Sacrament, you have been lacking in the spirit of faith, you've disedified your companions and you've also sinned against poverty."

Soeur Vincent's lack of fastidiousness must often have set Bernadette's teeth on edge, as for example on the day when she caught her cleaning out the mother mistress's room and, having forgotten to fill up the stoup with holy water, spitting into it instead. Bernadette insisted that she go and confess her fault to the mistress. One can imagine Mère Vauzou's irritation. "No, really!" she must have thought to herself. "My educated postulants would never have done a thing like that. How coarse, how disgusting!"

Soeur Vincent was not above telling a fib in order to get out of trouble. There was the day when she was looking after Bernadette in the infirmary and she brought her a cup of chocolate she had burnt. Soeur Vincent tasted it herself, and hoping thus to persuade Bernadette of its goodness, said: "It's excellent. It's simply delicious." And when Bernadette drank it, she remarked, dryly, "So it is—much better than usual." Mischievously, one day Bernadette gave her a lesson in austerity. When it was Soeur Vincent's turn to be in the infirmary, Bernadette announced to her, "I am going to give you a good tea." She brought some food and in particular some candied fruit. She was just about to give it to her friend, who was holding out her hand, when Bernadette took it away again, saying, "Today is Saturday. We won't eat it, after all. We'll offer this little mortification to Our Lady."

When Soeur Vincent first came, she brought in her trunk some chocolate for Bernadette from the Lourdes nuns. When she told Bernadette that she had handed her trunk over to the mistress of novices, Bernadette exclaimed: "Oh, you silly thing! We won't see any of it again." And Soeur Vincent asked woefully, "Do they take everything here?"

When eventually Soeur Vincent became aide-infirmarian to Bernadette, she learnt many a lesson on how to overcome squeamishness. There was one poor nun who was blind and who also had cancer of the breast. The wound was so revolting that Soeur Vincent could not even look at it, but Bernadette used to dress it with great care, and with due respect for the nun's modesty. She would lecture Soeur Vincent: "What a Sister of Charity you'd make, you who have so little faith." And when she was frightened to help her lay out a corpse, Bernadette used to say to her, "Coward. You'll never make a Sister of Charity."

When she asked Soeur Vincent to take the poor blind nun for a little stroll, she said to her, "Look after her as if she were *le Bon Dieu* himself." Soeur Vincent eventually became the Superior of a hospital. No doubt, in her old age, she often remembered what Bernadette had said to her. "If they send you to a hospital, don't forget to see Our Lord in the poor, and the more disgusting they are, the more you must love them."

Bernadette used to advise her about her prayers. Poor Soeur Vincent found it very difficult to meditate. In fact, getting up early in the morning suited her so little that one day she went off into a dead faint. When she complained to Bernadette of her inability to pray, Bernadette said to her: "Go to the Garden of Olives or to the foot of the Cross and remain there. Our Lord will speak to you. You will listen to Him."

When Soeur Vincent returned she said to her, quite frankly, "I went there, but Our Lord said nothing to me."

When she complained to Bernadette that she found it so difficult to overcome distractions during her thanksgiving after Communion, Bernadette said to her: "You must receive God well. It is to our own advantage to give Him a loving welcome, for then He has to pay us the rent."

The mistress of novices had tried to inculcate into her novices devotion to their guardian angels. Bernadette tried to pass this on to Soeur Vincent. She gave her this advice when she was in the novitiate: "When you pass by the chapel and haven't time to stop there, ask your guardian angel to carry your messages to Our Lord in the Tabernacle. He will take them and still have time to catch you up again."

Thirty years later, Soeur Vincent was still observing this practice.

But more than any words, Bernadette's attitude during prayer was a living sermon to all of them: many of the distracted ones learnt to pray by looking at her.

We learn many interesting little things from Soeur Vincent. Bernadette used to draw her veil over her face so that she couldn't be seen when she was saying her prayers. Soeur Vincent said to her one day: "You hide very well, almost as though you were wearing your shepherdess's hood," and Bernadette replied, "I like to be alone when I visit God."

She tells us how exceedingly clean Bernadette was, and how orderly in her appearance—*"Tirée à quatre èpingles"* (neat as a new pin). And how thoughtful she was for the feelings of her patients, observing due modesty when she was dressing their wounds or looking after the aged nuns, who might not have liked a young novice to be present.

It is Soeur Vincent who tells us about a miracle. A sick child had been brought by his mother to St. Gildard's. Bernadette was told to carry him through the cloisters. When she brought him back to his mother, he was completely cured.

17

"UNLESS THE GRAIN
OF WHEAT..."

"Why? That my chaff might fly;
my grain lie sheer and clear."[1]

Round 1872 there are signs that Bernadette was entering into what mystical theologians call "the dark night of the soul." Bernadette herself had no idea that this was so: had she not been told again and again by Mère Vauzou that her way was quite ordinary? Ecstasies were a thing of the past. Gradually, prayer became more of an effort. True, her physical condition helped in this, and she felt so tired in the morning, after sleepless nights, that it was almost heroic to pray at all at that early hour. All her delight in heavenly things had gone. She longed to love Our Lord more, yet she found that her heart felt frozen.

One day, when Mère Imbert was going to Paris, she asked the novices what commissions she could undertake for them. Bernadette said: "Bring me back the love of God."

As Bernadette grew in virtue, she saw the chasm that yawned between the greatness of Our Lord's love and her own coldness, and this was anguish to her. "Oh," she would repeat again and again, "I've received so many graces," as if she were grieving that she could do nothing to lessen her unworthiness. Gradually Our Lord was making her love Him for Himself, and not for the consolations which His presence would bring.

Our Lord had said to doubting Thomas, "Blessed is the man who hath not seen and yet hath believed." Bernadette now needed to practise the virtue of hope with greater hero-

[1] "Carrion Comfort" in *The Complete Poems of Gerard Manley Hopkins* (New York, Oxford University Press, 1937).

ism than ever before. Formerly she had only to call to mind Massabielle. She knew it was not a dream, it was a reality, and the very remembrance would give her strength and joy. But as she was called to heroic sanctity, which is attained by the exercise of the three theological virtues of faith, hope and charity, she had particularly to be exercised in the virtue of hope.

She had to struggle on with her prayers when she felt that she was talking to a blank wall. She had also to practise a form of prayer which was suitable only for beginners, and to persevere with it, while feeling that it had come to mean nothing at all. She had to bear with herself and the feeling of her own inadequacy. Directors have said that it is almost a proof of drawing nearer to God, this growing sense of inadequacy. Terrible are the sufferings of contemplatives, more excruciating than the blackest neurasthenia.

When St. François de Sales was a young student in Paris, he bore a similar temptation against hope most heroically. He was overcome for some time by inward despair. He felt sure that God had turned His face away from him and that he would be damned. But he resolved to love Him all the same, whatever happened. One day, when he had prayed to Our Lady in a certain parish church, this frightful burden lifted.

St. Jeanne de Chantal also knew this anguish towards the end of her life. With her, the trial took the form of a frightful *ennui* or boredom. Holy things—anything to do with God—filled her with devastating distaste.

No one at St. Gildard's suspected Bernadette's agony of mind, for she was just as quietly cheerful and smiling as ever. Only her confessor, Père Douce, knew. She put down in her little notebook his advice to her:

"You must carry the cross hidden in your heart like Mary."

There was a day, however, when between two terrible attacks of asthma, she confessed to Soeur Vincent Garros, who was by her side: "It is very painful to be unable to breathe, but it is even more painful to be tortured by interior anguish. It is terrible."

Who would have suspected her state of mind? Witness this account by Soeur Joseph Vidal, of *"notre chère Bernadette"* in September 1873:

"What touches me is her gentle simplicity and serenity, and even her gaiety, which turns to mischievousness at recreation time . . . You can see that her soul is filled with consolations. What pleasant people the saints are! And how agreeable it will be, up above, to be in such good company!"

In her notebook Bernadette wrote a prayer to "Jesus in His desolation as the refuge of souls in their desolation," begging Him not to abandon her in her affliction, and praying that she should seek no other consoler than Himself.

Here is her beautiful prayer, "The Beggar's Prayer to Jesus" *(la prière d'une pauvre mendiante à Jésus)*:

"Oh Jesus, grant me I beg You
The bread of strength to break my will and to weld it to Yours.
The bread of interior mortification,
The bread of detachment from creatures.
The bread of patience to bear the pains which my heart suffers.
Oh Jesus, You wish me crucified, *fiat.*"

She offered her tears and her sighs for all those who forget Jesus. She made use of the divine economy of Christian fellowship whereby the suffering members offer their pains for their brethren in need.

"Oh, most compassionate heart of my Jesus, accept each one of my tears, each cry of my grief, as a supplication for all those who suffer, for all those who weep, for all those who forget You."

But as Christ Himself in His agony in the garden turned to His sleeping disciples for comfort, so Bernadette—but oh, so occasionally—would sigh in the presence of a remarkably sweet sister called Soeur Marthe du Rais, who was with her for long months in the infirmary. Soeur Marthe had swept into St. Gildard's one night in her crinoline ball gown, accompanied by her maid. She had run away from home during a reception, braving her father's anger, for he did not want her to be a nun. She became one of Bernadette's spiritual friends. During the official enquiry, she said:

"Sometimes I saw her dejected, and she would say to me, 'I am discouraged.' "

In her distress Bernadette composed a prayer to her heavenly Mother:

"Oh, Mary, oh Mother of Sorrows, at the foot of the cross you received the title of our Mother. I am the child of your sorrows, the child of Calvary. . . . Oh, Mary, my tender Mother, here is your child, who can do no more (*qui n'en peut plus*). Have pity on me. Grant that I may be in heaven one day with you.

"You who have seen and felt the terrible desolation of your dear Son, assist me now in mine."

If contemplatives entering this "dark night" only realized what was happening to them, they might feel more courageous in facing their trial. But they usually blame their own lukewarmness or their bad health. St. John of the Cross, in *The Dark Night of the Soul,* however, makes it quite clear that all those authentically suffering in this Dark Night become more and more anxious to please God in spite of everything. That is the one infallible sign. One has met people who, at the end of a long life of holiness, were suddenly overcome by a sense of unreality and futility: "Oh, has it all been worth anything at all?" And then their grim endurance becomes heroic.

Bernadette wrote again in her notebook:

"I feel so tired in the morning! I must remember the temptation of Père Avila, hesitating one day, because of fatigue, to continue on his way to say Mass. Our Lord appeared to him and showed him the place of His heart, reminding him that fatigue had not prevented Him from praying up to the very summit of Calvary. Courage! I also must know how to overcome my inclinations.

"After all, even if I am tired and exhausted, I can find rest in the heart of Jesus."

Dante has sung: "There is no greater sorrow than to remember former happy days in the hour of present misery." He is echoed by Tennyson:

"This is the truth the poet sings.
  That a sorrow's crown of sorrows is remembering happier
    things."

The pain of exile from the heaven glimpsed in the grotto
of Massabielle was greater for Bernadette than it is possible
for us to realize. Occasionally, some observant sister would
guess this, as for example the nun who caught sight of Bernadette when they sang a hymn to Our Lady, "I will see her,
my beloved Mother." She saw Bernadette lift her eyes, and
two tears trickled down her cheeks. Or again, the other nun
who overheard her whispering during recreation, near the
statue of Notre Dame des Eaux, "Ah, my dearest Mother,
alas, those days are passed and gone."

To be shown recent photographs of the grotto was very
painful to her. Once she exclaimed: "Oh, my poor grotto, I
wouldn't recognize it any more." Oh, that blessed grotto
which had belonged to her and her Lady, it was being spoilt.
She felt she could never bear to go back to Lourdes again.
However, in imagination, she paid a visit to her grotto every
day, "even without asking for permission," and she would
relive those cold winter dawns of 1858. Asked by a nun if
she ever forgot the apparition, she exclaimed, "Oh no!" and
she struck her brow with her right hand and said, "I keep
it here." The roses in the convent garden or on the altars
must have seemed tawdry to her, compared with the golden
roses on her Lady's feet. She told Soeur Vincent Garros
that such beautiful roses were not to be found on earth.

Yes, she had been "knee-deep in violets," she had seen
that love of which Dante sings:

"Sweet heavenly love, which dost array thyself in smiles"

and now she was alone, sick and exiled.

All the statues of Our Lady which she saw at St. Gildard's
were not only completely unsatisfying, but they even pained
her. Once, overhearing a young nun praising a statue, she
gave her a reproachful glance, as if to say: "How could
you!" She particularly disliked the statues which showed
Our Lady holding her head high. "I don't understand why

they give her a long, twisted neck; she was looking at
heaven, but she did not raise her head; she stood naturally.
. . . They give her a goitre, the Blessed Virgin was not like
that. They make her look forbidding, but she was kind and
gracious." She used to say that artists would be well caught
out when they got to heaven and compared their handiwork
with the reality.

The little notebook gives indications that Bernadette
emerged in the end towards serenity. Here is a magnificent
prayer which will bear comparison with some of the greatest
prayers of the saints:

"Rien ne m'est plus, plus ne m'est rien que Jésus. Nothing means anything, any more to me, but Jesus. Neither
places, nor things, nor persons, nor ideas, nor feelings nor
honours, nor sufferings, can turn me away from Jesus. For
me, He is all honour, and charm, and heart, and spirit. Him
whom I love is my native land, He is my Heaven already!
My treasure! My love! My happiness consists only in Jesus,
and in Jesus crucified . . . in an intimate union with Jesus,
heart to heart with Jesus like St. John, in purity and in love."

There is a mysterious kinship between some saints. Bernadette scribbled in her notebook, "M.M. victim." She must
have meant St. Margaret Mary, whose prayers she sometimes quotes. Her confessor had urged her, in her mental
anguish, to offer herself up, like Our Lord on the cross, as a
victim for sinners. Both Bernadette and Margaret Mary
chose St. Francis of Assisi as their spiritual brother, because
of his love for Christ crucified.

Armed with the prayers and examples of these two saints,
Bernadette took to her heart all those poor sinners who had
excited the compassion of her Lady in the grotto, on the day
when she had urged her to pray for sinners, when she had
said: *"Pénitence! Pénitence! Pénitence!"* Her companions in
the infirmary noticed that she would offer up some small
mortification, such as taking nauseating medicine, for *"le
gros pécheur"*—"the big sinner." When she was asked who
that might be, she would say, "Our Lady knows."

Once she asked for permission to perform some special
penance: it was surmised that it was for Père Loyson, the
priest who had snubbed her at Lourdes by saying: "Couldn't

the Virgin Mary have taught you to speak French?" He had already left two or three religious orders. He went to London and married a Protestant.

A chaplain of St. Gildard's, Père Lemaître, who became vice-postulator of the Cause of beatification, has recounted something very moving. "One day, in 1877, Soeur Marie Bernard, accompanied by Soeur Victoire, the choir mistress, came to see a young priest, M. L'Abbé Perreau, after his mass . . . Joining her hands and with her eyes full of tears, Bernadette said in a beseeching voice, *'Monsieur l'Abbé,* I have a great favour to ask you.'

" 'What is it?'

" 'Please promise me to pray every day for my sinners,' she said in a state of great emotion. This was the direct result of her determination in 1873 to become a saint. She had exclaimed in her notebook: "I will become a saint, Jesus desires it!" Heroic sanctity consists in loving God with all your heart and your neighbour as yourself. Bernadette found her neighbours, not only within the infirmary, in the persons of the sick nuns she served with such exquisite tenderness, but also beyond the convent walls amongst the sinful ones of the world, glimpsed in the visions of Massabielle. Her contemporary, Daumier, gives a vivid picture of the various forms of vice of nineteenth century France.

After the Franco-Prussian War, the crowds coming to pray at Massabielle increased in numbers. Sixty thousand pilgrims appeared at the grotto during three days in October 1872. This of course infuriated the freethinkers and Freemasons. Président Thiers announced that pilgrimages were "no longer in our customs." The first thing to do was to stop these processions, and the best method of doing so was to disparage the visions and the visionary. Dr. Auguste Voisin, lecturing to his students at the Salpêtrière, said that the miracle of Lourdes had been accepted on the evidence of a child suffering from hallucinations, now locked up in the Ursuline convent of Nevers. Hereupon Dr. Robert Saint-Cyr, who knew Bernadette intimately, took up his pen in her defence. To the doctor who had reported these words, he wrote that Soeur Marie Bernard was his infirmarian and that she looked after her patients very intelligently, following his prescriptions carefully. He added that she wielded great authority and enjoyed his entire confidence. . . .

". . . You can see, *mon cher confrère*," he goes on, "that this young Sister is very far from being out of her mind. On the contrary, her calm, simple, gentle nature is very far from being inclined towards that kind of thing."

For his part, Monseigneur Forcade, writing in the *Univers*, was able to affirm that, "far from being mad [Soeur Marie Bernard] was a person of rare wisdom and unshakeable calm."

Many years afterwards, Chanoine Guynot was questioning Mère Julienne Capmartin, a contemporary of Bernadette's, who had now become the head of a large home for mentally deficient children. She said: "You will recall that they wanted to pass her off as having hallucinations. . . . I am not a mental specialist, but through force of circumstances I have acquired a certain amount of experience. I have around me dozens of people suffering from hallucinations and I recognize them simply by the look in their eyes. *Eh bien*, I can tell you that I have never seen anyone with a more transparently luminous and peaceful look than my dear little Soeur Marie Bernard. It might be compared to a beautiful woodland spring, clear and deep. There was child-like candour there, and something very simple and straight-forward which it was a pleasure to see. But underlying all that was something more—serenity, clear-sightedness and good sense."

It is prudent to emphasize this good sense of Soeur Marie Bernard's, after describing her soul's troubles, to prove that they were not caused by melancholia.

Bernadette was very far from being lost in a dream-world. Her pursuit of virtue had its very practical side. Having so often been told by Mère Vauzou that she was too touchy (when she was in reality only over-sensitive), she made up her mind to attack this touchiness of hers, and on the advice of her confessor she kept a record of her faults. But she found this very difficult to do, and quite soon she left off using notebooks. Her way obviously did not lie in certain rather too fussy practices which have been described as "licking the tonsure."

Some other little manuscripts at St. Gildard's prove how very seriously she took her duties as infirmarian. She wrote out comparative charts of weights and measures for making up medicines, and there were long lists of plants and pharmaceutical products, recipes for tisanes and potions. It is interesting to read how she treated *"les humeures froides"*—scrofula—with iron iodide and cod-liver oil, fortifying baths of nutmeg and quinine. There is also a gland pomade composed of marshmallow root and distilled mint water. For rheumatism pains, "three cups of elder flower, add five drops of aromatic spirits of alconite."

What a good infirmarian she was! You never had to wait if you called her. She would never stay to receive thanks. She didn't like to be thanked. She thought it was honour enough to look after an invalid, in whom she saw the person of Jesus Christ. She had a special gift for consoling, and she looked after her sisters, not only with devotion, but with real affection. She tried to make her patients lift their pains on to a supernatural plane and bear them for the love of God.

18

SOEUR MARIE BERNARD
SURROUNDED BY HER FRIENDS

*In November 1872, the head infirmarian died of consump-*tion and Bernadette took her place. But, alas, in 1873, her heart began to fail, and she was ill for the first part of that year. In April she got up, and in May, Mère Imbert took her for a drive in her carriage to the orphanage at Varennes: this seems to show a softening of heart on her part. On June the 2nd, Bernadette was so ill that she received Extreme Unction.

By 1874, Dr. Saint-Cyr at long last realized that the confined air of the infirmary was bad for Bernadette, so she left her work as infirmarian and was ordered to help in the sacristy. Before showing how she devoted herself to this most contemplative of occupations, it would be a good thing to see Bernadette surrounded by her friends, lest one be left with the impression that her life at St. Gildard's was one of unrelieved suffering.

Bernadette might be treated with frigidity by the Superior General and the mistress of novices. She might be snubbed by five or six satellites of the mistress, who wanted to curry favour, she might have trouble with the cantankerous kitchen sister, but on the whole, she was immensely loved by her fellow nuns.

An old nun told Chanoine Guynot about the postulant who, having noticed that Bernadette passed regularly down a certain staircase at a certain hour of the day, always tried to be there to meet her and quite simply, without any formality, used to hug her. What a charming picture!

Then there was Soeur Athanase, who wore felt slippers

during her time as a postulant. "But this did not prevent me from going to polish them—or pretending to do so—the brushes and the polish being near the infirmary, I then had an opportunity of seeing Bernadette."

Then there is the other nun who told Chanoine Guynot how she saw Bernadette making a pirouette with all the liveliness of a little girl, to escape being teased by some other nun, and she noted the familiar simplicity and the friendliness with which the other nuns used to tease her. She affirmed that "no nun had been more beloved at the convent than Bernadette." The happiness she radiated must have attracted them greatly. Mère Elisabeth has said: "Everything in her bespoke joy, a great and deep joy."

Soeur Alphonse says that she was always "gracious, lively. . . . I never remember having seen her in a melancholy mood." Soeur Eléonore said, "She was so kind! As kind as she was joyful. I never saw her sad."

It is the self-same Soeur Eléonore who tells us a little anecdote which shows us Bernadette in all the delightfulness of her charming ways.

One All Saints Day, Soeur Eléonore heard that Bernadette was ill, and she was grieved about it, because she was very fond of her. "As I knew she loved flowers, I picked a few violets and sent them by a novice who worked in the infirmary.

"The novice was commissioned to tell her from me, 'My dear Sister, to-day is your feast, as it is the feast of All Saints."

"The answer came to me the following evening by the same messenger. 'Since it is my feast,' said Soeur Marie Bernard, 'it is also yours. Please accept half my cakes, and don't have any scruples about it. I have Mother Assistant's permission.' "

Soeur Bernard Dalias, when she first came to Nevers, had all sorts of preconceived ideas of what Bernadette would look like. The story of how she found Bernadette amongst her companions has too often been quoted out of its context, thus losing its original flavour. It will be quoted here in full, from the *Souvenirs Inédits*, by Chanoine Guynot. When she first came to St. Gildard's, Soeur Bernard Dalias jumped to the conclusion that Bernadette couldn't be that little nun who was on the left of the mistress of novices.

"She was charming, no doubt. Tiny, rather pretty. The prettiest, perhaps, of all the group. . . .

"She appeared to me then very pleasant to look at, but she was so tiny, so youthful, so much a child, so lively, so spontaneous. There was about her so great a simplicity, she seemed so convinced of being such a small thing, or even nothing at all."

Soeur Dalias would never have thought that she was *the* Bernadette of the apparitions. After a while she said to the mistress, "My dear Mother, it is really rather extraordinary. I've been here three days and I haven't yet been able to discover which is Bernadette. It's quite disconcerting." And then the mistress turned towards her little neighbour, and exclaimed, "Bernadette? Here she is."

"What was my amazement to discover that the sister who interested me so much, the one I was looking at, whom I loved already but whom I eliminated completely from my suppositions—well! It was she. This was the confidante, the messenger of the Virgin; this was Heaven's chosen one, Bernadette. I was so much abashed that the unfortunate word sprang from my lips without giving me time to stop it:

"' '. . . *That!*' . . .

"You know the rest. Bernadette's smile, her self-possession, her marvellous aptness, her little hand stretched out to mine and this answer which has been repeated so many times:

"'But yes, mademoiselle, it is only *that.*'

"I can't tell you how confused, humiliated and uncomfortable I felt."

Mère Elisabeth has spoken about Bernadette at recreation:

"She came amongst us, and with complete simplicity made herself quite at home, telling us amusing stories which made us laugh as one can only laugh at that age. How many happy hours I owe her! And what a provision of good humour she would bring us!"

The laughter of saints! Soeur Eléonore describes a very amusing community scene.

"The Mother General, surrounded by her nuns, was making newcomers pass a singing examination. The little new sisters were very shy at having to sing in front of everybody. In spite of Mère Joséphine's encouragements, there were always some breakdowns. One forgot her notes, another sang out of tune, and, as you can well imagine, the sisters felt no obligation to keep a straight face.

"My neighbour especially was laughing heartily. She was a little brunette with an agreeable face, and with very beautiful eyes, as lustrous as porcelain."

Bernadette was completely spontaneous and lacking in self-consciousness. There are at least two stories about her eating a hen's egg at recreation. Once she found that a hen had laid an egg in the community carriage. She wanted to show her friends how easy it was to swallow an egg, and before they could prevent her, she had swallowed it. Then she realized that she had done so without permission, and accused herself to the assistant.

Soeur Bernard Dalias used to come and see her every half holiday in the infirmary in order to lay up a store of joy for the rest of the week—"a little of that joy which radiated from her whole person." And then she adds: "But one used to get a provision of something else beside gaiety." Soeur Bernard Dalias used to get relics! One day, when Soeur Marie Bernard was mending her flannel underwear, Soeur Bernard Dalias filched a handful of snippets and put them in her pocket. But in the evening, when she was reading aloud in the community room, she took her handkerchief from her pocket, having quite forgotten what was inside, and all the little flannel pieces were scattered all over the floor, to the great astonishment of the Superior. She had to explain, and the bits were promptly thrown into the fire. If Mère Vauzou was present she must have been exasperated.

Soeur Julienne describes an amusing little scene, fresh and concise, like an exquisite miniature. The Bishop of Moulins, Monseigneur de Dreux-Brézé, who had already met Bernadette, wished to see her again, and asked the Superiors to find some discreet way which would allow this without her being presented to him personally.

"They drew up a plan which would satisfy the prelate

without endangering the humility of the saint, and I was charged with carrying it out.

"One of our mistresses, Soeur Mélanie, told me to go to the infirmary and ask Soeur Marie Bernard to fetch some napkins. Then she added with a mysterious air, 'You will be sure to go with her. Make her pass near the flower bed, and stop in front of Monseigneur's room to show her a flower, or a stone, or an insect, or anything you like, but arrange everything so that she will turn towards the *salon*. Monseigneur de Moulins will be there and he will be able to see her without being seen.' The plan was very simple theoretically, but not so easy in practice.

"I replied that Soeur Marie Bernard was very strict about silence and that she would probably only call me a chatterbox for my pains.

"However, I went to the infirmary and gave the message. Soeur Marie Bernard left her work and followed me. When we were in front of the *salon*, I looked furtively through the window and could make out, framed in the door, the vague shape of somebody trying to see without being seen. This was the moment when I needed all my self-possession. I took my companion by the arm, and pointing to a daisy said to her in a whisper, 'Oh, my dear sister, isn't that little wild flower entrancing? It's more beautiful than any garden flower. God does things far better than men, don't you think?'

"I was prepared for resistance, but to my great surprise she stopped, looked at the simple little flower and, half leaning over, touched it gently, as if wishing to give a caress of friendship to this little creature of God.

"But then, finding my discourse too long, she detached herself from me with the single word: 'Chatterbox!' "

Many people still wanted to see Bernadette, but were always turned away by the extern sister. However, the bishop could not refuse these requests from fellow bishops. There is a story of how, when a bishop called on Bernadette in the infirmary, she was not as gracious as usual; in fact a little gruff! As he was speaking to her, by design aforethought, he allowed his violet skull-cap to fall on to her bed. No doubt, he hoped that Soeur Marie Bernard would pick it up for him and he would thus be able to treat his skull-cap as a relic. But through long practice, Soeur Marie Bernard had become more crafty than her admirers. The cap remained on the bed; the bishop made no movement to pick it up, nor did Bernadette. In the end, obliged to take the offensive, he said, 'Sister, would you give me back my skull-cap?' She replied, 'Monseigneur, I did not ask for it. You can pick it up yourself.' The mother assistant, who was looking on at this little scene, intervened and said, "Come now, my dear Sister, give Monseigneur back his skull-cap." And Bernadette obeyed.

When the Bishop of Nevers noticed that a prelate looked at Bernadette ecstatically during an interview and feared she might have noticed it herself, he said to her brusquely, "What are you waiting for? You've been seen, and that is enough; we don't need you any more." She went away immediately without looking at all hurt. She was even smiling.

As we have seen, Bernadette's fellow nuns at St. Gildard's were absolutely forbidden to mention the apparitions to her again. But sometimes a sign, a glance, a word revealed to them that her heart was at the grotto. Mère Joséphine Forestier was one day reminding her of a ceremony at Lourdes. Bernadette exclaimed, "Lourdes!" She did not say any more, but Mère Joséphine felt that her whole heart was filled with the visions of the grotto.

Soeur Bernard Dalias told Chanoine Guynot a story about the poplar trees. Near the kitchens there was a place called St. Zita's in honour of the patron saint of maidservants. The novices had gone down there to peel vegetables, and were all sitting in groups round their baskets. Soeur Marie Bernard and Soeur Bernard Dalias were next to one another. The half-open door allowed one to see the tall poplars beyond the enclosure. Bernadette looked at them, and then she said: "Oh those poplars, they make me quiver."

"And why do they make you quiver, my dear Sister?"

"Because they remind me of those by the Gave."

One day, Soeur Bernard Dalias found Bernadette in tears. It appeared that Mère Vauzou, about to leave for Lourdes, had told Bernadette, and then had added a word which had reduced her to tears.

"And when you think mother mistress asked me if I would be happy to see Lourdes again!"

"Oh, no doubt, my dear Sister, you would be very happy to see Lourdes again."

"On one condition, and that is that I should be alone there, or that I should be there without anybody knowing it, like a little bird hidden in the trees or on the rocks." Then she repeated gently, sweetly, "the grotto . . . to see the grotto again."

One of her childhood friends said that "she was attached to that little corner of the earth by all the fibres of her heart. The grotto, the Virgin, prayer. That was Bernadette."

When her companions would show their admiration for her too much, she had a way of putting them in their place. She compared herself to the ox of the shrine of Bétharram which had unearthed the statue of the Virgin whilst plough-ing a field. And then, once when she caught somebody's admiring glance, she said to her, "What do you do with a broom when you've finished using it?"

"You put it in a corner."

"Yes, indeed," she replied. "And that is what the Virgin has done with me."

It is a marvel that she survived the admiration of her companions without losing her perfect humility. To be treated like a saint during one's lifetime, and yet to emerge with such robust matter-of-factness and gaiety—what a miracle!

19.

SOEUR MARIE BERNARD,
THE CONTEMPLATIVE

Soeur Marie Bernard was employed to help in the sacristy from early 1874 until October of 1875, when her active life in the community ended. In the following November, lung haemorrhages began again, and she was continuously ill.

In her work, she showed great respect for holy things, and as she was so neat and tidy her appointment to be assistant sacristan was particularly suitable. In her free time she tended flowers destined for the altars. It seems she was very careful about the correct arrangement of flowers in bouquets and most critical about blending the colours rightly. Then she would read the lives of the saints, especially St. Bernard; she has left several notebooks with extracts from his life. If it was not too cold, she would go into a corner of the cloister, where she would embroider an alb for Monseigneur Forcade, who had now become Archbishop of Aix-en-Provence.

All her life Bernadette had a burning love for the Blessed Sacrament, so here she was able to pour out her love in care for the altar linen and altar vessels. On Christmas Eve, when the crib was ready, she took the Infant Jesus to place him in it, and she was heard to whisper, "You must have been very cold, my poor little Jesus, in the stable at Bethlehem. The inhabitants must have been heartless not to want to give you hospitality. I am so happy to prepare your crib for you." She had a great devotion to the Holy Child. At recreation one day her companions were telling the well-known story of a nun in ecstasy who had a vision of the Holy Child, but who left Him when she heard the bell ring for Office. Bernadette exclaimed, "I would not have behaved like that. I would have left when the bell rang, but I would have taken the Holy Child with me. He was not heavy. I would have taken Him too, and in that way He would not have left me." In addition to St. Margaret Mary and St. Francis of Assisi, one of her favourite saints was St. Joseph. She used to call him her father. She loved to go and pray in the little chapel of St. Joseph in the garden, and used to say, "Now I am going to see my father." By her bed in the infirmary she had a small statue of St. Joseph. In front of it she would put paper flowers and little candles. She said that she obtained many graces through St. Joseph, and she told Soeur Marthe du Rais, *"Il faut se metre bien avec lui"*—"You have to get on good terms with him." She and Soeur Marthe together used to recite his litany and all the prayers to him that they knew.

Then in the month of May, the month of her "tender Mother," as she called her, she would place a little statue against the curtains of her bed, also with its two tiny candlesticks and its minute basket filled with the paper flowers she had made herself. These are still to be seen in the museum in the Infirmerie Ste. Croix at St. Gildard's.

By a word dropped here and there, her companions would glean how one should love Our Lady. One day she was looking at an engraving which represented Our Lady with a child kneeling in front of her and gazing up at her with a look of great happiness. When she saw that picture, Soeur Marie Bernard raised her eyes to heaven and said, "That is the way we should always be with the Blessed Virgin."

Of St. Bernard, her patron, she would say, "I pray to him a great deal, but I don't imitate him. He loved suffering and I do all I can to avoid it." And then: "I should try to imitate him. He loved the Virgin Mary so much."

Soeur Marthe du Rais often saw her kiss the key of the tabernacle devoutly, and also the base of the holy ciborium which housed the consecrated Hosts.

In those days, when one could not break one's fast before Holy Communion, often she would go the whole night through, coughing ceaselessly, without taking a drop of water, because she did not want to miss her Communion the next morning.

The nuns who caught a glimpse of her either in chapel or in the infirmary when she made her thanksgiving after Communion were impressed by her expression of serenity. She seemed to be in ecstasy. She brought an atmosphere of prayer to the infirmary just by her example, and no nun would have interrupted her preparation or thanksgiving.

She had read the four Gospels so often that she knew them practically by heart.

If she were too ill to make the Stations of the Cross in the chapel, she would make them sitting up in her bed. There is still in the infirmary showcase a little yellow paper which unfolds, and on which are set down all the Stations of the Cross. Even if she had reached "the prayer of quiet," as it is called, she made use of all the great traditional devotions of the Catholic Church. When she said the rosary in chapel her friends felt that she was indeed speaking to Our Lady, and they learned much by seeing her make the wonderful sign of the cross which she had learnt at Bartrès and at the grotto—slow, majestic and full of awe.

Bernadette might be becoming more ethereal every day through illness, but she did not become too ethereal in her orisons. She knew that the mind is apt to have distractions in prayer and that it is healthy to focus its attention by certain traditional devotions. And so she was greatly devoted to the Sacred Heart of Jesus. She had learnt this love from St. Margaret Mary. By her singleness of heart, she was well-prepared to respond to Jesus, when He said: "My daughter, give Me thy heart. I want it undivided," for she had guarded against that great danger of the cloister, the making of private friendships.

In 1877, in the month of June, a statue of the Sacred Heart had been placed on a table in the novitiate. Soeur Marie Bernard had made a crown of thorns and placed it near the statue. In her sickbed she had already made some tiny roses of gilt paper. All these she put at the foot of the statue in a basket. Each week she asked the novices to practise some special virtue, beginning of course with the virtue of humility. And after one had made seven acts of each virtue one had the right to take a rose from the basket and to prick it on to the Crown of Thorns. This might sound trivial and childish to Platonists and nebulous intellectuals, but it is very practical, and rather on a par with St. Thérèse de Lisieux's "little way."

On the evening of the feast, there was a terrible storm. The lightning flashed down the curtain near Soeur Marie Bernard's bed, and the sacristy caught fire.

"Oh," exclaimed Bernadette with her usual calm, "it is the *'grappin'* who is not pleased with our beautiful feast." (Grappin, of course, is the Devil.)

Her tenderness towards the heart of Jesus was exquisite and childlike. In the sacristy she helped to make the little white doves which were to be scattered all over the convent, for the feast of the Sacred Heart. The head sacristan admired an especially beautiful dove, and said that she would put it on the arm of the statue. "Oh," cried Soeur Marie Bernard, "if such is the case, I will kiss its wings, so that she will bring the kiss to the Sacred Heart."

The age which produced Bernadette and Thérèse of Lisieux produced also the Victorian drawing-room, and if we feel tempted to jeer at practices which awaken no sense of religious fervour in our own days we should remember that they reflect a certain taste in other spheres besides the religious—clothes, furniture, buildings, all show a preoccupation with the non-essential, with the ornamentation, or over-ornamentation, of objects, and this not only in France. That its flowering in religious matters should have shown much that was good may be a matter for surprise, but also for admiration, and we should hesitate before condemning such practices as those mentioned here. Amongst simple souls they are rather the sign of that "holy liberty of God's children" than ridiculous trivialities invented by people with nothing better to do.

Abbé Febvre, her confessor after Père Douce, has affirmed that her greatest ambition, which she strove to her utmost to hide, had been "to be a victim of love for the heart of Jesus." And her other great ambition, according to Mère Joséphine Forestier, had been "to see the Virgin Mary glorified and loved." These two aims were nurtured by the great traditional devotions of the Church, which by visible means draws men to the love of invisible things.

20

LAST ILLNESS AND DEATH

The tumour on her right knee which had begun in the year 1867, was now more badly abscessed, and the knee had swollen to enormous proportions. Bernadette was given crutches. Occasionally the pain would lessen, and she could manage on two sticks. Then she had an abscess under her arm, which was operated on without morphia. She had abscesses in her ears which resulted in temporary deafness, and of course there were continual haemorrhages of the lung and continual attacks of asthma. She was ill until the end of May 1876. In that year, on September 15th, she had the consolation of seeing Abbé Pomian, her old confessor. He brought her some Lourdes snuff, for it was more finely ground than the snuff of Nevers. It must have been a great joy to see this good and kindly priest, who had been the first priest ever to hear her account of that first apparition of February the 11th. She was able to discuss the careers of her two brothers, about whom she was always anxious. Jean-Pierre, her godson, had neglected her so much, that one suspects he did not appreciate her at all, and she was very much hurt by his long silence. Her letters to her relations at Lourdes are all full of practical spiritual advice. How she dreaded that they should become rich, and how she dreaded to see them disregarding the laws of the Church, or keeping open shop on Sundays!

On September the 21st she received a present she had longed for, a crucifix. This is how she thanked the giver, Mère Sophie Cresseil, the Superior of a boarding school at Cahors:

"I do not know how to show you my deep gratitude for the beautiful crucifix which you have been so kind as to send me. I cannot express the happiness which I felt when I saw it. For a long time I had longed for a big crucifix to put by the side of my bed. And so, when I saw it, I exclaimed, as I took it in my arms and kissed it, that my dear Mère Sophie had had an excellent inspiration. I have been allowed to keep it and I am happier on my bed with my crucifix than a queen on her throne."

The new Bishop of Nevers, Monseigneur de Ladoue, was on the eve of his first journey to Rome, the journey which is called *"ad limina,"* when bishops treat of the affairs of their dioceses. He wanted to bring a letter from Bernadette to the Pope. So on December the 16th, he came to the infirmary and asked for one, emphasizing especially that she should not be helped with its composition. Her infirmarian, Soeur de Vigouroux, held the blotting pad to help her to write. A rough copy was made which had to be looked over by the sisters (and they cut out one expression which they thought too bold).[1]

In this letter she says that she is the "Zouave" of His Holiness. "My arms are prayer and sacrifice which I will keep until my last breath."

"It seems to me when I pray according to the intentions of your Holiness, that from Heaven Our Lady looks down on you with motherly affection, most holy Father, because you have proclaimed her Immaculate. I love to think that you are most particularly beloved by this good Mother because four years afterwards she came herself to say,

" 'I am the Immaculate Conception.'

"I did not know what that meant. I had never heard that word; but since, in thinking of it, I have said to myself often, 'How good Our Lady is.' It is as though she had come to confirm the word of our most Holy Father." In gratitude, the Pope sent her a small crucifix. This she was clasping at the moment of her death.

---

[1] "Since God comes to me, why should I be afraid to go to him who represents Him on earth? I am weak and need God, the Strong-One, and with your blessing, Most Holy Father, I shall receive the strength I need."

In the following year, 1877, from spring until autumn, she was not ill. On September the 8th, on the Feast of the Nativity of the Virgin Mary, she had the great grief of hearing the news of Abbé Peyramale's death. She tugged the sleeve of another sister from Lourdes and left recreation with her, so that the others should not see her tears. Oh, the memories that went with the death of that good pastor who had at first been so gruff to her, and then, after the testing period, had believed in her! How far away those Lourdes days began to seem!

On the following November 21st she renewed her vows.

1878, the year before her death, was momentous in that on January the 28th Mère Joséphine Imbert, Superior General, died of consumption after being ill for six years. Bernadette was seen by some onlookers to be in tears in the chapel.

The next day Mère Adélaide Dons was elected, a nun with powerful masculine features, a robust frame and the kindest of hearts. She was sixty-six years of age, and with her advent the era of snubbing and cold reserve was over for Bernadette. She knew her well, and she knew that she had never been proud. Chanoine Guynot has gleaned a charming story about them both. This good Superior used to take Bernadette for walks in the garden, during the last year of her life. The chaplain, Abbé Febvre, received a visit from his young cousin, who was studying to become a priest, on the first Tuesday of October, 1878, six months before Soeur Marie Bernard was to die. (The chaplain's house is still just as it was, surrounded by its little garden.)

The chaplain said: "Jean-Marie, you know that Bernadette is here with the Sisters of Nevers. There are many people who come and who want to speak to her. They go away again without even having caught a glimpse of her. At this moment, she must be taking a stroll in the garden with the Superior General. I can take you there, just by chance, and give you the opportunity of meeting her." So they went off together to the vast kitchen garden, to the west of the terrace on the slope of the little hillock. And there she was, leaning on her Superior's arm. The little nun was enjoying the air and sun of this peaceful autumn evening, after anoth-

er bout of grave illness. The chaplain left his cousin behind,
the Superior left Bernadette behind, and the young man and
Bernadette had a little confabulation on the path. After a
while the Superior returned to Bernadette and said: *"Ma
Soeur* Marie Bernard, would you pick some grapes from the
arbours on the wall? You might offer them to this young
student. He has been travelling and it would refresh him."

Bernadette did as she was told, and then walked up the
little hillock again, rather painfully and slowly, for no doubt
her bad knee was hurting her dreadfully. As she carried the
grapes, which always reminded her of the Blessed Eucharist,
she thought of this future priest and his first Mass. She
reached him, she drew herself up and looked at him. He
recalled:

"I do not remember her features very clearly. I only recall a tired face, a matt complexion, a charming smile and
the beautiful clear eyes in which the Virgin had left, as it
were, a reflection of Heaven."

Now Jean-Marie, though very tall, was only seventeen
years of age and Bernadette saw him still as a child and,
moreover, a child of the people.

"Eh bien, mon petit gars (my little lad)—So you're going
to the seminary?"

"I am, Sister."

"You're going to become a priest?"

"Yes, if God allows it."

Then she paused, looked towards the chapel, looked at
him again and said these words, very clearly:

"Yes, you will be a priest, but you will have to work very
hard and suffer a great deal."

(In fact, these prophecies came true.) Then she looked at
him intensely and said:

"A priest! It is such a wonderful thing to be a priest, a
priest at the altar. It is Jesus on the cross all over again.
Good-bye, *mon petit gars*."

Chanoine Lemaître has a delicious account of Soeur
Bernadette's last outing before the grape harvest:

"On one of those mysterious autumn days when everything seems to slip into changeless peace, from the sun,
which helps to warm you without burning you, to the mo-

tionless leaf hanging precariously on the tree without falling, she noticed in the stripped trellis a solitary forgotten grape . . . Her companions crossed their hands to make her a little step-ladder. She jumped up in spite of her small stature and her bad knee, and picked the fruit."

Alas, this was a foreshadowing of how her infirmarians would have to carry her, for very soon she lost the use of her legs. Decay of the bones had set in, accompanied by a terrible throbbing pain like a constant toothache. She used to apologize to her infirmarians for the trouble she was, but they laughed and said that she was not heavy and they could carry four nuns of her size.

On October 30th she was moved into the Infirmerie Sainte Croix. There are two windows opposite the door. On the left-hand side is the chimney piece in front of which she died, in an armchair. And on the right of the window was her bed, placed against the wall.

One of her Superiors, whose name we are not told, asked her playfully when she saw her in bed:

"What are you doing in bed there, you lazy thing?"

"But, my dear Mother, I am doing my job."

"And what is your job?"

"To be ill."

Bernadette wrote in her notebook: "What folly to turn back, when Our Lord asks for our hand to nail it. Henceforward, the more I am crucified, the more I shall rejoice."

Mère Bordenave has written: "Her sufferings were so excruciating that the nuns tried in vain by all the means which charity could devise to lessen the torture. Her face was like that of a corpse. She seemed to be dead. She spent entire nights without sleep, and if she happened to drop off for a few moments, acute pains would waken her again, making her endure her martyrdom almost without respite."

One would think they would now leave the poor creature alone. But no. Père Sempé was sent by Monseigneur de Tarbes with the Pope's authorization, to question her yet once more on the apparitions before it was too late—and that lasted for two days, the 12th and 13th of December, 1878. Père Sempé said: "Soeur Marie Bernard showed at that time very great joy, which was not usual with her on

these occasions . . . She repeated, with charm, in her sweet
Pyrenean tongue, the words which had fallen from the lips
of Mary. More than twenty-one years after the events, in
the presence of death and eternity, the nun affirmed what
she had said when she was still a child. She was the ever
faithful echo of the Mother of the Divine Word."

And then on December 18th her brother, Jean-Marie,
came to see her. He was now aged twenty-seven.

"Oh, Jean-Marie!" she exclaimed when she saw him.

They were both extremely moved at this interview.

On January the 7th, 1879, she was thirty-five years old.
She was now able to eat only a very small amount. All the
night through, the nun who watched by her side would hear
the abrupt, gasping moans. Soeur Philomène Roques, who
had been called to watch by her bedside on one of those
last nights, told her story to Chanoine Guynot:

" 'If I need you, I will call,' [Bernadette said] for she
wanted to spare us all fatigue. I therefore tried to obey her
and to rest, but without much success. During the night she
had a nightmare which woke her up. I heard her ask,
'Whom have they given me to watch by me?' I rushed forward at once. Perspiration was pouring from her brow.
'My dear Sister,' I said, 'do you need anything?' She moaned
a little, as if she were still under the impression of a terrifying dream. And then she said in a broken voice, 'I was far
away at Massabielle.' She continued, 'There was . . . a little
boy . . . who was throwing stones into the torrent.' As I
wiped her brow and her face, I said a few words to make her
forget this painful obsession."

This horror of anything that might profane the holy spot
at Lourdes which obsessed Bernadette that night shows to
what an extent the thought of the grotto and the apparitions
was with her. The idea of profanation drew from her cries
as though the stones of the boy in her dream struck her
personally.

Whenever she was able to, she took part in all the community exercises from her bed. Even when she was utterly
exhausted, during the Lent of that last year 1879, she would
do some work in the evenings by the inadequate light of a
small oil lamp. With a little pen-knife she would scratch

hearts on rose-coloured Easter eggs. She would joke and say with a smile, "Men have no hearts, and so I put them on eggs instead."

In His providence, God had seen fit to remove one last trial. Mère Vauzou fell ill in January, and so Bernadette was spared her sharp tongue at the last. And a month before Bernadette died, Mère Vauzou left St. Gildard's to go to Neuilly near Paris, to recover her health. So she was not present when Bernadette was on her deathbed.

Bernadette had said to Soeur Vincent Garros: "When you are in bed, you must lie still and think of yourself as if you were Our Lord on the cross." But now, to stay motionless was quite beyond her, for her pains were intolerable. She had given away the three devotional pictures hanging on her curtains, and kept only her crucifix, saying, "Now I need only Him." Then she took the crucifix in her arms and said, "I am like Him."

On March the 18th her sister Toinette and her husband came to visit her. She was so ill that she could not speak to them. She could hardly lift her head.

She received the last sacraments again on Friday, March the 28th, the Feast of the Compassion of the Virgin Mary. Abbé Febvre recounts that in a loud and distinct voice, which surprised them all, she said: "My dear Mother, I beg your forgiveness for all the trouble which I have caused you by my unfaithfulness in the religious life, and I also ask pardon from my companions for the bad examples which I have given them." And then she added, "And especially for my pride."

Abbé Febvre found words to cheer her. He said, "Very soon you will be enjoying Heaven. You will see the beauty and the glory of Our Lord, of which the Blessed Virgin has given you some idea." She said, "Oh, that is a very helpful thought."

By Holy Week, her poor body was one living wound. Even to move her slightly in bed caused her atrocious sufferings. She said, "Oh, if you could only find something to soothe my back. My skin is raw."

On Easter Monday she said to Soeur Léontine Villaret: "Haven't you got anything to strengthen my heart and help

me to breathe? . . . I am ground up like a grain of wheat . . .
I should never have thought that one had to suffer so much
to die."

On that same Easter Monday, Soeur Bernard Dalias, accompanied by some other nuns, had come up to say good-
bye to her during the midday recreation. They had come in
very quietly because she was asleep, or seemed to be. Soeur
Bernard Dalias came closer than the others and looked
down at her in silence.

"She seemed to feel our presence. I saw her turn her head
very slightly, open her eyes and look at me. She recognized
me at once, as I realized from a facial expression which I
could not describe, but which I can call a smile of the eyes.
She looked at me, closing one eye in a playful manner. I
saw from this that she had remained till the last moment the
simple, charming creature she had always been."

Bernadette put out her hot little hand and said: *"Adieu,*
Bernard, this time it is the end."

On the night of Easter Monday until the Tuesday, she
seemed very much afraid and kept crying out: "Go away,
Satan! Go away, Satan!" She confessed afterwards to the
chaplain that the Devil had tried to throw himself on her,
but that she had invoked the name of Jesus and recovered
her trust. Her last night was really horrible. We have an
account of it from Mère Alphonse, who when she saw her
decided not to go to bed but to sit in an armchair by her
side all night.

"From time to time, suffering would wrest a low moan
from her, which made me start in my chair. She asked me
quite often to help her to turn, so that she could find a little
relief for her poor body, which was flayed alive. She was
lying on her wounds, as it were.

"And then we would try to come to an arrangement between us, to effect these manoeuvres, which was very difficult. I would take the foot of the bad leg . . . and I would
try to follow, very carefully, the movement of the body, so
that she should be able to turn all of a piece, without there
being any need for the leg joints to function."

Wednesday, April the 16th, dawned, the day of her release. She had written in her little notebook, "I will do every-

thing for Heaven. . . . There I will find my Mother in all the brightness of her glory."

Her sufferings became more intense. A little after eleven in the morning, they put her in the armchair with her legs on the foot rest, in front of the fireplace where a fire was burning. Between twelve-thirty and one o'clock, Mère Joséphine Forestier went to see her, and found that she was trying with trembling hands to lift a bowl to her lips but not succeeding. Mère Joséphine thought she should warn the infirmarian and the rest of the community that the end was near.

In the meantime, Mère Eléonore Cassagnes, who had been her spiritual friend, knelt down beside her, and said to her:

"My dear Sister, at this moment you are on the cross."

Bernadette stretched out her arms and, looking at the crucifix, cried out: "My Jesus, oh how I love Him!"

Mère Eléonore continued: "I will ask our Immaculate Mother to give you some consolation."

Bernadette replied, "No, no consolations but strength and patience. All this can be used for Heaven." And then she added, "I saw her!" She was looking at that moment at the statue of the Virgin Mary. "I saw her. Oh, how beautiful she was and how I long to see her again!"

Chanoine Lemaître has given a striking account of what happened after the chaplain, M. Febvre, had come in.

"She raised her left hand to her brow. With glowing eyes she looked upwards, and her gaze was fixed immovably on a certain point. Her face was calm, serene, tinged with melancholy. And then, with an expression not of fear but of surprise, on an ever increasing, very emphatic note, she uttered this triple exclamation: 'Oh! Oh! Oh!' her voice firm and growing stronger.

"A sort of quivering seemed to seize her whole body. Then she gently let her hand fall on heart. Her eyes were gradually lowered, and then, in a very distinct tone, in a voice full of love, she said: 'My God, I love You with all my heart, with all my soul and with all my strength.' "

A little before three o'clock, Mère Nathalie Portat, who was in the chapel, felt drawn to go up again to the infirmary.

"The patient seemed to be enduring terrible interior sufferings. The infirmarians, alarmed, sprinkled some holy water several times on the dying nun, and suggested various invocations to her. She grasped her crucifix, the one from Rome. She looked at it lovingly, kissed the wounds one by one. All of a sudden she raised her head, stretched out her arms towards Mère Nathalie. She looked at her and said, 'My dear Sister, forgive me. Pray for me, pray for me.' "

Mère Nathalie and the two infirmarians knelt down by her. Then she gave a loud cry, and with her eyes looking up to heaven and her arms stretched out as on a cross, she said, "My God." A tremor of reverence mingled with fear passed through the three nuns, who were still kneeling. One of them was supporting the upstretched arms of the dying nun, for she was holding her arms out all the time. At last she let them drop and again joined in the prayers of her companions. She repeated twice: "Holy Mary, Mother of God, pray for me, poor sinner." And then she looked troubled again and twice renewed in silence her moving supplication to Mère Nathalie, stretching out her arms, with her eyes fixed on her.

"Why are you stretching your arms towards me like that? What do you want me to do for you?" said Mère Nathalie.

"I want you to help me."

"Poor sinner—" were her last two words. Whilst her companions were repeating, "Jesus, Mary, Joseph, have pity on her, protect her," at about quarter past three, clutching her crucifix against her heart, Bernadette died. Two great tears had fallen on her cheeks, and her head was leaning to one side.

As Monseigneur Lelong was to say at her funeral: "Her sufferings were a chalice of which she drank deeply. Her whole existence may be described as one long martyrdom, nailed with her Master to the cross. She had written: 'Oh Jesus, I don't feel my cross when I think of Yours.' Her death bears many similarities with the death, in agony and darkness, of her beloved Master."

She had written: "Come now, my soul, courage. One more day in the footsteps of Jesus and Mary climbing Calvary, and then with Jesus and Mary, Happiness, *Allégresse*, Eternity."

Soeur Bernard Dalias, who came to look at her before they put her in her coffin, said that her face was young and peaceful again, with a wondrous expression of purity and beatitude.

In spite of the continual rain, great crowds began to move towards St. Gildard's. A working woman of the people, meeting one of the sisters in the park, asked her at what time the funeral procession would take place. The sister replied: "But she's not being taken to the cemetery, we're keeping her."

"You're keeping her? Oh! How glad I am! My good dear Sister, this isn't just idle chatter, everyone feels that she is not only the model of a Christian but certainly the model of a saint."

The funeral was fixed for Saturday. None of her relations came, alas. Mère Adélaide Dons, the Superior, as if foreseeing the future, did not have her buried in the town cemetery, but in the little oratory of St. Joseph in the convent vineyards, the oratory she had loved. It is almost ironical to think that this chapel had been built on the initiative of Mère Vauzou, as a thank-offering to God for the recovery of a former bishop of Nevers! It was a good thing that Mère Vauzou was safely away at Neuilly, for she would never have approved of this chapel being used for Bernadette.

The coffin was not covered, so everybody saw her when she was brought into the chapel. Her beautiful eyes were only half shut, and her hands and nails were still pink, as if she were alive. A workman who had eventually to close the coffin whispered as he looked at her face, "Oh, what a pity." A very small boy, who brought a daisy crown, could only with difficulty be dragged away from her tomb, where he was lost in prayer!

Mère Vauzou returned from Neuilly, and eventually became Superior General in her turn. Towards the end of her term of office, her conscience began to prick her, after hearing of the miraculous cures due to Bernadette's intercession. So one day, when she was travelling in the south in company with Mère Joséphine Forestier, she went to visit a priest of great holiness, who was credited with the discernment of spirits and the ability to read souls—Père Jean was a Cistercian of the Abbey of Fontfroide near Narbonne. He was by then very old, very infirm; he lived on a celestial plane. He was very kind, and his aim was to restore confidence to troubled souls. Mère Joséphine has written:

"She spoke to him alone for quite a long time in the parlour, and then she followed him immediately to the confessional. When she left the abbey, she was beaming, and during the journey from Fontfroide to Narbonne, eight kilometres, she said to me, 'I'm very happy to have seen that holy man. . . . I was frightened that I'd been too severe to *ma Soeur* Marie Bernard. That was tormenting me. I told him why I acted as I did. Père Jean completely reassured me, and I am now very much at peace.' "

Worn by a life of labour, Mère Vauzou retired in 1899, and again, by the irony of circumstances, in August 1901, she was sent to Lourdes and stayed in the orphanage of Marie Immaculée, facing the grotto and the basilicas. Occasionally, when the crowds outside got too noisy, she looked as if she were on edge, and she would brusquely close the shutters of her room. When Mère Joséphine Forestier, returning from a pilgrimage to Rome, went to see her, and told her that at Rome they had talked of introducing Bernadette's beatification Cause, Mère Vauzou replied, "Wait till I'm dead." When she died at eighty-two, on February the 15th, 1907, she prayed to Our Lady of Lourdes to watch over her in her death agony. On the 16th or 17th of February when Mère Joséphine came to kneel by her bier, she prayed this prayer:

"Ma bonne mère, in Heaven one does not always see things in the same light as on earth, and now that you are, I hope, enjoying this light from above, I beg you to take in hand the Cause of Bernadette. I will leave you the initiative in this affair. I will not act. I will wait for a sign from Heaven." And she told this to Mère Henri Fabre and Mère Marie-Thérèse Bordenave.

The sign came on the 5th of March, in a letter from Monseigneur Gauthey, Bishop of Nevers, writing from Rome.

He said that the Cause of Bernadette's beatification should now be prepared.

The official enquiry began in August 1908, and by October 1909, the Congregation of Rites was in possession of all the documents. The month before, they had opened her coffin and had found her body completely incorrupt. Her attitude reminded Monseigneur Gauthey of the young virgins of the first centuries represented in the catacombs. She was finally canonized on Friday December the 8th, 1933, in St. Peter's, Rome, in the presence of Mère Marie Alphonse Crapard, Superior General of Nevers, a hundred and sixty of her nuns and forty thousand pilgrims, ten thousand being French. In his homily, Pope Pius XI accentuated the humility of this "ignorant daughter of simple millers, who possessed for all riches, the candour of her exquisite soul."

A miller's child indeed, a grain of wheat ground to powder and now united to the white sacrificial Host, the victim on the altar. She it was who, listening to her Lady and obeying her behests, had unsealed a fountain of healing for men's bodies, and a cure for their souls' ills. And now the time of travail is over. As we gaze at the golden roses on the Lady's feet, we can dream with Dante of the angels who disseminate the sweetness in the celestail air of the *Paradiso*. They pass like bees from petal to petal of the great Rose of Paradise. We also recall his description of the Virgin Mother smiling with so much beauty at games and songs, "as to make gladness in the eyes of the beholders."

And the laughter! The laughter of Our Lady in the grotto . . . It recalls the vision that Dante epitomized in his immortal line,

> "Eternal light that loves and smiles.
> (*O Luce eterna che . . . ami ed arridi.*)"

Now Bernadette will share in that *riso de l'universo* of which the Florentine sings—the laughter of the universe as it adores the Eternal Light.

In the late nineteenth century a nearly blind priest, the priest of the Paris ragpickers, Père Lamy, was one day scrubbing his church floor on hands and knees, garbed in an old apron, when suddenly he saw the Archangel Gabriel, who said to him: "Our Lady is here." As Père Lamy tried vainly to tear off his apron, Our Lady turned laughing to the angels in her train and said, "What fierce humility!"

What joy for fiercely humble Bernadette to see again those eyes of Mary—"Those eyes loved and venerated by God," said Dante. Those eyes, now, every year, during the great pilgrimages to her grotto, look down upon the multitudes of sinners with such great kindness, that many repent of their evil deeds. The heart of the message of Lourdes is that the Immaculate has come to call sinners to repentance, so that she may offer them again to her Son. And the eternal miracle of Lourdes is that no pilgrim returns home unconsoled.

St. Catherine of Siena says that the sight of an immortal soul in a state of friendship with God would be enough to make one die of joy. What rapture, then, shall we feel at the sight of Mary's soul, which is the delight of God and the paradise, as it were, of the blessed Trinity!

Pope Pius IX tells us that when he was contemplating the beauty of Mary's soul as he proclaimed the Dogma of the Immaculate Conception, he was so overwhelmed with divine light that, but for a special grace, he would have died of joy. As the Dominican Père Philipon has written in his great book on the Mother of God, "Next to Christ, the Immaculate is the masterpiece of God." . . . "She is the created image that most nearly resembles the Blessed Trinity."

Much has been written about the miracles of physical healing which Mary accomplishes in Lourdes, not enough of the spiritual resurrections.

Many of us will remember the *Journal of Elisabeth Leseur,* written by a very spiritual and firmly convinced Catholic who had married an unbeliever to whom she was utterly devoted. After her death, in the year 1912, her husband recounted, in his little book *My Conversion at Lourdes,* how he had come upon his wife absorbed in prayer at the grotto:

"I had before me something which escaped me, which I did not understand. It was, however, clearly something supernatural and I could not take my eyes off the sight."

After her death, as he was travelling in the direction of Lourdes on a train (though with no plan of going to the shrine), he heard a voice say to him: "It has all been arranged to make it possible for you to get to Lourdes, where God awaits you." The voice kept repeating again and again, "You must go to Lourdes, go to Lourdes," and he realized that it was the voice of Elisabeth. He went to the grotto, accompanied in spirit by his wife. And there he implored Our Lady for the gift of faith. He received it. And then he entered the Dominican order, where the ardour of his faith redeemed all his former scepticism and unbelief.

The fascinating book *Three White Veils for Alessandra* tells how a beautiful Italian Countess, the Marchese di Garda, who had lost her faith, her health and her lover— d'Annunzio—was moved, at Lourdes, in August 1910, to repeat Fénelon's prayer: "O Being of infinite perfections, if it is true that Thou art and that Thou dost understand the desires of my heart, show Thyself to me. Raise the veil that covers Thy countenance . . . O truth, O wisdom, O supreme goodness, if it is true that Thou hast made me for Thyself, do not suffer me to belong to myself so that Thou possessest not thine own work. Open my eyes, show Thyself to Thy creature."

At Lourdes that day, in the Rosary church, Alessandra gazed at the painting of Our Lady which seemed to look at her wherever she was. And she prayed: "Oh Mary, work your greatest miracle in me. Let my life belong to you, be consecrated to you entirely and for always." She then heard someone close at hand saying: "I confess to Thee . . . because Thou hast hidden these things from the wise, the prudent and revealed them to little ones."

Torn between anguish and joy, she heard the voice again, sweet, loud and penetrating: "I am here. Look for me in thyself."

That very afternoon she made a confession of the sins of her whole life. Then she received Holy Communion at the Carmelites' and went to pray at the grotto, which was her Tabor, "shining with all the splendour of the Incarnate Word, inflaming the heart." Oblivious of all her surroundings, she said: "Yes, I will follow You."

She left her family, the world, her riches, and became a Carmelite at the very poor convent at Paray-le-Monial, and there she died in great holiness. Her Cause of beatification has been introduced at Rome.

Eve Lavallière, the renowned French actress, came to Lourdes after her conversion. She renounced her lover and her riches, keeping but the bare necessities for living. She went to Mass every day in the orphanage of the Sisters of Nevers where St. Bernadette had learnt how to read. She loved to walk in the footpaths of the saint, picking firewood along the banks of the Gave. Every day she went to pray in the *cachot,* in the rue des Petits-Fossés.

O Saint Bernadette, what strange penitents you gather from the far ends of the earth! And how beautiful these shriven souls become, who have listened to the Lady's call: *"Pénitence. Pénitence. Pénitence,"* and who have turned to her Son who desires to forgive more than they desire to be forgiven. O shepherdess of souls, what a garnering for your Father's barns!

Lourdes is the Heaven of penitents. Hundreds come who have not been to confession for years. After unburdening themselves of the sins of a lifetime, they rise up and are given the ring and the white robe, and the Father leads them to the banquet of His true lovers. And all because a poor miller's child of a hundred years ago showed them the path which leads to the festal hall.

Lourdes)
Nevers)   1956–7.
London)